The Priority of the Other

The Priority of the Other

Thinking and Living Beyond the Self

MARK FREEMAN

OXFORD
UNIVERSITY PRESS

OXFORD
UNIVERSITY PRESS

Oxford University Press is a department of the University of Oxford.
It furthers the University's objective of excellence in research, scholarship,
and education by publishing worldwide.

Oxford   New York
Auckland   Cape Town   Dar es Salaam   Hong Kong   Karachi
Kuala Lumpur   Madrid   Melbourne   Mexico City   Nairobi
New Delhi   Shanghai   Taipei   Toronto

With offices in
Argentina   Austria   Brazil   Chile   Czech Republic   France   Greece
Guatemala   Hungary   Italy   Japan   Poland   Portugal   Singapore
South Korea   Switzerland   Thailand   Turkey   Ukraine   Vietnam

Oxford is a registered trademark of Oxford University Press
in the UK and certain other countries.

Published in the United States of America by
Oxford University Press
198 Madison Avenue, New York, NY 10016

© Oxford University Press 2014

All rights reserved. No part of this publication may be reproduced, stored in a
retrieval system, or transmitted, in any form or by any means, without the prior
permission in writing of Oxford University Press, or as expressly permitted by law,
by license, or under terms agreed with the appropriate reproduction rights organization.
Inquiries concerning reproduction outside the scope of the above should be sent to the
Rights Department, Oxford University Press, at the address above.

You must not circulate this work in any other form
and you must impose this same condition on any acquirer.

Library of Congress Cataloging-in-Publication Data
Freeman, Mark Philip, 1955–
The priority of the other : living and thinking beyond the self / Mark Freeman.
pages cm
Includes bibliographical references and index.
ISBN 978–0–19–975930–9 (alk. paper)
1. Attention.   2. Consciousness.   I. Title.
BF321.F817 2013
126—dc23
2013008388

1 3 5 7 9 8 6 4 2
Printed in the United States of America
on acid-free paper

To Deborah, Brenna, and Justine, for all that you are

To my mother, Marian, whose presence beckons

To Jody, John, and Kim, in warm memory

Contents

Acknowledgments	ix
Introduction: Thinking and Being Otherwise	1
1. From Self to Other	19
2. Oblivion and Attention	52
3. For the Other	77
4. Beyond the Human	113
5. The Possibility of Transcendence	144
6. Living Ex-centrically	180
Coda: A New Language for Psychology and Beyond	216
References	225
Index	235

Acknowledgments

WORKING ON THIS book for more than a decade has brought me into dialogue with numerous people, and I am extremely grateful for their wisdom, counsel, and friendship. These include Molly Andrews, Michael Bamberg, Robert Bishop, Jeff Bloechl, Art Bochner, Jacob Belzen, Jens Brockmeier, Scott Churchill, Carolyn Ellis, Michelle Fine, Blaine Fowers, Roger Frie, Ken Gergen, Mary Gergen, David Goodman, Ruthellen Josselson, Amia Lieblich, Jack Martin, Dan McAdams, Lisa Osbeck, Bill Randall, Jeff Reber, Danny Schouela, Kate Slaney, Jeff Sugarman, and Fred Wertz. I also want to give special thanks to Frank Richardson and Brent Slife, who have been not only quite wonderful conversation partners in recent years but fellow travelers and explorers, committed to charting new intellectual and spiritual territory. I would be remiss if I didn't acknowledge as well those persons from my graduate years at the University of Chicago who were formative in my thinking about the issues at hand. These include Bert Cohler, Mihaly Csikszentmihalyi, Peter Homans, Paul Ricoeur, and David Tracy. Some of these fine people are no longer with us. I very much hope this book serves to preserve their memory in some way.

In addition to acknowledging specific persons, I want to acknowledge several intellectual communities I have been fortunate to be a part of while writing this book. These include the Society for Qualitative Inquiry in Psychology, the Society for Theoretical and Philosophical Psychology, the Society for Personology, the Narrative Study Group, and, most recently, the Psychology and the Other Institute, which, under the able direction of David Goodman, has been instrumental in furthering the cause of bringing the Other to bear upon the discipline of psychology.

I also want to acknowledge those on the home front, that is, the College of the Holy Cross, where I have had the privilege of teaching and learning for some 27 years. Among the many people who have helped shape this work, I give thanks to Jeff Bernstein, Bob Cording, Chris Dustin, Margaret Freije, Andy Futterman, Bob Garvey, Jim Kee, Suzanne Kirschner, Joe Lawrence, John Manoussakis, Bill Morse, Denise Schaeffer, Vicki Swigert, Steve Vineberg, and Chick Weiss. In addition to these, I want to recognize and remember several friends and colleagues from Holy Cross who have passed on but whose spirit very much lives on in the pages of this book: Kim McElaney, John Wilson, and Jody Ziegler. What a gift it has been to work and live alongside these people. They have my deepest gratitude. I am also grateful to the Department of Psychology and to the College itself—to Stephen Ainlay (now at Union College), Tim Austin, Philip Boroughs, SJ, Michael McFarlane, SJ, and Frank Vellaccio, in particular—not only for having let me do what I do, as a teacher and writer, for more than a quarter-century, but for providing an unusually hospitable and fertile environment for pursuing those "basic human questions" (as the College's Mission Statement puts it) that are central both to liberal arts education and to human existence itself. The fact of the matter is, I would have never written this book if I hadn't landed at Holy Cross.

Consider some of the questions and ideas found in our mission statement: "What is the moral character of teaching and learning? How do we find meaning in life and history? What are our obligations to one another? What is our special responsibility to the world's poor and powerless?" There is more: "Because the search for meaning and value is at the heart of the intellectual life, critical examination of fundamental religious and philosophical questions is integral to liberal arts education. Dialogue about these questions among people from diverse academic disciplines and religious traditions requires everyone to acknowledge and respect differences. Dialogue also requires us to remain open to that sense of the whole which calls us to transcend ourselves and challenges us to seek that which might constitute our common humanity." As shall become clear in the pages to follow, these words very much speak to the priority of the Other.

Last but not least, this book is a product of the efforts of a number of individuals at Oxford University Press, including Catharine Carlin, Abby Gross, Mallory Jensen, Joanna Ng, and Suzanne Walker. I am grateful to them too and thank them for their support for the project, their helpful commentary, and their hard work in helping to bring it into its current form.

The Priority of the Other represents a synthesis of much of the work I have done over the course of the last fifteen or so years. Although none of the chapters found here reproduce in full pieces that have been published elsewhere, a number of them do in fact make significant contact with this earlier work. Articles and chapters drawn upon include "Thinking and Being Otherwise: Aesthetics, Ethics, Erotics" (*Journal of Theoretical and Philosophical Psychology, 32*, 2012, pp. 196–208, by permission of the American Psychological Association); "Listening to the Claims of Experience: Psychology and the Question of Transcendence" (*Pastoral Psychology,* 2013, DOI: 10.1007/s11089-013-0528-6, by permission of Springer); "The Priority of the Other: Mysticism's Challenge to the Legacy of the Self," in *Mysticism: A Variety of Psychological Approaches* (J. Belzen & A. Geels, Eds., 2004, pp. 213–234, by permission of Rodopi); and "The Personal and Beyond: Simone Weil and the Necessity/Limits of Biography," in *Autobiography and the Psychological Study of Religious Lives* (J. A. Belzen & A. Geels, Eds., 2009, pp. 187–207, by permission of Rodopi). Grateful acknowledgment is also made to Taylor & Francis for permission to reprint copyrighted material from Iris Murdoch's *The Sovereignty of Good* (Routledge, 1970).

Official acknowledgments aside, I also express my deepest appreciation to the many others with whom I am in dialogue throughout the pages of this book. They don't, of course, speak back in quite the same way that flesh-and-blood interlocutors do, but their presence, as partners in dialogue, remains quite real. I am immensely grateful for their contributions to the cause.

Introduction

THINKING AND BEING OTHERWISE

THIS BOOK IS anomalous in the field of psychology by virtue of its focus on "the Other," which, in the present context, refers to both the human and the non-human spheres.[1] There is a very basic reason for this. Psychology, having come of age under the influence of Descartes and other champions of the *ego cogito*, the thinking "I," came to delimit its focus largely to what was happening inside the self, within the enclosure of the skin. This would expand with the emergence of social psychology and, more recently, cultural psychology, but by and large its purview has remained much the same. Put in the simplest of terms, it is essentially *ego-centric*.

This perspective is belied by much of our experience. What I therefore want to suggest in this book, cautiously, is that a portion of psychology would do well to shift its long-standing emphasis on the priority of the self—however relationally or dialogically conceived—to the priority of the Other.[2] In

---

1. I do not mean to suggest that this focus is mine alone; for other notable explorations, see, for example, Gantt and Williams (2002), Kunz (1998), Sampson (1993), and Simão and Valsiner (2007). Also significant in this context is the work by Gergen (2009), Gilligan (1982), and Slife (2004), among others, who have found in "relational" thinking an important corrective to the largely ego-centric perspective found in much contemporary psychology, as well as the work carried out in relational psychoanalysis (e.g., Aron and Mitchell, 1999; Mitchell, 1988; Orange, 2011; Stolorow, Atwood, and Orange, 2002). As for my decision to capitalize the "O" in "Other," I do so mainly to underscore both the "size" of the category (it is large, indeed) and the fact that it encompasses both the human and non-human spheres.

2. The phrase "the priority of the Other" (or "other") can be found elsewhere, mainly in the context of Emmanuel Levinas's work (e.g., 2000). Generally speaking, the "Other" (or "other") in question refers to the human other. As above, my own use of the phrase refers to both the human and the non-human. Moreover, I attempt to speak about "priority" in a somewhat different way than Levinas, focusing more on issues of concern to psychology.

speaking of the former, I refer to that broad tradition of thinking, in philosophy, psychology, and beyond, that looks to the self, variously conceived, as the primary locus, if not the originating source, of meaning and value. In speaking of the latter, I refer to the rather less broad tradition of thinking that looks instead to the various "objects" outside ourselves—other people, nature, art, God—that draw us beyond our own borders and thereby open up the possibility of there emerging a larger, unbounded Self, one that knows, and feels, its kinship with the world.³ One might think of this perspective as *ex-centric* (Freeman, 2004b).⁴

Given that I am someone with a special interest in the narrative fashioning of identity, it might seem strange that I have come to move in this direction. Personal narratives issue from a self, a narrator: in a most basic and obvious sense, the story of my life is thus irrevocably *mine*. As I have suggested elsewhere, however (Freeman, 2007), this says nothing at all about the ultimate sources of my story, about the driving forces that propel it forward, giving it meaning and substance. If the philosopher/mystic/social critic Simone Weil is right, these forces cannot, and do not, derive from the self but instead derive from the Other. "Humility," she writes, "consists in knowing that in what we call 'I' there is no source of energy by which we can rise. Everything without exception which is of value in me

---

3. I use the word "object" in this book in the purely colloquial sense of "that to which I am drawn." In it, I include not only things but activities, ideas, principles, and whatever else, beyond me, that draws me outward. The word is not ideal. Following Gabriel Marcel (1950), the word "presence" comes closer to the meaning I want to convey, for "the very act by which we incline ourselves toward a presence"—a person, for instance—"is essentially different from that through which we grasp at any object." Indeed, "in the case of a presence, the very possibility of grasping at, of seizing, is excluded in principle." We are therefore considering a different kind of relationship. Grasping an object is something *I* do; "a presence," in contrast, "is something which can only be gathered to oneself or shut out from oneself, be welcomed or rebuffed" (p. 255). Jean-Luc Marion (2008) conveys a similar idea when he explains his preference for the word "phenomenon." Having established that both of these terms may be more appropriate than "object" for what I wish to convey in this book, I nevertheless maintain that, for all its objectifying connotations, the latter still works better colloquially than the former. Insofar as I use phrases such as "objects of attention," therefore, I simply ask your indulgence. In a semantically perfect world, it would be "presence" or "phenomenon" all the way. But in this one, "object" seems the better choice.

4. Especially important in this context is the work of Martin Buber (e.g., 1965, 1970, 1998 [1965]), which I draw upon extensively in the pages to come. Indeed, although he doesn't employ the term "ex-centric," I consider him the philosopher/psychologist of ex-centricity par excellence.. According to Buber, we cannot speak of the human person as a being unto itself but only in relation to all that is not-self. This idea of "relation" is absolutely central in Buber's work—more central, surely, than the idea of the Other. From my perspective, however, he is as much a theorist of the Other and of the fundamental ex-centricity of being as those who more readily use these terms.

comes from something other than myself, not as a gift but as a loan which must be ceaselessly renewed" (1997 [1952], p. 27). "I" am not the source of my inspiration or my enthusiasm, and whatever self-help books might say, I am emphatically not the source of the joy I may feel for the many experiences that come my way. I am thinking especially of those aesthetic experiences, broadly conceived—experiences of art or nature, for instance—that move us, take us out of ourselves. Central to Weil's perspective, and to the perspective offered in this book, is the idea of *attention*—which we might think of as that quality of responsively respectful consciousness that can allow the otherness of the Other, whatever it may be, to come our way.[5]

Also relevant to the perspective at hand is the idea of *devotion*, which we might think of as *sustained* attention, faithfully directed, in service to some worthy sphere of reality. As Charles Taylor (1989) has noted, "one of the most basic aspirations of human beings [is] the need to be connected to, or in contact with, what they see as good, or of crucial importance, or of fundamental value" (p. 42). This is nothing short of a "craving," Taylor insists, and the good to which he is referring is *outside* us, serving as a point of orientation and direction. "This sense of the good," he adds, "has to be woven into my understanding of my life as an unfolding story" (p. 47). Along these lines, whatever role I might play in fashioning the story of my life, "I" am not its origin. Indeed, it might plausibly be said that, while the *proximal* source of one's story is the self, the *distal* source is the Other. "Even the sense that the significance of my life comes from its being chosen...depends on the understanding that *independent of my will* there is something noble, courageous, and hence significant in giving shape to my own life" (1991, p. 39; see also Taylor, 1996). So: *attention* and *devotion*.

A third idea to be explored is the idea of *transcendence*. All I will suggest for now is that the "good" Taylor speaks of, far from being a mere matter of convention or consensus, instead points to something truly *other*, something beyond, that conditions and gives form to our existence. Having said this, we can and should ask, with Iris Murdoch, "Is there...any true transcendence, or is this idea always a consoling dream

---

[5]. The notion of attention is particularly important in the practice of "mindfulness" (e.g., Kabat-Zinn, 2005) as well as in other Buddhist-inspired modes of awakening to the world (e.g., Wallace, 2006). See also the classic statement on attention offered by William James in *The Principles of Psychology* (1950 [1890]) as well as more recent work (e.g., Gallagher, 2009) seeking to underscore its significance for living a focused, aware, purposeful life. For further comments on Weil, see Coles (2001), Du Plessix Gray (2001), and Freeman (2009).

projected by human need on to an empty sky?" (1970, p. 57). That it is frequently the latter is clear enough, and Murdoch—who is actually something of a skeptic in terms of religion—does well to caution us against succumbing to such illusion and folly. Nevertheless, she avows, "There is...something in the serious attempt to look compassionately at human things which...suggests that 'there is more than this.' The 'there is more than this,' if it is not to be corrupted by some sort of quasi-theological finality, must remain a tiny spark of insight, something with, as it were, a metaphysical position but not a metaphysical form. But it seems to me the spark is real" (1970, p. 71). For Murdoch, great art is clear evidence of the reality of this transcendent spark. So too is love. And, her own reticence notwithstanding, there also are those spiritual and religious experiences that, for many, are felt to be revelations of the divine, the sacred, the *wholly* Other (Otto, 1958 [1923]). I shall have much more to say about all of these—and about the challenge of adducing "evidence" for transcendence—in due time.[6]

Let me continue by offering a somewhat audacious assertion: it could very well be that the great quantity of attention devoted to the self, in psychology especially, is, in part, a *mistake*. Bear in mind that I have no interest here in "deconstructing" the self or exposing it as a bourgeois reification or wiping it off the face of the earth (etc.). Our selves, as we have come to know them, are here to stay, at least for a while; the direction of history doesn't change overnight. What's more, it is amply clear that our selves are important to us; so it is that we protest when our selves, or those of others, are denied, negated, or hurt, or when our creativity and freedom are not given room to grow and flourish. In addition, many people seek self-gratification and self-fulfillment and self-improvement. They try to be self-actualized; they seek to realize and develop their own unique potential as selves, as specific people, with specific arrays of interests, abilities, talents, and desires. But there is something extremely curious about the way all of this has been understood and framed for many years. What has been suggested thus far, with the help of Weil, Taylor, and Murdoch, is that, appearances notwithstanding, the experiences and things that generally provide the greatest yield of meaning of existential "nourishment" have

---

6. Among the many relevant texts, see Caputo and Scanlon (2007), Dupré (1976, 1998), Faulconer (2003), Forman (1990, 1998), Hollenback (1996), Kerr (1997), Nussbaum (1990), Steiner (1989), and Westphal (2004). For an especially provocative and quite different approach to the idea of the sacred, see Kripal (2011). Also important in this context is of course William James's classic work, *The Varieties of Religious Experience* (1982 [1902]).

little to do with our selves. They derive instead from what is *other* than self, outside of it.

One can of course give oneself some small measure of sexual "gratification." But it is a far cry from the gratification one can experience with another. One can also derive gratification and fulfillment, even "flow," when one rises to the occasion of a particular challenge, or when one's skills and capacities are tested and one prevails (Csikszentmihalyi, 1990). I can also be pleased at my own strength or personal growth, or the realization of my potential as the unique being I am. But it is difficult to understand what it means, or what it can mean, to find fulfillment in my*self,* apart from my relation to what is Other. If I am a painter, it is the act of painting and the work's coming into being that captivate me. And if I am a lover, it is the person before me who "catches my attention" and calls forth my desire.

Consider too the practice of psychotherapy. It seems fair to say that much of modern psychotherapy remains directed toward one's self. This, at any rate, is the way it is often talked about. There are self-esteem problems and distortions of self-image and disturbances in the sphere of self-regard. One's self can be weak or impaired or incomplete, and thus in need of being "restored." Often, however, it is not the *self* that needs to be restored, but the *world*—that is, the world within which one can live and thrive. Certain forms of anxiety and depression often lead people to excessive self-concerns. The self is exactly that which they cannot get out of, and as a result they can derive no sustenance from the world, no nourishment. Indeed, at an extreme, the world, the real world, is virtually absent, unavailable; the only world inhabited is thus the closed and often ugly one that has been fashioned by the self (see Leary, 2004). The therapeutic task, therefore, is to help bring this self back to the real world, the one with real people and places and things, the one that can nourish the self and feed its hunger to be. Again, none of what has been said thus far should be taken to imply that the self is unimportant or that it cannot make true gains during the course of therapy; the post-therapy self may very well be much stronger and more fully formed than the pre-therapy self. But the restoration or betterment of the self, I suggest, is ultimately a function of the restoration of the world. In this sense, *self is secondary; the Other comes first and is thus the primary source of meaning, value, and existential nourishment.* This is the first and most basic meaning of the priority of the Other.

Bearing this idea in mind, I want to argue further that the Other—in the form of other persons, the various objects found in the non-human world, and what Martin Buber refers to as "the mystery of being"[7]—is *ingredient* not only to human flourishing but to full human personhood, and that by shifting our attention from self to Other we will gain a more adequate, and indeed accurate, portrait of the human condition. I believe this shift is a significant one. As Robert Bellah and his colleagues have pointed out in their well-known book *Habits of the Heart: Individualism and Commitment in American Life* (1985), we have been bequeathed a language for understanding our aspirations and goals that is fundamentally individualistic in nature. This language, they suggest, is impoverished and inadequate; it simply doesn't do justice to the quite real commitments people often make, for instance, to community or church. It also fails to adequately acknowledge our *dependence* as persons and the profound vulnerability it entails.[8]

This situation has been exacerbated by the kind of pseudo-Darwinian thinking that finds in "selfish genes" and the like the key to human nature, the assumption being that, finally, we—solitary individuals in harsh competition with others for our very survival—are self-seeking monads. Why "pseudo-Darwinian"? As Mary Midgley argues compellingly in her recent book *The Solitary Self: Darwin and the Selfish Gene* (2010), much of the work that moves in this self-ish direction runs counter to Darwin's actual views, which "simply do not fit with the solipsistic tendencies of our age" (p. 49). Such "social atomism," Midgley maintains, "is not really an essential part of the idea of evolution. It is essentially political: an ideology shaped by Enlightenment individualism, one that takes different forms according to the political and social pressures of the day" (p. 55). What Midgley most wants to underscore in her work is "our need for each other" and the idea that this need "is not a weakness but a strength." Indeed, it is our very "lifeline, our essential passport to the real world," and "it is what points us outward to all the riches around us, the great stores of otherness in which we need to live" (p. 64).

---

7. Also important in this context is Gabriel Marcel's two-volume work *The Mystery of Being* (1950). Although I draw more explicitly on Buber's thinking in much of what follows, Marcel too finds his way into these pages, for his own reflections on the fundamental questions and issues explored herein represent a major contribution to both thinking and being Otherwise.

8. For related comments, see especially Ernest Becker's *The Denial of Death* (1973). Among the many questions and harsh realities explored in this seminal work is the idea that, appearances and wishful fantasies notwithstanding, we are in fact vulnerable, incomplete creatures. Becker even goes so far as to speak of "the lie of self-sufficiency, of free self-determination, of independent judgment and choice" (p. 129). In this respect, some of what he has to say represents a valuable check on our much-vaunted *in*dependence and autonomy.

If Midgley is right, much of the way we have come to think about ourselves is simply *wrong*, and it is imperative that we begin to craft a more truthful account, for "the image we have of our own nature has a deep effect on how we live." The fact is, "Most humans, throughout most of history, have surely seen themselves as parts of a greater whole, continuous both with the life around them and with whatever higher powers may be acting within it. They have not aimed to become independent of it, much less (as is now sometimes suggested) to run the whole universe" (Midgley, 2010, p. 125). This suggests that "the emphasis on competition in recent political and economic thinking—the constant insistence on tournaments between individuals as central to human life—is a pernicious myth and the supposedly scientific story about evolution that has been used to back it is just a fantasy" (p. 141), largely derived from those features of Enlightenment thinking that gave rise to the modern self, the Individual, autonomous and free, "something separate, something higher and extraneous, an alien spiritual tribe, called on to exploit and colonize matter for its own ends." That our shared self-image might be wrong is troubling enough. That "we have come to do so much damage without even noticing it and have ended up understanding so little about our own continuity with what we were destroying" (p. 143) makes it that much more so.[9]

The problem I am addressing here is not unrelated. In part, the problem is one of language. Despite the fact that much of what moves and nourishes people lies outside the self, we have persisted in assuming that it is a more internal matter. And despite our profound vulnerability and fragility, we have persisted in speaking of our independence and mastery, our power to shape the world as we wish. Even the most cursory glance at the psychology or self-help section of the local bookstore indicates that

---

9. See also Marilyn Robinson's important book *Absence of Mind: The Dispelling of Inwardness from the Modern Myth of the Self* (2010). As is clear from the title of the book, Robinson's main focus in this book is less "otherness" than "inwardness," or reflective interiority. But she, like Midgley, is eager to expose the mythical nature of those "parascientific," ego-centric perspectives on human nature that have led to the "disheartened cultural landscape" (p. 35) we have come to inhabit. As Robinson notes, "There is an odd, undeniable power in this defining of humankind by the exclusion of the things that in fact distinguish us as a species" (p. 37). But "there is no reason to assume our species resembles in any essential way the ancient primates whose genes we carry. It is a strategy of parascientific argument to strip away culture-making, as if it were a ruse and a concealment within which lurked the imagined primitive who is for them our true nature" (p. 134). The result is diminishment of both our inwardness and our essential connection to those features of otherness without which we would not, and could not, be human.

we are inundated with the language of "self." There is even a magazine called *Self*, and the font size of this magical word on its cover is very large indeed. (Whether there could ever be a magazine called *Other* remains open to question.) But the problem is not only one of language; it is one of attention and understanding. Not only do we *say* we are interested in the self, but the self is often what people look toward first when trying to figure out what's going on in their lives—why, for instance, they are as lonely and unhappy as they are. The word I used earlier to describe this situation, you will recall, is *mistake*. And what I mean by this is that it is a misdirection of attention and understanding, indeed a *misconstrual* of what matters most. By underscoring the priority of the Other in this first and most basic sense, I hope to redirect some of this attention and understanding and to re-construe what matters most. The task is a difficult one. The modern condition, through both its glorification of self and its deep-seated suspicion of goods beyond the self, seems to have left many people not only empty but empty-handed, devoid of a sense of direction and purpose—devoid, in fact, of the sense that meaningful priorities can even be established.[10] This bespeaks the urgency of meeting the task head-on.

THERE IS ANOTHER sense in which I address the priority of the Other in this book as well. Here I am referring to the *ethical* dimension—the responsibility, care, and love that may be called forth by the Other. The work of the philosopher Emmanuel Levinas looms especially large in this context.[11] According to Levinas, this calling-forth is primary, fundamental: the Other—the *face* of the Other—captivates and captures me, holds me hostage. This idea will serve as a vital site for thinking the priority of the Other in the pages to follow. I will not be valorizing it, however, for the fact of the matter is that much of our moral and ethical life is compromised and troubled. Hostage though I may be to the face of the Other, I can and do inflict serious damage too, and it is imperative, I believe, to

---

10. See especially Cushman's (1990) comments on the "emptiness" of the self. See also Cushman (1995); Goodman, Dueck, and Langdal (2010); Richardson, Fowers, and Guignon (1999); and Taylor (1989).

11. Levinas's oeuvre is large, and much of the work in it is likely to be rough going for the philosophically uninitiated. Bearing this in mind, *Ethics and Infinity* (1985) may be a good point of entry, as may some of the chapters found in *Alterity and Transcendence* (1999a). Those interested in exploring in greater detail the philosophical foundations of Levinas's work can also turn to *Totality and Infinity* (1969), often considered his "classic" text, as well as *Otherwise Than Being or Beyond Essence* (1998).

come to terms with this tragic fact. Our ethical energies run deep, to be sure—deeper, perhaps, than is sometimes assumed; we possess extraordinary "reserves" of responsiveness and care. But these reserves frequently remain untapped and unrealized. In addition, they are often buried under the weight of our aggressiveness and destructiveness.[12]

In reading Levinas, I also find myself asking about the scope of the ethical relation. What exactly does it mean to live for the Other? Is the poet or painter—or, for that matter, the psychologist or philosopher—living out the ethical relation? At Jesuit colleges such as my own, there is a good deal of attention given to the notion of service, especially to the poor and marginalized. Whatever their faith, students are educated to be "men and women for and with others" and are urged to become active agents of social justice. As a result, many of them work in soup kitchens or inner-city schools, or travel to Mexico or Kenya to be in solidarity with the poor, or look to the broader, structural bases of inequality and violence, in the hope that they might help to lessen some of society's most pervasive social ills. Some of them even elect to do these sorts of things for their entire life. It's quite wonderful. At the same time, I sometimes encounter students who feel that unless they are "service" people in this explicit justice-oriented way, they are not quite legitimate, not quite good enough. And what I tell them is that this focus on social justice, important though it surely is, doesn't exhaust the deep meaning of service to the Other. The idea of the greater good does not refer only to the social whole. Nor does it refer only to people. It refers instead to the whole of reality. And whatever brings us closer to this whole, in all of its profound otherness, cannot help but serve the wider world. Here, then, I offer a second working principle: *the Other, both human and non-human, is the primary source of our ethical energies, and being-for-the-Other is a key feature of our own Self-realization.*

Thus far, then, I have spoken of the Other in two distinct ways: first, as a source of meaning, value, and existential nourishment, and second, as a source of ethical energy and commitment—for simplicity's sake, *aesthetics* and *ethics*. What I also want to suggest, following Weil and Murdoch

---

12. After I had completed an initial draft of this book, I came across Jacob Needleman's interesting and provocative *Why Can't We Be Good?* (2007), which does well to underscore the challenge at hand. It does less well, in my view, in responding to the challenge. Moreover, it seems ultimately to affirm the priority of the self rather than the Other. Qualifications aside, Needleman's book is an honest, heartfelt exploration of both our vast potential for goodness and our limits in realizing it.

especially, is that there is a connection between the two, or at least a possible one.[13] "In enjoying great art," for instance, Murdoch (1993) writes, "we experience a clarification and concentration and perfection of our own consciousness.... [Art] inspires because it is separate, it is for nothing, it is for itself" (p. 8). In this sense, it "teaches us how real things can be looked at and loved without being seized and used, without being appropriated into the greedy organism of the self" (1970, p. 65). Murdoch goes on to speak of *eros* in this context, which she describes as "the continual operation of spiritual energy, desire, intellect, love, as it moves among and responds to particular objects of attention, the force of magnetism and attraction which joins us to the world, making it a better or worse [one]" (1993, p. 496).[14] Bearing this idea in mind, alongside aesthetics and ethics I want to speak also of an *erotics*. This is because eros, as we have just considered it, not only includes and further embodies both the aesthetic and the ethical but moves beyond them, referring not only to my being moved *by* the other or my responsibility *for* the Other but to my passion and love, to the desiring energy that is both called forth from the world and binds us to it.[15]

Plato comes to mind here, as does Freud. In the case of the former, I am thinking especially of *Phaedrus* (1995), his wonderful meditation on beauty and love. In the case of the latter, I am thinking of *Civilization and*

---

13. For related comments, see Elaine Scarry's *On Beauty and Being Just* (1999), which also draws on Weil's and Murdoch's ideas regarding the connection between the aesthetic and ethical realms.

14. Wendy Farley's *Eros for the Other* (1996) pursues a related line of thinking and has served as a valuable point of reference during the course of my musings about eros, the idea of the Other, and the connection between the two. Farley also makes significant contact in her book with the idea of attention, recognizing the importance of discrete practices in which "the self steps back and focuses on some subject matter other than itself" (p. 191). As Farley notes in this context, rightly in my view, such refocusing of attention entails a certain measure of "self-effacement." But this self-effacement, rather than referring to a wholesale absenting or "purging," refers instead to a kind of quieting, a being-present, such that the Other can have its say.

15. For Farley too, the Other is not to be restricted to the human. Focusing mainly on the ethical, she insists upon the need "to articulate the claims imposed by ethical existence in such a way that all reality is understood to be included. It is not only other persons that are real, beautiful, and vulnerable to wrongful destruction or exploitation. It is the mark of all reality to be beautiful and vulnerable. This is true of persons, of other creatures, of ecosystems, of streams, oceans, deserts—realities that are not particular creatures and yet are real and can be wrongfully harmed" (1996, p. 11). Here, as elsewhere, Farley's thinking is incisive and important. See also my friend Robert (Bob) Cording's book of poems, *What Binds Us To This World* (1991). It's a great read and touches on many of the concerns addressed throughout this book.

Its Discontents (1962 [1930]), when Freud considers the battle between Eros and Thanatos, love and death, the two "giants," vying for dominion. In terms of more recent work, I also think of what Jean-Luc Marion (2007) has had to say about "the erotic phenomenon"—especially about the idea that we are lovers *first* (*ego amans*)—and his more general aim of moving beyond the constituting, conceptualizing, and constructing "I." It is very difficult to think this way—for psychology, in particular. In fact, truly thinking Otherwise, in the way that Marion and others have tried to do, would, on some level, mean the *end* of psychology, as we know it. One important question, therefore, is whether we might know it differently. More on this later.

NOW THAT I have offered some introductory words about the task of *thinking* the priority of the Other, I want to speak briefly to the task of *living* the priority of the Other. As I have already suggested, doing so is much easier said than done. Thanatos, Freudian-style, is one reason. What Iris Murdoch (1970) refers to as the "fat relentless ego" is surely another. So too is the fact that it has been fed, all too abundantly, by the ego-centric and at times positively narcissistic nature of much of contemporary life. But there is also what might simply be termed "ordinary oblivion," the condition of our being caught up, mindlessly, in the frantic movement of our lives. The result is twofold: our existential undernourishment (or even *mal*nourishment) and our ethical impoverishment, our incapacity to summon the ethical energies that might otherwise be called forth. Instead of an erotic relation to the world, there can be a sterile and alienated one.

How, then, shall we live? More specifically, what can be done to tip the balance from Thanatos to Eros and thereby live the priority of the Other? A short while ago, we noted that there is a connection between being attentively or devotionally present to the Other and becoming "morally better."[16] This connection is by no means necessary, however; one can be highly attentive to this or that object and still behave quite badly. Hitler

---

16. Here, I refer again especially to the work of Simone Weil and Iris Murdoch, both of whom are interested in drawing the connection between attending to the Other and the nature of moral life. For Weil, see especially *Waiting for God* (1973 [1951]) and *Gravity and Grace* (1997 [1952]). For Murdoch, see *The Sovereignty of Good* (1970), *Metaphysics as a Guide to Morals* (1993), and *Existentialists and Mystics: Writings on Philosophy and Literature* (1998). See also Antonaccio (2000) and Antonaccio and Schweiker (1996) for helpful treatments of Murdoch's work, particularly as it bears upon the nature of moral life.

was apparently very attentive to works of art, and the pedophile priest may be strenuously devoted to God (though one could argue that neither of their respective orientations to the Other could possibly be "full"). It should also be noted that the extent to which we may become morally better is a function of the specific objects at hand, that some of these objects may be quite bad, and that our moral life may in turn contract rather than expand, leading more in the direction of evil than of good. Is there a way to gauge the value of these objects? Are there measures one can take to ensure that the Other in question is *worthy* of our attention or devotion? One would think so. But history suggests that this task is difficult, indeed. These difficulties aside for the time being, I maintain that being attentively or devotionally present to the (worthy) Other, in the way that has been described thus far, does in fact up the chances of behaving—and living—well.

Particularly important in this context are discrete *practices*, regimens of attention, oriented either toward one's own internal processes (as, for instance, in mindfulness and other meditative practices) or toward objects outside the self.[17] Also important, in turn, are those devotional *projects* that in their very sustainability can serve to direct and strengthen our ethical energies. For many, of course, God is an especially notable "object" of attention and devotion alike and serves well in this capacity. But there are countless other objects as well, and the nature, quality, and intensity of our relation to them bear significantly upon how we lead our lives.

The Plan of the Book

Chapter One charts the movement from self to Other largely through Martin Buber's (1970) consideration of the "I–Thou" relation, focusing especially on the idea of attention. Buber himself rarely refers to attention, but it is clear, on the basis of what he does say, that how we attend to the

---

17. Meditative practices are frequently portrayed as oriented purely inward, and the language used to describe them frequently reflects this perspective. My own view is that even as these practices focus inward, they involve a kind of "decoupling," such that one can attend to one's own internal processes *as other*. In doing so, moreover, one is simultaneously working toward letting more *world* in, less occluded by one's own distractions, projections, and meanderings. In this respect, while my own focus in this book marks an important difference in perspective, much of what I discuss in the pages to follow is quite compatible with the fundamental principles from which such practices derive.

world is of the utmost significance in determining what we are able to draw from it. His primary concern in addressing the I–Thou relation is the relationship—or, as he puts it, the *dialogue*—between people. But the Thou need not be a person at all. I can, and often do, treat a tree as a mere thing, an "It," part of all the inert stuff I navigate through as I go about my business. "But it can also happen," Buber (1970) writes, "if will and grace are joined, that as I contemplate the tree I am drawn into a relation, and the tree ceases to be an It. The power of exclusiveness has seized me" (p. 58). There has been a shift of attention, and what had heretofore been relegated to the world of mere things has come alive. What we see in this simple example is not only that the priority of the Other can be encountered in both the human and the non-human world, but that much of the world is capable of being enlivened, even *enchanted*, through the attention we give it. I say "much" of the world here rather than all of it mainly for the sake of realism. There are some who would probably want to include it all. It could, for instance, be argued that virtually any object or pursuit can be an occasion for the discovery of meaning or the taking in of existential nourishment, no matter how routine or mundane it may be; it all depends on one's "attitude." There is something very optimistic about this perspective: the world, it's sometimes said, is what you make it. But the fact is, the specific object of one's attention or devotion *matters*. This qualification notwithstanding, much of the world can be rendered decidedly more enchantingly Thou-like than we often take it to be, and it is important to know how this can happen.

In addition to the spheres of others and of things, there is that sphere of otherness tied to what had earlier been referred to as "the mystery of being," especially, but by no means exclusively, as it emerges in spiritual and religious life. Along these lines, Buber (1965) speaks of our "threefold living relation" and maintains that "[we] can bring [our] nature and situation to full reality...if all [our] living relations become essential." Moreover, we "can let elements of [our] nature and situation remain in unreality by letting only single living relations become essential, while considering and treating the others as inessential" (p. 178). We can become thoroughly committed to others, for instance, without making contact with the mystery of being. Or we can become strenuously devoted to religion without living it "on the ground," for and with others. Buber's main point, in any case, is that the threefold living relation about which he speaks is ingredient, as I put it earlier, both to human flourishing and to full human personhood.

Chapter Two, "Oblivion and Attention," explores the fact that we often fall well short of this fully formed mode of being. It begins by addressing a decidedly tragic feature of the human condition: even though it is well within our capacity as humans to be attentively present to both the human and the non-human world, and even though such attentiveness generally yields a desirable measure of meaning, fulfillment, and care, we have a marked tendency to short-circuit this very attentiveness, even an "inherent proneness to alienation" (Dupré, 1976, p. 42). Also tragic is the fact that, oftentimes, it takes calamity or catastrophe to awaken us from the inattentive slumber we live. Witnessing the imminent death of a loved one, for instance, we may be drawn to see her and to care for her anew. In the aftermath of a disaster, we see not only the devastation it has wrought but the perishable beauty of human life. Our own oblivious "caughtupness" is interrupted, and in its place is an opening, and an openness, to the Other.[18] Real priorities become clearer; vows may even be made to keep hold of these priorities and to live them, *before* the next catastrophe comes along. These vows are often short-lived. It is as if there is a force that intervenes, drawing us backward, inward, returning us, once again, to just that state of ego-centric oblivion we had sworn to transcend. Indeed, as I suggest in Chapter Two, there is a distinct sense in which both centripetal and centrifugal forces are at work in the human condition: we are pulled both inward, by the ego and its sundry needs and wishes, and outward, by the Other. There is no getting around this play of forces. But again, there may be a way of tipping the balance. My hope is that the pages to follow will give us some clues about how this might happen.

Chapter Three, "For the Other," addresses more explicitly the ethical dimension of the priority of the Other, focusing on the qualities of care, responsiveness, and responsibility. The work of Buber and, especially, Levinas is focal in this chapter. As noted earlier, for Levinas, the human face is the living embodiment of the priority of the Other. Indeed, the face is not only "straightaway ethical" (Levinas, 1985, p. 85), directly revealing

---

18. Becker's *The Denial of Death* (1973) is relevant in this context as well. Following his line of thinking, it might be said that the "repression of death" is lifted in such circumstances, if only temporarily. For Becker, fear is at the root of this repression. As stated above, however, I tend to see it more as a kind of oblivion or forgetfulness, rooted in our being inattentively caught up in the movement of our lives. This difference notwithstanding, Becker's work is a must-read for thinking through these issues, along with numerous others.

its meaning and its compelling power to call forth our own sense of responsibility, it is the very "locus of the word of God," sacred in its presence and commanding in its gaze, providing a kind of "testimony" that is unassailable (Levinas, 1999a). In this respect, the face, for Levinas, is the priority among priorities; it comes before any and all other claims that might be made upon us—but only, I would add, if we are attentive enough to be witnesses to the testimony provided. I have already confessed to being unsure of how far to go with Levinas's perspective. There are other Others than our fellow human beings and other claims made upon us. But there is no overestimating Levinas's importance for conceptualizing the priority of the Other, and working through his ideas will do much to advance the cause at hand.

Chapter Four moves our exploration of the Other beyond the human and draws heavily on the work of Simone Weil and Iris Murdoch. It is in this chapter that I address in still greater depth and detail the idea of attention and the concrete ways in which it might be mobilized, in the service of strengthening and deepening moral life. For Weil, there is no question but that God was the primary object of her attention and devotion. For Murdoch, it was the beauty of nature and, especially, art. One might find it curious that Murdoch, who remained decidedly skeptical about theological claims, was as inspired as she was by Weil, a believer through and through. But again, it may be that religious impulses, of a sort, exist even among those who would reject any and all creedal or dogmatic religious claims. Such impulses, Murdoch insists, issue from the very fabric of experience, permeated as it is with intimations of goodness and perfection. Marion (2008), in a similar vein, speaks of the "saturated phenomenon," the kind of phenomenon that "exceeds the categories and principles of understanding" (p. 34) and thereby *arrests* us, stops us in our well-laid tracks. "Far from being able to constitute this phenomenon," Marion writes, "the *I* experiences itself as constituted by it." This is "because it no longer has at its disposal any dominant point of view over the intuition that overwhelms it" (p. 44). Saturated phenomena are thus vehicles of what Murdoch (1970) terms *unselfing*—and *reselfing*—par excellence. The good news is that they are actually quite readily available to us in the course of everyday being and need not be "exceptional" in quality. Indeed, according to Marion, *"the majority of phenomena, if not all* can undergo saturation" (2008, p. 126). I have already expressed some uncertainty about this idea, my own perspective being that the specific objects of one's attention or devotion matter. But Marion's general point still stands: we do not need exceptional phenomena for the Other to come into being, for there is vast potential within the fabric of ordinary experience for such saturation to emerge.

It is a short step from this set of issues to the question of transcendence, the focus of Chapter Five. The magnetic pull of the Other—in a work of art, for instance—calls forth our own spiritual movement, our own propulsion forward and upward, in the direction of a kind of wide-openness in which the world seems to burst and bloom. Of some of the work by Bach, Haydn, Mozart, and Beethoven, George Steiner (1989) has written, there are "felt intimations of open horizons, of well-springs of recuperation and self-surpassing for a constricted and worn humanity" (p. 63). These kinds of works, he believes, bring us "closer to the border-crossing into 'otherness,' into the *terra incognita* of a humanity beyond itself than, perhaps, any experience else. Song leads us home to where we have not yet been" (p. 75). For Steiner, this "home" cannot be wholly earthly; its very beyond-ness signals the existence of something else, something *more*. William James, who plays a central role in Chapter Five, says something similar in *The Varieties of Religious Experience* (1982 [1902]) when considering the distinct possibility that religious experience could bring human beings into contact with a "higher part" of themselves, perhaps even "an altogether other dimension of existence from the sensible and merely 'understandable' world" (p. 515). For both Steiner and James, this dimension, whether encountered through aesthetic experience or religious experience, bespeaks the existence of a higher, transcendent realm, one that is somehow both *continuous with* and *other than* the ordinary one we inhabit. James is more cautious about positing this realm than Steiner. It seems harder for him to completely break away from the "sensible" world; transcendence thus remains a possibility—a good possibility, in fact, but only that. But what is it we mean when we speak of the word "transcendence"? Chapter Five seeks to explore this very question.

Chapter Six, "Living Ex-centrically," looks toward our prospects for living our lives in such a way that the priority of the Other is made real. I have already acknowledged that there are a great many forces, internal as well as external, that conspire to make living in this way extraordinarily difficult. I will not try to solve this "problem" in this book. This is because what we are considering here, far from being a problem to be solved, is an enduring feature of the human condition, ever in need of our concern and care. Moreover, certain aspects of contemporary life have intensified this feature: put together the "culture of narcissism" with the age of technologically based distraction and *in*attention, and you've got a near-unbeatable combination.[19] *Near.* I will put the matter in the simplest of terms: We have the capacity to live ex-centrically, such that we recognize and uphold the priority of the Other. We see this with radiant clarity when our loved ones fall ill, when catastrophes consume the lives of the innocent, or when a book or piece of music or scene in nature takes our breath away and reminds us what is most real. But we often stop short of living in this way. One might call it a failure of *memory*. Can we live differently? My foremost aim, in the end, is simply to take this question seriously, by resisting pat solutions and promises of redemption, by looking candidly at our own contradictions, and by imagining small ways of opening ourselves to what is *there* in the world.

I close the book with a Coda, which has as its primary aim the fashioning of a new language for psychology and for thinking about human experience more generally. Why this new language? As indicated at the outset of this Introduction, the language currently employed tends to be ego-centric in orientation, and the fact is, this language is frequently belied by experience. One task of an Other-oriented psychology is thus to translate some of this language into different terms, ones more fitting, more adequate to the lives we actually live. But there are other tasks too. Foremost among these, for the discipline of psychology especially, is the task of devising ways of better preserving the otherness of other people. So much of what gets done in psychology hides from view the person before us, the flesh-and-blood being who precedes all of our scales and tests, categories and constructs. These can be useful, to be sure; but they can also obscure and distort the very reality they were designed to disclose. Preserving the otherness of other people is therefore a matter not only of *respect* but of *truth*. A further, related task, for psychology and beyond, is to explore in greater depth precisely those regions of otherness—in art and religion, most notably—that are, arguably, beyond the

---

19. See especially Christopher Lasch's seminal book, *The Culture of Narcissism: American Life in an Age of Diminishing Expectations* (1991). See also Twenge and Campbell (2009), for whom this sort of culturally induced narcissism has reached "epidemic" proportions.

purview of our "comprehension," our conceptual grasp. This too, I suggest, will require a new language, one that is more poetic in nature, more prepared to speak what cannot ever fully be spoken. The challenges at hand are large and daunting. My hope is that once we rise to them we will have in hand a surer sense of what it might mean to both think and live the priority of the Other.

I

From Self to Other

Disruption

The semester had recently ended, I had just completed a lengthy term as an administrator, and I was heading into Cambridge to do some bicycling along the Charles. The stereo was on and I felt good, ready for a change. But concerns of one sort or another were still racing through my mind. "I didn't do this." "I ought to have done that." "Do I really have the time to bike around in the sunshine today?" " Do I have the *right*?" "Let it go," I said to myself. "Get over it." "*Stop.*" But how? I could try to put up a wall and bar all these nagging thoughts from entry. As a general rule, though, this doesn't work very well. I could also go into more of an "observer" mode, mindfully witnessing the parade without getting caught up in the frenzy. This can be helpful, and if memory serves me well, I did try to get closer to this more open, welcoming frame of mind. But the path of my release came from elsewhere. At one point, the music I was listening to took hold of me. With it, the day appeared, and I literally felt my concerns recede, move backward, the way water moves back out to sea after it hits the shoreline. I was *disrupted*, and while this disruption was partly a matter of my own doing, of my getting myself to a place where I could let reality *in*, it was reality itself—the music, the day, the *world,* in all of its wondrous otherness—that was the source. That's really what allowed me to "let it go."

There are other, quite different forms of disruption as well. My mother is a 90-year-old woman with dementia, chronic obstructive pulmonary disease, and some other maladies who lives in a nursing home close by. It wasn't an easy decision to have her move there, but it was a necessary one, particularly given her medical problems. Her short-term memory is pretty much shot, and she has only the most minimal sense of time. So, days can go by—days *have* gone by—when I don't see her, and that's just fine; out of sight, out of mind. She also forgets that I've seen her when I have, so it's not as if I go there to stock and restock her memory. Why *do* I see her, if not every day, then at least a few times a week? I have no interest whatsoever in making myself out to be some sort of caregiver-hero. There are times when I think about going over to her place and I don't do it: Should I go to see Mom? Or should I take a nap? Or go outside and have a margarita? She doesn't always win! But she generally does. Why?

There are multiple reasons, some quite mundane. I go to see her because that's what you're supposed to do, or so she knows what a good son I am, or to assuage some of my own guilt. But I also go to see her for *her*—because she is alone and in need and my visit brings her one of her few moments of pleasure in life. It's not easy. I often dread going up in the elevator to her floor; there is always something disturbing or depressing going on. Leaving is no better: I go marching off to work or dinner while she sits in a circle with fading, withered, like-minded others, watching some awful TV show or tapping a balloon into the air during the "recreation" period. But in the middle is...*her*, her simple presence, disrupting me, drawing me forward, outward. She is sitting in a wheelchair, slouched, eyes closed. I walk over and tap her lightly on her shoulder or fiddle playfully with her hair. Her eyes crawl open, she turns her head toward me, and she smiles a faint but radiant smile. I so want her to feel whatever joy she can.

Just as the music had been the primary source of my letting go of those anxious concerns, my mother—in *her* wondrous otherness—is the primary source of my care, my desire to be there, with her and for her. In a very real sense, she is, at that moment, the source of my very being, now expanded and extended, beyond its former borders. She is also the source of some of my *own* joy, and her existence, in its very infirmity, has brought a measure of depth and meaning to my life that I could not have otherwise attained. Why should it be? I also want to know why, more generally, it frequently seems to take *severe* disruptions—dreadful diseases and myriad other calamities and catastrophes—to awaken us to what is *there*, in the world. I will have much more to say about this in the chapter to follow. For now, I want to focus more on the idea of the Other, and why "thinking Otherwise" can serve as a useful corrective to prevailing ways of thinking about the human condition, in psychology and beyond.

To Be Moved

In the Introduction, I proposed that the primary source of meaning, value, and existential nourishment in life lies not in the self but in the Other. The idea seems simple enough. The self, we can say, ordinarily occupies a certain "place" in the world. This place can be at the dinner table, or at one's job, or in the family room; one is eating or carrying out a task or watching a movie. As we have just seen, however, at times we find ourselves disrupted and in turn *dis*-placed from these very places, transported elsewhere. Someone or something has taken hold of us, such that we have been *moved*. For better or worse, we cannot move ourselves; we can only be moved by what is *other* than ourselves. The Other thus has priority.

But what is it that we mean when we speak of being moved? And in what kinds of contexts does it occur? To be moved, I suggest, means to be affected by something in such a way that there is released in us a strong element of sympathetic feeling. We are held spellbound; we are captured and enraptured. At the same time, we are in motion; we are transported elsewhere. How can this be? To be moved is also to find oneself rendered vulnerable, affected-by, such that something is "released" in us, something that calls forth a deeper region of being, to which we belong. Jean-Luc Marion's (2000a, 2008) notion of the saturated phenomenon, mentioned in the Introduction, is one significant way of framing the experience of being moved. In contrast to those phenomena that are more or less "containable" within thought, or that may be traced to a discrete intention, saturated phenomena bespeak "an excess of intuition, and thus of givenness, over the intention, the concept, and the aim" (p. 33). Regarding the dimension of vulnerability, Marion goes on to note that in the face of such phenomena, "The *I* loses its anteriority and finds itself, so to speak, deprived of the duties of constitution, and is thus constituted: it becomes a *me* rather than an *I*" (p. 44).[1] It is thus rendered *secondary*.

To be moved is to be overwhelmed by the Other, in vulnerability, and thereby to be brought into its fold. Consider in this context a little story Martin Buber (1965) tells about one particularly special horse:

> When I was eleven years of age, spending the summer at my grandparents' estate, I used, as often as I could do it unobserved, to steal

---

[1]. For a further, detailed treatment of the notion of "excess," along with rich examples of saturated phenomena, see also Marion (2002b).

into the stable and gently stroke the neck of my darling, a broad dapple-grey horse. It was not a casual delight but a great, certainly friendly, but also deeply stirring happening. If I am to explain it now, beginning from the still very fresh memory of my hand, I must say that what I experienced in touch with the animal was the Other, the immense otherness of the Other, which, however, did not remain strange like the otherness of the ox or the ram, but rather let me draw near and touch it. When I stroked the mighty mane, sometimes marvellously smooth-combed, at other times just as astonishingly wild, and felt the life beneath my hand, it was as though the element of vitality itself bordered on my skin, something that was not I, was certainly not akin to me, palpably the other, not just another, really the Other itself; and yet it let me approach, confided itself to me, placed itself elementally in the relation of *Thou* and *Thou* with me. The horse, even when I had not begun pouring oats for him into the manger, very gently raised his massive head, ears flicking, then snorted quietly, as a conspirator gives a signal meant to be recognizable only by his fellow-conspirator; and I was approved. But once—I do not know what came over the child, at any rate it was childlike enough—it struck me about the stroking, what fun it gave me, and suddenly I became conscious of my hand. The game went on as before, but something had changed, it was no longer the same thing. And the next day, after giving him a rich feed, when I stroked my friend's head he did not raise his head. A few years later, when I thought back to the incident, I no longer supposed that the animal had noticed my defection. But at the time I considered myself judged. (pp. 22–23)

There is much to unpack in this wonderful, deceptively simple passage. This horse, unlike the ox or ram, whose otherness remained "strange," was for Buber the *Other*, whose otherness allowed him "to draw near and touch it." Buber also speaks of the "element of vitality" he felt when he stroked the horse, and the great excitement of encountering "something that was not I," indeed, "not akin to me," and yet, at the very same time, "let me approach" and "confided itself" to him. The very combination of the creature's radical *difference* from him and its willingness to allow him *near* this difference and thereby grow familiar with it had been nothing short of electrifying: the Other *existed*, and it was possible to move closer to it. There is a remarkable sense of affirmation as well. The horse is a "conspirator" who gives the little boy "signals" and, through him, "approval." A beautiful horse that confides and conspires and affirms—quite a horse! But that is not all. In some mysterious way, the horse also seemed able to *withdraw*, to abandon its status as the Other. Rather than truly being in relation with the horse, the little boy had begun to have "fun," the horse in turn becoming a plaything, an object, to be assimilated to his designs. In that very moment, the boy had also become conscious of his hand. The magnetic pull of the Other was suddenly suspended, broken; there was a movement backward, toward the ego, the constituting *I*, with its hands and its wishes.

Things were "no longer the same" afterward, or so it had seemed. As Buber recalls it, his own "defection" had led to the withdrawal of the Other: in place of a *Thou* was...a horse—and a not especially happy one at that. Whether the animal had truly noticed his defection was unclear. The implication is an interesting one. Perhaps, in the face of his own guilt for having turned his friend into a mere thing, an It, he had projected an element of displeasure and disappointment. Whatever the horse itself might have done, Buber had thus for a time felt himself "judged." There is of course a mythical quality to the story: The Beautiful Horse Who Stopped Raising His Head (Because of the Boy Who Stopped Truly Relating to It). And, again, the story—part of it, at any rate—might not even be true. For all (the adult) Buber knows, the horse hadn't noticed a blessed thing. But the point still stands: the quality of our attention to the Other, including horses, affects the quality of the relationship in which one is engaged and, in turn, the satisfaction one can derive from it.

Moving encounters with horses aside, there are many other kinds of events and experiences that bring us face to face with the priority of the Other. As Mihaly Csikszentmihalyi (1990) has suggested in his exploration of the "flow" experience, numerous activities, from dancing to rock-climbing, can serve this function. Such activities present opportunities for what Diane Ackerman (1999) calls "deep play," wherein "one becomes fascinated by an 'other,' in whose presence one feels exaltation."[2] "The other," she notes, "can be a person or a god, but it can just as easily be

---

2. Christopher Bollas (1992) also makes reference to the idea of play but speaks instead of "being played upon" *by the object*, "transformed by the particularity specific to [it]" (p. 31). Bollas also speaks of the special power of those objects that are unbidden: "we are played upon by the inspiring arrival of the unselected, which often yields a very special type of pleasure—that of surprise" (p. 37). Awkward though this sort of language may sound, it is, perhaps, better suited to what actually transpires in our relation to the world.

a war, a mountain, or a bicycle. The relationship is no less devotional and obsessive" (p. 87). As Ackerman notes, "some activities are more conducive to deep play than others, but what matters is the mood, not the activity. One can hunt mushrooms with an enthusiasm bordering on mania, find bliss in building a wall of perfectly balanced fieldstone, lose the world while performing complex surgery.... On the other hand," she continues, "one can turn bronco riding into drudgery. One can create mildly. One can live at a low flame. Most people do. We're afraid to look foolish, or feel too extravagantly, or make a mistake, or risk unnecessary pain" (p. 196).[3]

In these last few pages, we have moved from the spirited connection between a boy and a horse all the way to the mania of mushroom hunting. On the face of it, there is little in common between these phenomena; at the level of concrete experience, they are in fact utterly disparate. In each, however, there has been a process of displacement, in which one is taken out of oneself, drawn forward by the magnetic pull of the Other. What is the significance of this curious correlation?

Relationality

As Buber writes in *I and Thou* (1970), "In the beginning is the relation" (p. 69). As such, "We may suppose that relations and concepts, as well as the notions of persons and things, have gradually crystallized out of notions of relational processes and states" (p. 70). Buber even offers an account of how the self comes into being through these relational processes and states:

> Man becomes an I through a You. What confronts us comes and vanishes, relational events take shape and scatter, and through these changes crystallizes, more and more each time, the consciousness of the constant partner, the I-consciousness. To be sure, for a long time it appears only woven into the relation to a You, discernible as that which reaches for but is not a You; but it comes closer and closer to the bursting point until one day the bonds are broken and

---

[3]. I have already expressed some uncertainty about the notion that virtually anything—any object or activity—can move us in the way Ackerman suggests. The issue is a difficult one. On the one hand, Ackerman notes, rightly in my view, that "some activities are more conducive to deep play than others." On the other, "what matters is the mood, not that activity." I return to this issue later. For now, let's call it a draw. Both clearly matter, and in so mattering they underscore exactly that aspect of relationality which Buber seeks to explore.

the I confronts its detached self for a moment like a You—and then it takes possession of itself and henceforth enters into relations in full consciousness. (p. 80)[4]

Whether this process happens "one day" is surely open to question; there is a mythical dimension to Buber's account here too that renders it too neat, too pat. But the main idea—that the relation to what is other occurs *prior* to the emergence of the *I*—is an important one.[5]

More important for present purposes is the notion that this original state of relationality remains the primary source of meaning and significance. "Spirit," Buber (1970) insists,

is not in the I but between I and You. It is not like the blood that circulates in you but like the air in which you breathe. Man lives in the spirit when he is able to respond to his You. He is able to do that when he enters into this relation with his whole being. It is solely by virtue of his power to be related that man is able to live in the spirit. (p. 89)

Oftentimes, Buber goes on to say, this state of affairs goes unrecognized. "That feelings," for instance, "yield no personal life has been recognized by few so far; for they seem to be the home of what is most personal. And once one has learnt, like modern man, to become greatly preoccupied with one's own feelings, even despair over their unreality will not easily open one's eyes; after all, such despair is a feeling and quite interesting" (p. 94). According to Buber, in other words, our own interiority and inwardness lead us astray by convincing us that we ourselves, the feelings that are "in" us, are the source and foundation of our interests, excitements, and passions. But

---

4. In a related vein, Midgley (2010) urges us to recognize the profound state of *dependence* in which we begin our lives. "The Enlightenment message about the need to be adult—to take full responsibility for our own lives—is a sound one. But to exaggerate it into a rejection of all dependence is to lose touch with the human situation altogether. If we try to do that, we lose as adults the vital, realistic sense of our entirely dependent situation that we gained as small children. We then risk ceasing to be properly human at all" (p. 64).

5. This idea is also in keeping with certain strands of classic developmental theory, as exemplified, for instance, by Freud and Piaget. Acknowledging their differences, both consider the kind of "bursting" point—or what I sometimes think of as "fissioning"—that Buber is referring to. Neither, of course, is a theorist of the Other per se. And yet there is ample room, I believe, for translating some of their central concerns into the kind of language being used herein.

this is simply wrong, he insists. Not unlike what Simone Weil (1997 [1952]) told us earlier, the self cannot be its own source of energy and value. Nor can it be its own source of inspiration. Inspired though "I" may be, inspiration itself must come from elsewhere.

It might be interesting to note in this context that the idea of "inspiration" is not unrelated to the process of breathing. One might therefore ask how the kind of inspiration considered here relates to the kind of breathing processes that are frequently the focus of meditation and other such practices. Seen from one angle, these practices remain entirely internal, self-focused. Seen from another angle, however, there is a distinct sense in which one is indeed receiving energy and nourishment from without, from some sphere of otherness beyond the perimeter of the self. So it is that Jon Kabat-Zinn (2005) speaks of "tuning in to...breath sensations...gently, with a lightness of touch, allowing our attention to approach the breath...as if we were coming upon a shy animal sunning itself on a tree stump in a forest clearing—with that kind of gentleness and interest, not so much in stealth as in love" (p. 283). Kabat-Zinn also speaks of "giving yourself over" to these sensations:

> In giving yourself over to breathing, in aiming and sustaining your attention moment by moment, you invite the sense of an observer observing the breath to dissolve into just breathing. The subject (you) and the object (the breath or even "my breath") dissolve into breath*ing*, pure and simple, and into an awareness that needs no "you" to generate it, that already knows breathing as it is unfolding, beyond thinking, underneath thinking, before thinking. (p. 284)

Here too, "The *I* loses its anteriority," as Marion (2008) had put it, and is given over to pure relation.[6]

In *Between Man and Man* (1965), Buber underscores the importance of "the life in which the individual...is essentially related to something other than himself" (p. 166). This is the only path toward the absolute, toward that state of wholeness and integrity which draws us forward: "Human life

---

6. As a discrete practice, such breathing processes involve a measure of purposeful intentionality—of "aiming"—that is somewhat different from the process of being moved. Moreover, strictly speaking, there is no Other; the "object," Kabat-Zinn (2005) acknowledges, remains "my own." These (significant) differences notwithstanding, there is, again, much about practices of this sort that is in keeping with the priority of the Other, for ultimately they are about letting in the world and thereby awakening to it. The relevant literature on these practices is vast and varied, and others know it far better than I do. It is well worth exploring.

touches on absoluteness in virtue of its dialogical character, for in spite of his uniqueness man can never find, when he plunges to the depth of his life, a being that is whole in itself and as such touches on the absolute" (p. 168). According to Buber, the dialogical character of human life bears within it a "threefold living relation": to other people, to the world and things, and, last but not least, "to the mystery of being—which is dimly apparent through all this but infinitely transcends it—which the philosopher calls the Absolute and the believer calls God, and which cannot in fact be eliminated from the situation even by a man who rejects both designations" (p. 177). This last point is an especially important one: the connection about which Buber speaks would seem to be critical, even for the atheist. To put the matter more baldly and boldly, we are spiritual beings, with spiritual impulses, needs, and yearnings, and even if these impulses, needs, and yearnings lead us away from God and religion—as they frequently do—there nevertheless remains a very real sense in which they bespeak a kind of primordial religiosity.[7]

As Buber (1965) goes on to suggest, certain aspects of the threefold relation he has identified have come to be held in profound suspicion. For Kierkegaard and Heidegger, for instance (we can add Sartre as well), the "crowd," the "they," is largely to be left behind; only when one frees oneself from the pressure and, indeed, bondage of the social world, with its countless norms and demands, does there exist the possibility of authenticity and self-realization. "In itself this is true," Buber acknowledges, "that nameless human all and nothing in which we are immersed is in fact like a negative womb from which we have to emerge in order to come into the world as a self. But it is only one side of the truth, and without the other side it becomes untrue." Ultimately, "[t]he genuineness and adequacy of the self cannot stand the test in self-commerce, but only in communication with the whole of otherness" (p. 178). As noted earlier, the

---

[7]. One might ask why I speak of "religiosity" here rather than "spirituality." The reason is that the latter generally connotes the "within" more than the "without" (i.e., the *Other*). Insofar as our spiritual impulses, needs, and yearnings point in the direction of otherness—of some sphere of being and energy that transcends us—they warrant being called "religious." This perspective is largely in keeping with James's conception as articulated in *The Varieties of Religious Experience* (1982 [1902]). For a recent treatment of the seemingly primordial nature of this religiosity, see Keen (2010), who, especially in light of communism's failed attempts to root out religion, argues that "human beings are innately religious animals who demand a spiritual horizon that extends beyond patriotism and the promise of economic happiness" and that, consequently, "[a]nyone who bets that religion will vanish in the near future should be prepared to lose the wager" (p. 157).

burgeoning of dialogical and relational thinking has done well to counteract the more monological perspectives Buber is referring to here.[8] At the same time, even in these movements there can remain a certain mistrust, especially in our relation to the world and to things. The world, many claim, is "socially constructed." Far from having access to reality in itself, therefore, we can only encounter a world fashioned and mediated by our own human designs. Much the same situation obtains in our relation to what Buber refers to as "the mystery of being." In the wake of thinkers such as Marx, Nietzsche, and Freud—perhaps the foremost practitioners of what has been called the "hermeneutics of suspicion" (see Ricoeur, 1970, 1974)—many have come to mistrust notions like the Absolute and God; these, it is frequently held, are merely ideas we have created in order to stem the tide of meaninglessness and to convince ourselves that there is some greater order, some greater purpose.

There is unquestionably some validity to these critiques. There is little doubt that much of what we take to be reality "in itself" is in fact socially constructed, at least in part; if there is anything we have learned throughout the course of the past century, it is that we often mistake culture for nature, thereby transforming what is mutable into ostensibly immovable stuff, static and unchanging. There is also little doubt that people often turn to notions like the Absolute and God for the sake of comfort and consolation. The partial validity of these critiques notwithstanding, what each of them has done in its own way is occlude, and perhaps undermine, the very condition of relatedness that is at the heart of human existence.[9]

If we wish to speak at all about "living relations," some might claim that surely the primary one is to oneself, alone. In the end, I must

---

8. I don't know that Kierkegaard and Heidegger are quite as "solitary" as Buber makes them out to be. Indeed, each of them has served as an important source of inspiration for many thinkers whose primary concern is in fact the relational dimension of being. Buber's main point nevertheless stands. If only as a function of the cloistering constriction the "they" frequently provides, there have been significant attempts to think beyond the primacy of the social and to imagine what a more "authentic" existence might be.

9. There are certainly social constructionists who wish to highlight this relatedness. This is why Kenneth Gergen, one of the foremost proponents of the constructionist worldview (e.g., Gergen, 1992), was able to write a (good and important) book called *Relational Being* (2009) that makes significant reference to Buber and even has a chapter on "approaching the sacred." At the same time, he is less comfortable with the notion of "objects" that are somehow beyond the sphere of the socially constructed. Can one have it both ways? Is the "sacred" socially constructed? Insofar as it always assumes its specific form in a social world, yes. But this very idea of "assuming its form" also suggests that it is, on some level, beyond this world, thus referring to a dimension of otherness that cannot be contained by our constructions.

live with *me*, and I had better do everything in my power to make sure the household is a harmonious one. "This relation, however, unlike the others," Buber (1965) maintains, "cannot be regarded as one that is real as such, since the necessary presupposition of a real duality is lacking. Hence it cannot in reality be raised to the level of an essential living relation" (p. 180). The implication is an interesting one: the very relation some assume to be the realest of all is actually *un*real.

I am not sure Buber is right about this. Even though, materially speaking, there is no living relation to ourselves that compares to that which we can have with beings outside ourselves, there still remains a distinct duality involved, particularly in the context of self-reflection and evaluation.[10] This is likely what Buber (1965) has in mind when he speaks about lyric poetry, which would seem to embody a "completion and transfiguration" in relation to the self of the sort made possible by our living relations with beings outside the self. But lyric poetry, he argues, is about "the tremendous refusal of the soul to be satisfied with self-commerce. Poetry is the soul's announcement that even when it is alone with itself on the narrowest ridge it is thinking not of itself but of the Being which is not itself, and that this Being...is visiting it there, perplexing and blessing it" (p. 180). The main issue, therefore, isn't so much the unreality of our relation to ourselves but its primacy and importance within the fabric of human experience. Even if something like dialogue with oneself is possible, it cannot, by its very nature, provide that element of nourishment and sustenance that may be found in dialogue with the Other.[11]

The bottom line, for Buber (1965), is that it is a mistake to try to determine what human beings "are" apart from their living relations to what lies outside them: "The question of what man is cannot be answered by a consideration of existence or of self-being as such, but only by a consideration of the essential connexion of the human person and his relations with all being" (p. 180). It is also a mistake to try to *understand* human beings apart from their living relations: "Only when we try to understand the human person in his whole situation, in the possibilities of his

---

10. For the classic statement of just this duality, see James's chapter on the consciousness of self in *The Principles of Psychology* (1950 [1890]).

11. In this respect, I sometimes wonder about the internality of many meditative practices. In accordance with what was said earlier about inspiration, there is surely a kind of otherness encountered in such practices. But it is an otherness that remains located essentially within. Can this more internal form of otherness provide the kind of nourishment and sustenance found through engagement with what is outside the self? Perhaps. Following Buber, however, the dynamic at hand would seem to be a quite different one.

relation to all that is not himself, do we understand man" (p. 181). Finally, it is a mistake to *evaluate* the human condition in itself, as if the Other were a mere extension or appendage of one's own separate, essentially solitary existence: "Only the man who realizes in his whole life with his whole being the relations possible to him helps us to know man truly" (p. 199). Put simply, the human person is not merely a "being," but a "being-in-relation." As such, any attempt to subtract the element of relatedness from our picture of the human person will yield an image that is not only incomplete but distorted and deformed.

Buber has unquestionably helped us cast into question the legacy of the monadic and monologic self. Human existence is *dialogic* through and through, he insists, and with this insistence we find before us an entirely different image of human nature and an entirely different conception of what it might mean to live well. Judging from the increasing emphasis on dialogical thinking, in psychology and beyond,[12] Buber's work was very much ahead of its time. In a distinct sense, he sought to "deconstruct" and dismantle the sovereign self, the Individual, fundamentally alone in the world. In the same basic movement of critique, he also sought to underscore the inherently relational nature of human reality and the deep difference between "I–It" and "I–Thou" relations. And yet, he may not have gone quite far enough in his thinking about these matters. That the "dialogic" represents an advance over the "monologic" is clear enough. But it is only a kind of halfway point in the movement from self to Other. Rather than "being" and "self," we have "being-in-relation" and "self-in-relation." So far, so good: the priority of the self, qua ego-centric monad, is being undermined. But undermining the priority of the self is not quite the same as establishing the priority of the Other. We need to go farther.

Toward the Other

Let us return to Simone Weil (1997 [1952]) for a moment. Weil, you will recall, maintained that all sources of meaning and value lie wholly outside the self. It is certainly true that we may find ourselves "in relation" to such sources, and these relationships may be vitally important to us. But what

---

12. For dialogical work in psychology, see especially Hermans (1996) and Hermans and Kempen (1993); see also Sampson (1993). In the background of many such efforts is the work of Mikhail Bakhtin (e.g., 1981, 1986). Also important in this context, though less well known, is the work of Hans Robert Jauss (e.g., 1989).

have priority are the sources themselves. "All men are ready to die for what they love," she proclaims. "They differ only through the level of the thing loved and the concentration or diffusion of their love." And, contrary to popular belief, "[n]o one loves himself." The way she frames this issue is curious and provocative: "Man would like to be an egoist and cannot. This is the most striking characteristic of his wretchedness and the source of his greatness" (p. 54). Self-interested though we may often be, we are, Weil suggests, a perpetual going-beyond. We are disturbed, disrupted and moved, brought out of our in-ness by the otherness of the Other.[13]

Evidence in support of this idea may be found in those who are overly self-centered. The self-centered person, Gabriel Marcel (1950) has written, "remains incapable of responding to calls made upon him by life.... He remains shut up in himself, in the petty circle of his private experience, which forms a kind of hard shell round him that he is incapable of breaking through" (p. 201). According to Marcel, it is therefore "essential to human life not only...to orientate itself towards something other than itself, but also to be inwardly conjoined and adapted—rather as the joints of the skeleton are conjoined and adapted to the other bones—to that reality transcending the individual life which gives the individual life its point and, in a certain sense, its justification" (p. 212).

Weil and Marcel would thus seem to be of a piece in their consideration of the centrality of the Other, the beyond-self, in human life: we are neither self-enclosed nor self-sufficient but require for our very sustenance—indeed, our very *humanity*—the presence of something outside ourselves, something that will in fact draw us out of ourselves. Are they right about this? A good portion of contemporary thought seems to suggest something quite different. What is most important, many believe, is to be true to *oneself*, to one's own ideals and aspirations. The time has passed, the argument might go, for adhering to directives from without. Whether we like it or not, we ourselves are responsible for our lives, and, consequently, we must carry them out in such a way that we embrace this responsibility and develop our own unique capacities and potentialities to the fullest. William James (1950 [1890]) even crafted something of a psychological formula that sought to express this idea. Self-esteem, he

---

13. The term "in-ness" is a bit awkward. In fact, I had initially used the term "inwardness" here. But as Marilyn Robinson (2010) and others have pointed out, true inwardness, seen as a kind of reflective interiority, may be thoroughly in keeping with the otherness being considered herein. Awkward though it may be, in-ness, therefore, serves as a more apt counterpoint.

suggested, is essentially a function of one's actualities divided by one's potentialities—that is, what one actually does in the world set against what one could do or should do. If in fact the two terms led to a fraction close to one, all would basically be well; one would have made good use of one's own capacities and potentialities and therefore feel tolerably good about one's life. If, however, the fraction was much smaller, there could emerge a sense not only of lost opportunities but of shame or even despair.

Tolstoy's novella *The Death of Ivan Ilych* (1960 [1886]) readily comes to mind in this context. Having considered his duty "to be what was considered so by those in authority," having been "attracted to people of high station as a fly is drawn to the light, assimilating their ways and views of life and establishing friendly relations with them" (p. 105), and having "performed his official tasks, made his career, and at the same time amused himself pleasantly and decorously" (p. 106), Ivan Ilych had crafted what appeared to be a good and successful life. He also managed to collect a Good Wife, a Nice House, and many of the other accoutrements of a successful life. As a result, "everything progressed and progressed and approached the ideal he had set himself: even when things were only half completed, they exceeded his expectations" (p. 115). Judging by what happened subsequently, however—he had suffered an injury while doing a bit of household work, and his pain and suffering "began to mar the agreeable, easy, and correct life that had established itself" (p. 120)—he had shot entirely too low: the "ideal" he had set for himself, he eventually realized, was flimsy, superficial, and just plain wrong. The "awful truth" would eventually be faced. Ivan Ilych had mistaken for real that which "was not real at all, but a terrible and huge deception which had hidden both life and death" (p. 152). Rather than basking in the glow of a life well lived, Ilych therefore suffers the deep despair of having sacrificed this very life in the name of cheap and false ideals. In the terms of the aforementioned Jamesian formula, Ilych's actualities had fallen sorely short of his potentialities—of *life's* potentialities—and this very realization, brought on by the face of death, led to his horrible demise.[14]

Tolstoy's story would appear to support the idea that what is most important in life is to be true to oneself, to one's own ideals and aspirations. There is some sense, in fact, in which Tolstoy's brand of existentialism seems not unlike that which is often associated with Kierkegaard,

---

14. Ernest Becker's *The Denial of Death* (1973) is again relevant in this context, and well worth exploring.

Heidegger, and Sartre: rather than listening to the inner truth of the self, Ilych had listened to the demands and directives of others, especially those who were well placed and respected, and it was this social susceptibility that had done him in. Ilych had thus lived not only superficially but *inauthentically*. This idea of authenticity would seem to support the primacy of being true to oneself, of following one's own inner lights.

There is, however, another way of understanding this idea. Charles Taylor (1991) has argued forcefully that the discourse of authenticity and self-fulfillment bears within it a "powerful moral ideal" that goes well beyond the confines of the solitary self. The problem is that this ideal has been debased, with the result that it has lost some of its force. In times past, Taylor tells us, being in touch with realities and sources of inspiration outside the self had been considered integral to the development of full personhood. Eventually, there would emerge a process of "subjectivation," a turning inward, such that the notion of being true to oneself acquired currency: "Being true to myself," Taylor writes, "means being true to my own originality, and that is something only I can articulate and discover. In articulating it, I am also defining myself. I am realizing a potential that is properly my own" (p. 29). But this very project of potentiation and self-realization, he insists, cannot stand completely on its own. Indeed, the ideal of authenticity, shorn of demands issuing from outside the self, cannot help but be self-defeating. Things acquire meaning and significance, Taylor explains, against a background of value, a horizon of intelligibility. However important it may be that my life be *mine*, that I remain true to myself, that I choose my own destiny, I cannot possibly do so in a moral vacuum. Some of my choices will be more meaningful and significant than others; without this, "the very idea of self-choice falls into triviality and hence incoherence" (p. 39). For Taylor, therefore, "To shut out demands emanating beyond the self is precisely to suppress the conditions of significance, and hence to court trivialization" (p. 40). Authenticity, in turn, far from being the "enemy" of such demands, in fact presupposes them.[15]

Let us return for a moment to the story of Ivan Ilych (Tolstoy, 1960 [1886]) with Taylor's important corrective in mind. Just as Ilych's despair over the sorry state of his life reached a fever pitch, a mysterious force

---

15. See also Guignon (2004) for a wide-ranging historical and philosophical exploration of the idea of authenticity, with special attention to the modern "industry" as found in self-help books, television shows, and other such arbiters of self-realization and fulfillment.

came upon him and suddenly freed him from his torment. He "caught sight of the light, and it was revealed to him that though his life had not been what it should have been, this could still be rectified" (p. 155). He suddenly felt sympathy for his wife and son; in Buber's terms, "It" had become "You." He would no longer hurt them or treat them as mere extensions of his own sorry wishes and fantasies. More significant still, however, was Ilych's realization that his life itself had been self-enclosed and shut up, and that his own sources of "inspiration" had been nothing more than the thinnest niceties of bourgeois propriety and taste. Simply put, he had in fact been *wrong* about his life, and it was exactly this realization that paved the way to a moment of redemption in his final hours. "What is the right thing?" Ilych asked shortly before his death. He then "grew still, listening" (p. 155).[16]

Ivan Ilych had fallen prey to a kind of autism, a state of self-enclosure. Things could be related to one another—his title to his job, his job to his wife, his wife to his house, and so on—but the entire structure within which he had "lived" had been *self*-defining, tied exclusively to his own fantastic images of what constituted a good and worthwhile life. Ilych's main problem, then, wasn't so much his failure to be true to himself as his failure to locate something *outside* himself—devotional objects, as I have called them (1997)—that might have served to orient him more meaningfully. Even if Ilych had been able to find such objects, he might still have articulated his own project of self-potentiation via the discourse of authenticity. We may do so as well; it is difficult to avoid its powerful pull. Following Taylor, however, this is only a problem if one's drive for authenticity negates and cuts off those outside sources without which this drive itself would be meaningless and trivial. Put differently, it is only a problem if one's drive for authenticity occludes, or for that matter obliterates, the priority of the Other.

From Taylor's perspective, the aim of living authentically remains a viable one. Within this aim, moreover, there is an inescapable reference to self: my interest is in determining how to make *my life* meaningful and significant. But this says nothing whatsoever about what will serve

---

16. Tolstoy's story is, admittedly, something of an obsession of mine. For clues about the substance of this obsession, see Freeman (1997, 2007, 2010). Most of this work is about memory, narrative, and related issues. But it is also about the nature and sources of ethical and moral life. Indeed, in addition to being (what I regard as) *the* classic work on hindsight, it is also one of the great works on the priority of the Other as it emerges in inverted form.

to make it so. If Taylor is right, only that "which has significance independent of us or our desires" will fit the bill (1991, p. 82); the energy that fuels the very project of authenticity can only derive from without. I might note that Taylor, along with Buber, acknowledges that certain forms of poetry would appear to present an exception to this rule. Given that much of it is clearly marked by the arduous journey inward, toward the interior of the self, it would seem that the movement of meaning takes place essentially from within. But this, Taylor argues, is to confuse the "manner" through which the poet gains access to the world and the specific "matter" that he or she seeks to disclose through the work itself. Ultimately, and again, meaning and significance can only derive from without.

Just in case this seems too tidy a solution to the problem at hand, it should also be noted that the "confusion" to which Taylor refers may be an unavoidable, and even productive, one. Robert Hass (1984), for instance, in a wonderful essay on Rilke, suggests that "within" and "without" are not as far apart as we might imagine. Indeed, "[t]hat voice of Rilke's poems, calling us out of ourselves, or calling us into the deepest places in ourselves, is very near to what people mean by poetry" (p. 230). The priority of the Other does not negate the project of authenticity. Nor does it remove us from the "deepest places" in ourselves. On the contrary: our encounter with the Other—whether in the form of a treasured horse or a poem by Rilke—frequently brings us to dimensions of our own inner life that we may never have known before. For, insofar as we can open ourselves to the Other and draw meaning, value, and nourishment from the encounter, we become enlarged. So it is that I spoke in the opening pages of this book about the emergence of a larger Self, one that knows and feels its kinship with the world. I address this issue in greater detail in the chapter to follow. For now, I simply wish to underscore the idea that embracing the priority of the Other, far from negating or denying our own interiority, is precisely the condition for deepening it, bringing it into fuller being.[17]

---

17. An important qualification is to be made here, one that I will also address in greater detail in the chapter to come. In speaking of enlarging, deepening, and so on, I am assuming that the Other in question is *good* and nourishing. But of course that isn't always the case. Sometimes the Other can be downright demonic, corrupting and undermining whatever depth and humanity we might have. It is perhaps the existence of this "bad Other" that has led some very smart philosophers to question the very place of the Other in our lives.

Devotion, Redux

Our brief excursions into Tolstoy and Taylor appear to serve as a confirmation of the idea that we require, for our humanity and sustenance, the presence of extra-personal "objects" to call us outward. As we have also seen, this process of calling us outward is often, at the same time, one of calling us deeply inward. But it is not "we" who do the calling. Rather, it is the Other. How are we to understand this process?

According to Simone Weil (1997 [1952]), "If we suspend the filling up of the imagination and fix our attention on the relationship of things, a necessity becomes apparent which we cannot help obeying." Obedience, therefore, "is the only pure motive, the only one which does not in the slightest seek a reward for the action" (p. 43). Murdoch (1970), following Weil, also highlights the connection between necessity and obedience. "This is something of which saints speak and which any artist will readily understand. The idea of a patient, loving regard, directed upon a person, a thing, a situation, presents the will not as unimpeded movement but as something very much more like 'obedience' " (p. 39). For both Weil and Murdoch, therefore, we don't so much "will" to be attracted to this or that feature of the world. Rather, we are pulled outward, as if by force. Valuable though this idea is, I am not quite sure how far to go with it. Am I "obedient" to a poem of Rilke's? In the sense of being utterly and completely compelled, even transfixed, the answer is *yes*: the poem *commands* me, *moves* me. For my part, there is nevertheless something too authoritarian-sounding about the idea of obedience for me to fully embrace it. This could just be my own 21st century, individualistic, knee-jerk response to the supposition that I am to "obey" anything at all besides the law (if that). But it could also be that the idea of obedience, in connection with that of necessity, is too mechanical and too reminiscent of a kind of force that moves down a hierarchy, from those with power to those without.[18]

Another term that could be used to understand the process we are considering is *responsiveness* (see Kerr, 1997). This is, in essence, a softer and perhaps more palatable version of the idea of obedience. Its

---

18. I find myself more able and willing to embrace the idea of obedience in the encounter with other people. On encountering someone suffering, for instance, my response can be quite spontaneous and direct; my concern and care are immediately called forth. I return to this issue in Chapter Three when I consider Levinas's work.

main asset, however, is also its main liability. As human beings, we are responsive, or at least potentially so; there is no doubt about it. But this idea doesn't quite get us to that state of being compelled (not to mention being forcibly "yanked out" of our composure or being "blown away" by this or that person or thing) that often characterizes our encounter with the Other. Responsive though we are, the term therefore seems both too generic and too weak to accommodate the phenomenology of experiencing the priority of the Other. There is a particular kind of responsiveness at work, a particular way in which we "are" when we are under the Other's spell.

Closer to the mark is the idea of *surrender*, which is in some sense midway between obedience and responsiveness. I am not obedient to Rilke's poem; nor am I merely responsive to it. When I let it wash over me or take hold of me, I surrender to its spell, not so much "giving up" (as in "I surrender") or "giving in" as "being-given-by."[19] Phenomenologically speaking, in fact, the idea of surrender comes closest to what I want to convey here in this particular moment of encounter. But as is the case with the idea of attention, I also want to include another moment in the encounter, another aspect of the phenomenology at hand. This brings me once more to the idea of *devotion*, for in being-given-by—a person, a poem, or what have you—I also *give-myself-over-to*, "pledging," as it were, a certain allegiance and fidelity. Strictly speaking, I am not "devoted" to a particular poem. I have not given myself over to it with the kind of steady, long-term attentiveness that the term ordinarily connotes. At the same time, there is something decidedly long term, even permanent, about my own "stance" in relation to an object of this sort, especially when I have surrendered to its call. Oftentimes, I am compelled by the priority of the Other in such a way that I know it embodies a meaning and a value that transcend the singularity of the occasion. Even if I am not devoted to *this* person or to *that* poem or song or painting, I am indeed devoted to the spirit "behind" it, the spirit that allows it to become an instantiation, an embodiment, of something beyond itself. I am emphatically not claiming that these beings are merely images or stand-ins; they are as real and concrete as can be. But in their very concreteness there is something *more*. And in the very

---

19. Up until the point of formulating this idea, I hadn't fully appreciated (or understood) Marion's notion of "being given," which is addressed in his (aptly titled) book *Being Given: Toward a Phenomenology of Givenness* (2002a). It's still not crystal clear, but I'm closer than I was.

moment when I encounter them, I know that, somehow, I will need to find a place in my existence for this more, this surplus.

The poet and critic Yves Bonnefoy, on the occasion of presenting his inaugural address to the College de France (in December 1981), recollected his initial attraction with the "excess in words" highlighted in surrealist writing.

> What a call, as if from an unknown heaven, in these clusters of lawless tropes! What energy, it seemed, in this unpredictable bubbling up from the depths of language! But once the initial fascination was over, I took no joy in these words which I was told were free. I had before my eyes another kind of evidence, nourished by other poets, the evidence of running water, of a fire burning peacefully in our daily existence, and of time and chance of which these realities are made, and it seemed to me fairly soon that the transgressions of automatic writing were less the desired surreality, existing beyond the too superficial realisms of controlled thought whose signifieds remain fixed, than a reluctance to raise the question of the self, whose richest potentiality is perhaps in the life that one takes on day after day, without illusions, in the midst of what is simple. What are all the subtleties of language, after all, even turned upside down in a thousand different ways, next to the perception one can have, directly, mysteriously, of the movement of the leaves against the sky, or of the noise fruit makes when it falls into the grass? And always throughout this whole time I kept in mind, as an encouragement and even as a proof, the moment when the young reader opens passionately a great book and finds words, of course, but also things and people, and the horizon, and the sky: in short, a whole world given all at once to his thirst. (1989, p. 162)

"Words are there for him, of course," Bonnefoy continues; "he can feel the vibrations of the signifiers which lead him toward other words in the labyrinths of the signifiers, but he knows that there is a signified amongst them, a signified which depends on no one of them in particular and on all of them at once, which is intensity as such." For Bonnefoy, therefore, "[t]he reader of poetry does not analyze—he pledges to the author, his brother, that he too will remain in intensity. And soon he closes up his book, anxious to go and live out the promise. He has rediscovered a hope. And this is what gives us the right to think that one should not give up hope in poetry" (p. 162). In this hope, something has been *realized*, made real. This realization *is* the realization of the priority of the Other. It is also the realization that my life must, on some level, be a *devotional* one, in which I *attend to* and perhaps *serve* a cause greater than me.[20]

Such causes are abundant. As noted in the Introduction, some of them take the explicit form of service, in which people devote their lives to others' well-being, social justice, or the greater good. This is one vitally important way of giving-oneself-over-to and thereby living the priority of the Other. There is also, of course, religious devotion, wherein one gives oneself over not so much to a specific cause as to a sacred source, an object of devotion—a *god*, perhaps. In certain quarters of Jesuit thinking, these two modes of devotion are intimately related through the notion of "faith serving justice." As we have just observed, however, these more explicit forms of devotion in no way exhaust the idea. As noted briefly in the Introduction, and as is discussed further in Chapter Four, great works of art, by virtue of bringing us closer to the whole of reality, are very much in service of attuning us to the wider world as well. Great art, Murdoch had said, often leads to "unselfing," to helping us shed those aspects of egoistic existence that get in the way of our seeing things clearly and for what they are. In addition, it teaches us how to behold things without seizing or using them, without appropriating them for our own needs and wishes. Our attentiveness to great art may even help attune us to the otherness of other people and thereby make it more difficult for us to objectify them, to treat them as mere things.

But there is still more that art, and beauty more generally, can do with regard to bringing us closer to reality and, in turn, serving the wider world. "Beauty quickens," Elaine Scarry (1999) has written; "[i]t adrenalizes. It makes the heart beat faster. It makes life more vivid, animated, living, worth living" (pp. 24–25).[21] There is even a kind of "invitational"

---

20. There are, again, dangers here. As Weil (1997 [1952]) has argued, "Man always devotes himself to an order. Only, unless there is supernatural illumination, this order has as its centre either himself or some particular being or thing (possibly an abstraction) with which he has identified himself (e.g. Napoleon, for his soldiers, Science, or some political party, etc.)" (p. 54). Her point is an interesting and provocative one: without supernatural inspiration, devotion is likely to devolve into idolatry of one sort or another. It is also a questionable one. Among other reasons, it is painfully clear that supernaturally inspired devotion hardly immunizes one against idolatry.

21. As Jean-Luc Nancy (2011) adds, "The beautiful awakens in us an attraction, a desire that is stronger than simple pleasure" (p. 105). Nancy also speaks of eros in this context: "our relation to beauty is always one of love, because a relation of love goes beyond the simple pleasures of attraction or gratification" (p. 117).

aspect to our encounter with beauty: "At the moment one comes into the presence of something beautiful, it greets you. It lifts away from the neutral background as though coming forward to welcome you—as though the object were designed to 'fit' your perception" (p. 25). At the same time, Scarry notes, there is also built into our encounter with beauty a seemingly inevitable experience of "being in error," of somehow being cognizant of the distance and gulf between the earthly phenomenon at hand at and its spiritual source.

> On the one hand, something beautiful—a blossom, a friend, a poem, a sky—makes a clear and self-evident appearance before one.... The beauty of the thing at once fills the perceiver with a sense of conviction about that beauty, a wordless certainty.... On the other hand, the act of perceiving that seemingly self-evident beauty has a built-in liability to self-correction and self-adjustment, so much so that it appears to be a key element in whatever beauty is.... Something beautiful fills the mind yet invites the search for something beyond itself, something larger or something of the same scale with which it needs to be brought into relation. (pp. 28–29)

In some strange way, "beautiful things...always carry greetings from other worlds within them" (p. 47). Scarry even speaks of the link between beauty and an "immortal realm." This link will not exist for everyone; ultimately, she implies, it is a function of one's faith in the existence of such a realm. But this is a secondary matter in any case, for phenomenologically speaking, the result is much the same: "the perceiver is led to a more capacious regard for the world" (p. 48).

Beautiful things, Scarry (1999) adds, also carry intimations of *truth*. As she explains,

> It is not that a poem or painting or a palm tree or a person is "true," but rather that it ignites the desire for truth by giving us, with an electric brightness shared by almost no other uninvited, freely arriving perceptual event, the experience of conviction and the experience, as well, of error. This liability to error, contestation, and plurality—for which "beauty" over the centuries has so often been belittled—has sometimes been cited as evidence of its falsehood and distance from "truth," when it is instead the case that our very aspiration for truth is its legacy. It creates, without itself

fulfilling, the aspiration for enduring certitude. It comes to us, with no work of our own; then leaves us prepared to undergo a giant labor. (pp. 52–53)[22]

For Scarry, therefore, beautiful things or people, in and through their very finitude, signal not only the immortal and the infinite but also that never-to-be-fully-reached realm of certainty in which earthly errors have been erased, left behind. The perceiver's "more capacious regard for the world" is thus a function of the deep and abiding connection between beauty and truth.

This "regard" is not to be construed only in aesthetic terms or as a kind of appreciation. It is that, to be sure. But if Scarry is right, it is also much more. Not unlike Murdoch, Scarry wants to suggest that through our encounter with beauty, wherever it is found, we are led to a more respectful, caring, and indeed *just* relationship to the world. "It is as though beautiful things have been placed here and there throughout the world to serve as small wake-up calls to perception, spurring lapsed alertness back to its most acute level. Through its beauty, the world continually recommits us to a rigorous standard of perceptual care: if we do not search it out, it comes and finds us" (Scarry, 1999, p. 81). This rigorous standard of perceptual care can make its way, finally, to people. Specifically, Scarry explains, "beautiful things give rise to the notion of distribution, to a life-saving reciprocity, to fairness not just in the sense of loveliness of aspect but in the sense of 'a symmetry of everyone's relation to one another' " (p. 95).

In short order, Scarry has moved from beauty to truth to justice—and indeed *goodness*—and beyond. For this, she is surely to be commended. But I am not sure whether her recourse to the notions of distribution and reciprocity are adequate to the matters at hand. Is it "symmetry of everyone's relation to one another" that is brought forth by beautiful things, or is it the *dis*-symmetry of our relation to the Other?[23] Scarry acknowledges that "[a]t the moment we see something beautiful, we undergo a radical

---

22. See especially Hans-Georg Gadamer's *The Relevance of the Beautiful and Other Essays* (1986); see also Heidegger's *Poetry, Language, Thought* (1971) and Vattimo's *Art's Claim to Truth* (2010).

23. This issue is explored more fully in Chapter Three, when we consider some differences between Buber's and Levinas's thought. Whereas the former tends to use the language of reciprocity and mutuality, hence of symmetry, the latter wishes to speak more of the essential *dis*-symmetry between self and Other. Why this is so is also addressed later on.

decentering" (1999, p. 111). But this decentering, rather than revealing the priority of the Other, would seem to lead us down the path of the Same, toward "fairness," equity of regard. Don't get me wrong: I have nothing against fairness and equity! But what Scarry has said up until this point leads to a different conclusion, one that takes us beyond distribution and reciprocity, toward the priority of the Other.

One might well ask in this context, what is it that one actually *feels* when in the presence of the beautiful? What *kind* of regard for the world is brought about? Following up on the aforementioned idea of devotion, I suggest that our encounter with the beautiful frequently brings with it a distinct feeling of *reverence*, which is to say, a kind of regard that has the priority of the Other figured into its very form. Let me be more explicit about this claim. As Scarry herself notes, beautiful things often serve as "wake-up calls" to perception, "spurring lapsed alertness" into a more acute state. This seems true enough. But what also happens in the course of our encounters with the beautiful has to do with the *objects* that embody it. Scarry acknowledged this as well. These objects seem to point beyond themselves, in the direction of *truth*. Somehow, the world becomes *illuminated*, brought into clearer and more radiant view.

As Marcel (1973) has pointed out, the idea of illumination requires that there be some source of light. Just as for Weil there is no source of energy within the "I" to sustain itself, for Marcel the story is much the same: we are not our own sources of light; illumination must derive from elsewhere. And this aspect of being-from-elsewhere has, as its correlate, the priority of the Other. In order for me to receive the wake-up call to perception, in other words, I first have to experience the otherness of the beautiful thing itself. There is thus not only a *reverential* dimension to this encounter, as I have suggested, but a *referential* one as well. Indeed, Marcel (1973) writes, "it is only to the extent that we take life in its spontaneous upsurge, in its freshness, and thus in a kind of referential quality—the reference being to a primordial, secret, and, as it were, inviolable integrity—that we can, as in a flash of lightning, once again see its sacred value" (p. 210). For Marcel, whose consideration of these issues goes well beyond the domain of beauty into the whole of reality, there is, once more, a kind of "invitation" at work: "I think that each of us is invited, as it were, apart from any appeal to faith, which does not concern us here, to restore the traces of a world which is not superimposed from without ours, but is rather this very world grasped in a richness of dimensions which ordinarily we are simply unaware of" (p. 212). It is in "this very world," therefore, with its reference to "a primordial, secret, and...inviolable integrity," that we locate the priority of the Other. Returning to Buber, it is also in this world that we encounter the mystery of being—but only if we are attentive enough to its objects and devoted enough to the causes and purposes they call forth to accept the invitation being given.

Eclipsing the Other

It can be difficult. As Marcel goes on to suggest, the person who says he or she doesn't love life anymore can no longer experience the world in its "spontaneous upsurge" and "freshness." Far from being a place of sacred value, it can become a place with no value at all. More to the point still, it can become a kind of *non*-place, an empty extension of the person's alienation and misery. There will be no beauty and no wake-up calls to perception—only, perhaps, a perpetual sleepiness. For these people, the world may be essentially dead, a lunar landscape through which they roam interminably and without purpose. There are no sources of sustenance and nourishment, no sources of light. Aspects of this landscape are, arguably, uniquely modern: in the absence of those gods and goods to which we might once have turned, there remains the lonely, empty self.

As I indicated in the Introduction, it is curious, and problematic, that so much of contemporary therapy is oriented toward the self, for in a great many situations, it is precisely the Other—the living, bountiful world—that most needs to be restored. The self, I suggested, is frequently the main problem, as evidenced especially in those forms of anxiety and depression in which there is an excess of self-consciousness and self-concern, resulting in the occlusion and exclusion of reality. At an extreme, again, the world becomes essentially dead, a non-place, an emptiness filled in by one's own bleak desires and designs. The therapeutic task in such situations is to help bring this self back to the world, the living world, possessed of people and things that can once again nourish one's life.

The use and abuse of (self-altering) drugs is relevant in this context as well. Acknowledging the fact that such pharmaceutically induced self-alterations are sometimes necessary and valuable, there is reason to question them from the perspective being advanced here. This is hardly the first place they have been questioned. Critics have, for instance, complained that many drugs deal only with surface behaviors rather than underlying causes and that, consequently, they are at best a stopgap measure. Other critics have complained that such drugs can and often do prevent people from working through their experience; they can numb the sting of suffering but can also block the process of coming to terms with one's afflictions and deriving some measure of meaning from them. In addition, there is the related problem of the "medicalization" of experience, the notion that this or that behavior is a symptom to be removed or alleviated rather than a difficult piece of life to be endured and perhaps transcended. But there is another problem involved in using drugs to alter the self, and that is that what is *outside* the self—which we have regarded as a potentially profound source of sustenance and nourishment—may not be changed one whit. If only there were world-altering substances!

Some of the modern "miracle" drugs, it may be countered, are exactly this. As some people might claim, they—their selves—may not feel like they have changed much at all; the world, on the other hand, may feel like a better, more hospitable place. Insofar as one becomes able to derive sustenance and nourishment from this newly found world, whether pharmaceutically fashioned or not, this form of therapy can be valuable and worthwhile. If it becomes possible to build a bridge between the pharmaceutically fashioned world and the "natural" one, all the better. Given the relief that some of these drugs sometimes provide to people, I would not be one to withhold them. But to the extent that they are directed primarily toward repairing or rebuilding or restoring the self, toward shoring up its inner resources to the exclusion of outer ones, they cannot help but prolong the alienation in question.

To return to the more general problem of psychotherapy, what is most important to emphasize is the relationship—or *non*-relationship—between self and world that frequently characterizes certain forms of psychopathology. As philosopher and psychoanalyst Jonathan Lear (1998) has argued in his own reflections on psychoanalytic practice, "The only way to effect a profound shift in the psyche is via the transformation of the world in which it lives" (p. 78). For many people, Lear explains, the private world they have fashioned has held them captive, locked within the cramped walls of their own psyches, and the only way to help them to free themselves is to somehow devise ways to allow the world in. He writes:

> The real world—that is, the world as it is undistorted by powerful phantasies—had become for the analysand a transcendent realm. The world had become inaccessible because it was hidden behind a veil of phantastic distortions. Thus genuine communication with the world had become impossible, for the analysand was, in effect,

"communicating" with himself. That is, what he took to be communication with others was in fact an interaction with his own phantasies, projected onto the external world. Through repeated interpretations of transference distortions, through proper handling of the transference neurosis, the analyst is able to communicate an objective world—a world of objects rather than phantastic facsimiles—to the analysand. The analysand becomes ever more able to live in a world which is not dominated by phantasy and repetition. What has hitherto been a transcendent realm becomes immanent and inhabitable. (pp. 141–142)

It should be clear that, for Lear, the idea of a "transcendent realm" has an entirely different meaning than the one we touched upon in the Introduction. In the present context, it refers largely to a realm that is temporarily beyond the reach of the analysand. It is a realm that has become veiled, covered over, and therefore unable to supply that sort of "energy" and "light" of which we have spoken. As a result, there is no possibility of true dialogue with the world. In Buber's terms, I–Thou relations have essentially been obviated, stopped in their tracks, replaced by what might plausibly be called "I–I" relations, wherein the entire world becomes bathed in one's own deformed designs. Rather than real objects of attention, there are pseudo-objects, the world having become populated with split-off parts of the self. The task is thus clear: somehow, the world must be made real, and available, once more. Only then can it become a place in which to truly live and thrive. Indeed, only then can it become a *place* rather than an abyss.

Christopher Bollas (1992) provides some important additional details about the self–world relationship as understood through psychoanalysis. Certain objects (by which he means, very broadly, phenomena in the world to which we can relate, such as books or friends) are like "psychic 'keys' [that] open doors to unconsciously intense—and rich—experience in which we articulate the self that we are through the elaborating character of our response" (p. 17). Bollas refers to this process as a kind of "lifting," wherein a dimension of self is made available for knowing. "We shall have sensed in each such unit of experience an idiom of the self we are by virtue of the character of the evoked. As each encounter solicits us, lifts us up from our unconscious nuclearity, it shows an aspect of our self to the I and thus reveals some feature of our sensibility" (p. 28). As noted earlier (see Footnote 2), Bollas also speaks in this context of being "played upon" by objects: "The particularity specific to the object...transforms me" (p. 31), allowing me to discover a deeper, richer field of experience.

Interestingly enough, Bollas (1992), along with Scarry and Marcel, goes on to consider the "invitational" moment of the self–world relationship. Some people, he suggests, welcome the various invitations the world provides and are able to enter into a dialogue with things and with people that nourishes them: "Persons rich in self experiencing, who take pleasure in the dialectics of the human paradox, seek objects with evocative integrity that challenge and stretch the self." Others, however—such as those about whom Lear spoke—cannot help but decline the invitation: "They impose their view on the object world and blunt the evocative—transformational—facet of objects in the field" (p. 31). From this perspective, therefore, it is essential not only that human beings have authentic life projects through which they can define and articulate their existence in an ethically meaningful way, but that they, *we*, live in the real world, the one comprising objects filled with enough evocative potential, enough *energy*, to move us. Such objects, we have noted, are sources of light as well, serving both to illuminate the world and enlighten us along the way.

Relatedness and Otherness

Psycho-dynamics of the sort considered by Lear and Bollas help to underscore, in yet another way, the priority of the Other in human life. For Lear, the Other is nothing less than the world itself, unoccluded and unconcealed. To live in the absence of this world is to remain shut up within the privacy of the self and thus removed from the possibility of intimacy with what is real. For Bollas, likewise, the Other is the array of living objects that are able to "lift" us out of ourselves—if we are open and attentive enough to let them. And yet, the self, again, is by no means to be left out of the picture. Recall what Robert Hass had said about the "voice" present in Rilke's poetry: that which calls us out of ourselves may also call us into our deepest places. The very path toward this deeper Self thus lies along the route of the Other. Too often, I have suggested, this simple truth has been forgotten. That is, we have imagined that we are self-contained and self-sustaining and that, consequently, we can find meaning and value by merely turning inward. We have even imagined that our arrival at this condition represents a process of evolution, a coming-of-age of the human spirit. But this turning inward, shorn of its ties to the Other, represents a process of *in*volution and, ultimately, a shrinking of our innermost potentialities. I am not so much interested in decrying "narcissism" or "individualism" in these pages; that has already been done, and well, by many others. My interest is rather to bring to light a way of thinking about human life that is pervasive and highly problematic and that needs to be replaced by one that is more adequate to both the lives we lead and the ones we ought to.

The fact is, some of the effects that have been wrought by positing the priority of the self have been devastating—for our relationships with people and things, for our environment, for our spiritual life, and for ourselves. What is every bit as problematic, I have suggested, is the fact that in positing the priority of the self, we have simply gotten it *wrong*. If we wish to thrive as human beings, the self cannot be the priority; only the Other can. Along the lines being drawn here, perhaps it is time to *give* greater priority to the Other. I mean this not only as a moral injunction, having to do with fashioning better, more Other-directed conduct, but as an ethical imperative, having to do with fashioning better lives.

It is not my purpose in this book to give the self a bad name. I myself have written extensively about the self and will continue to do so. Indeed, much of my work has sought to preserve a place for the self in the face of intellectual currents that are suspicious of, or even hostile toward, the very idea (e.g, Freeman, 1993). However "insubstantial" we may be (because the self is not a substance-like thing, it is difficult to pin down exactly what it is) and however much we may be "socially constructed" (many of the so-called essential attributes of the self turn out to be social products, tied to time and place), our selves remain *important* to us. We want to feel good about who and what we are, we want our selves to grow and develop, and, as Taylor suggested, we want to live out in authentic fashion those life projects that are nearest to our hearts and souls. It should also be emphasized that there is no specifying ahead of time whether the "I" is to be indicted for its egoism or praised for its richness and depth of feeling. As Buber writes in *I and Thou* (1970),

> How dissonant the I of the ego sounds! When it issues from tragic lips, tense with some self-contradiction that they try to hold back, it can move us to great pity. When it issues from chaotic lips that savagely, heedlessly, unconsciously represent contradiction, it can make us shudder. When the lips are vain and smooth, it sounds embarrassing or disgusting.

> Those who pronounce the severed I, wallowing in the capital letter, uncover the shame of the world spirit that has been debased to mere spirituality.
>
> But how beautiful and legitimate the vivid and emphatic I of Socrates sounds! It is the I of infinite conversation, and the air of conversation is present on all its ways, even before his judges, even in the final hour in prison....
>
> How beautiful and legitimate the full I of Goethe sounds! It is the I of pure intercourse with nature. Nature yields to it and speaks ceaselessly with it; she reveals her mysteries to it and does not betray her mystery....
>
> And to anticipate and choose an image from the realm of unconditional relation: how powerful, even overpowering is Jesus' I-saying, and how legitimate to the point of being a matter of course! (pp. 115–116)

For Buber, therefore, the self remains not only important but fundamental. It can be corrupted, to be sure. In some people, moreover, it operates in such a way that the entire idea seems corrupted, rotten at the core. But there is no necessary contradiction or enmity between "I" and "You." This is so, Buber reminds us, even in the seemingly ego-less context of mysticism. "What has to be given up," he writes, "is not the I, as most mystics suppose; the I is indispensable for any relationship, including the highest, which always presupposes an I and You. What has to be given up is...that false drive for self-affirmation which impels man to flee from the unreliable, unsolid, unlasting, unpredictable, dangerous world of relation into the having of things" (p. 126). What has to be given up, in short, is the I of inattention, retreat, and self-enclosure, the I that is shut up and barricaded from the world in order to preserve the very integrity it cannot help but lose in the process.[24]

Louis Dupré (1976) goes even farther in his own reflections on the nature of selfhood in relation to mysticism. "[T]he ultimate message of the mystic about the nature of selfhood," he writes, "is that the self is

---

24. Karen Armstrong argues similarly that "[w]hen the masters of the spiritual life ask us to transcend the ego, they want us to get beyond the grasping, frightened, angry self that often seeks to destroy others in order to ensure its own survival, prosperity, and success" (2011, p. 86). Armstrong refers to this "me-first" mentality as "reptilian" and is well aware of just how difficult it is to move beyond it.

essentially more than a mere self, that transcendence belongs to its nature as much as the act through which it is immanent to itself, and that a total failure on the mind's part to realize this transcendence reduces the self to *less* than itself" (p. 104). As Dupré explains,

> The general trend of our civilization during the last centuries has not been favorable to this message. Its tendency has been to reduce the self to its most immediate and lowest common experiences. But for this restriction we pay the price of an all-pervading feeling of unfulfillment and, indeed, dehumanization. Deprived of its transcendent dimension selfhood lacks the very space it needs for full self-realization. With its scope thus limited freedom itself becomes jeopardized. Within such a restricted vision any possibility of meaning beyond the directly experienced is excluded. (p. 104)

There is much in these passages to reflect upon. First, there is the somewhat paradoxical idea that the self may be more than itself, that in its very nature it may be a going-beyond, a movement of transcendence—in the direction, I would add, of the Other. The second thing that Dupré tells us is that, in large measure, we have failed to recognize this transcendent dimension and have thereby imagined ourselves to be decidedly less than what we in fact are, or may be. Images proliferate: we are behaving bodies, or animals, or machines, or information-processing systems—anything, in other words, but what we are. We have become selves-reduced, our "immediate and lowest common experiences" serving for many to tell the whole story.

Dupré tells us still more. By virtue of the shrunken self-images that have been constructed during the course of recent centuries (and psychology, I'm afraid, must shoulder a portion of the blame), we have come to lead less meaningful and fulfilling lives. For some, the response has been to burrow farther and farther into the hole of the self in the hope recovering some of its lost depth. If Dupré is right, however, we need to move in the exact opposite direction. Only if we look *outward* will there exist the possibility of recovering the transcendent dimension. In saying this, it is not entirely clear whether Dupré is urging us to recognize the priority of the Other. At times, this seems to be the case. At other times, he seems to be imagining that we can in fact "find" this lost transcendent dimension somewhere within ourselves via "the rediscovery of the inner life" (the subtitle of the book I have been referring to, *Transcendent Selfhood*). What is most important in either case is that without the transcendent dimension of life the self suffers, depriving itself of the "space" it requires to grow and reach its own highest levels. It remains self rather than becoming Self—that is, that mode of being which is "given back," we might say, by living the priority of the Other.

Notice that for Dupré, the shrunken self-images we have come to possess spell a marked loss of *freedom*. The irony is a bitter one: the modern self, freer than ever of the "encumbrances" of times past, has apparently curtailed its *deep* freedom along the way by eliminating from view those very sources of sustenance that would allow for its full realization. This "restricted vision," in turn, virtually excludes "any possibility of meaning beyond the directly experienced." That is, it excludes the possibility of an encounter with the *Other*, with that which truly transcends the immanence of the self. There is another irony at work here as well. The shrunken state of the modern self is frequently seen in its grandiosity and its fantasies of self-sustenance. Its manifest largeness thus signifies its latent smallness, and its apparent gains signify its all too real losses. Given this state of affairs, it is clear that there is the need to recover a certain humility in our own way of thinking about who and what we are. This brings us all the way back to Weil, who, you will recall, told us that humility consists precisely in knowing that there is no source of energy within the "I" by which we can rise as human beings. It is only when we know this, and *live* it, she implies, that such "rising" is made possible. We only become *truly* large when we are willing to embrace our own real smallness in the total scheme of what is real.

To foreshadow an issue to be considered in greater detail in Chapter Three, there is a remarkable correlation at the heart of these ideas: the more humble and Other-directed we are, the more meaningful, gratifying, and fulfilling our lives are likely to be. This is emphatically not to say that Other-directedness is merely a means to the end of our own fulfillment. This would be a crude instrumentalism, and it would immediately strip away whatever moral and ethical impulses there may be in our own aspirations to goodness. Nor do I wish to say that the Other is simply the detour we need to take in order to get to ourselves. This too would be a kind of instrumentalism, and a rather crassly egocentric brand of it at that. What I am saying is that there is a remarkable, and remarkably fortunate, coincidence between being oriented to the Other—for instance, in the form of our responsibility to and for other people—and living a life characterized by fulfillment and self-realization. Indeed, it may very well be that living the priority of the Other is the surest path both to Self-realization and to the good life we seek, for others and for ourselves. In a very real sense, it is there for the asking. But as we shall see in the next chapter, living this way is no easy task. Let us turn to it.

2

Oblivion and Attention

Coming into Being

I've taken to riding my bicycle to work several times a week during the summertime. This morning was particularly beautiful, so rather than just try to get there as quickly as possible, I took a little side trip on a bicycle path for six or seven miles. There I was, cruising through trees and wildflowers, purple and orange and white, perched along the side of the path, the river below. What a great way to start the day! But I wasn't there. That, at least, is what I realized about midway through the trip, when I remembered where I was. And all of a sudden there they were—the trees, the flowers, the river, the *day*, that I had taken the time to be with only to have them recede from view. I was thinking about this very book, actually; that's where my attention was. The result had been oblivion. It was a pleasant oblivion, mind you; I was moving fast, feeling the wind, the whir of the tires. But for a good chunk of time I was all but absent to the world.

The same sort of oblivion frequently characterizes our relations with people. They are there, right before us, but we may not really see them; they're just part of the world we navigate through, moving on to this or that task or thought or preoccupation. There are of course times when the veil is removed—a birthday, or an anniversary, or a flight that takes loved ones far away. Like the trees and wildflowers, they may suddenly come into view: Oh, yes; that's who she is! Happy Birthday! Have a safe flight. There are other things that bring people into view too. A few years back my wife was diagnosed with leukemia—a quite treatable form of it, fortunately, but leukemia nonetheless. And immediately after the diagnosis she came into view in a way that she hadn't for some time. There are all kinds of dynamic reasons for why people grow closer—or farther apart—in circumstances such as this one. And, of course, there was the sheer fact of her, and our, finiteness staring us in the face. Whatever the sources may be, the phenomenology remains: I was attending to her in a way that I hadn't been, and with that attention *she* emerged. The situation is a most humbling one. She had been there all along. Why did it take leukemia for me to see her?

It wasn't only seeing that emerged at this point either but caring, loving, *being there* for her. The former, it would seem, was a requisite condition for the latter. At the same time, I only came to see her, in the fullness of her being, owing to the demand suddenly being made upon me.[1] Not that I didn't care for her or love her beforehand; I did—but not in the same way, with the same urgency and intensity and presence. Why? And is it possible to be present in this way in the absence of a devastating diagnosis or some other calamity or catastrophe? It can't be that these assaults are *required*. And yet without them we often fall sorely short of being fully there, for the Other. What is to be done?[2]

This phenomenon extends into the cultural sphere as well. About a decade ago, there was a terrible fire in Worcester, Massachusetts, where my family and I have lived for the past 25-plus years. Two firefighters had raced into a burning building, the Worcester Cold Storage and Warehouse Co. building, in order to search for homeless people thought to be living there. Not long after they entered, the fire intensified, leaving them disoriented, lost, consumed by smoke and heat and darkness. Upon receiving pleas for help, four more firefighters entered the building, now in the hope of finding their brothers. None returned.

The entire city fell into a state of shock and then profound grief. Worcester is a small city, and it seemed that nearly everyone had some

---

1. I have already mentioned the importance of Levinas's notion of the "face": "It demands me, requires me, summons me" (1999a, p. 27). In this sense, it is an originary source, calling forth my own sense of care and responsibility. As the example of my wife shows, however, my very capacity to truly *see* her face was, at one and the same time, a product—specifically, of my newfound awareness of her affliction. In this latter sense, therefore, it might plausibly be said that even as seeing may be understood as the requisite condition of my care and love, it is this very care and love that insists on my seeing. For an extended treatment of the idea of being demanded, see especially David Goodman's *The Demanded Self: Levinasian Ethics and Identity in Psychology* (2012).

2. It is tempting to maintain that we humans will remain in the proverbial "cave" unless someone or something drags us out. Absent this sort of jolt to the system, it will be perilously easy to bask in the illusory comfort of the shadows. Even with such a jolt, however, there will likely need to be reminders—"mnemonic devices," as it were, brought to bear on our situation. Otherwise, we can be quite sure that oblivion will return and have its way.

personal connection to one of the six fallen firefighters. In our case, one was a neighbor who had lived right across the street. In other cases, one might have been the father of a friend or someone's son or nephew, someone you knew or had heard about sometime. For many, there was a strange immediacy to the incident and its echoes; whether there was a personal connection or not, there was the sense that the six firefighters were familiar, that they were flesh-and-blood men, whom one probably passed at the supermarket or at the bank or in a car, taking their kids to school or soccer practice, just like you.

A feeling of senselessness, coupled with an awareness of the accidental nature of things, added to the misery. As it turned out, there were no homeless people in the building. We would later learn that after knocking over a candle, the one that started the inferno, two people—a couple, down and out and no doubt afraid and confused—had left the scene. *How could it be?* Two firefighters had gone in to find those people, to save them. And then four more had gone in, all of them now buried in smoking rubble, never to surface again, all in the name of a possibility, that there were people, living people, inside, who might be in need of their help. One day the six men were there and the next day they were not. *How could it be?* And how could it not be possible to undo it? The whole thing had literally been unbelievable.

The community's response was overwhelming. Amidst all the horror and grief, there was an incredible outpouring of care and love. On seeing the agonized face of one of the deceased firefighters' wives on television, or that of the fire chief, vowing, through his tears, to turn over every brick in that hellish warehouse until each of his men was brought home, you wanted to do anything and everything in your power to help, to *be there*, somehow, for these people, most of whom you didn't even know. Meals were sent to the homes of the families. Donations started pouring in, not only from Worcester but from all around the state and even beyond. And near the scene of the fire, where a fire engine remained, there emerged a shrine, filled with flowers and poems and photos of the dead. There was a ceaseless stream of visitors, from near and far, trying to catch a glimpse of the building, still smoking and in the process of being dismantled, or of one of the working firefighters, exhausted and grimy, searching around the clock for the charred bodies of his brothers. None of this seemed like it was for the sake of voyeuristic excitement either. It was for the sake of respect, of somehow making contact with the honorable dead, their families and friends, and their fellow firefighters, still doing their job, now as always.

For many days afterward, all eyes remained on the tragic event, and nearly everything else—all the daily stuff that gets people preoccupied and irritated and angry—receded from view. It was still possible to yell at your kids (just like it's still possible for me to squabble with my wife), but it was much tougher; more than anything, you wanted to take them and hold them. And when we all stood outside on the cold December day when a commemorative ceremony was held, watching thousands upon thousands of firefighters marching together in complete unison and silence, you couldn't help but feel that everyone was real and that they meant something important. There was a sense of a common orientation, a common project, and it was *good*. Hardly anyone cut people off in traffic. And some of the people whom you would ordinarily loathe or ignore or look down upon were suddenly worth recognizing, seeing. For those few days, there had come into view what I have herein been calling the priority of the Other—in this case, the priority of the other person, whether firefighter or familiar face or complete stranger, never to be seen again, but for now, briefly, one of my fellow human beings, trying, just like me, to be there, in the world.

In some ways, the tragedy became transformed into a true celebration, of the lives of firefighters, of the community of Worcester, and of humanity itself—or at least the *possibility* of humanity. As many a newspaper editorial or letter to the editor noted, it was amazing how people had come together. For a brief while, people had gotten their priorities straight. There was even the sense, for some, that through this tragedy they had discovered the true nature of things, especially the value of other people and of life: that person I've never seen before, standing over there in her otherness, her difference, really is my neighbor. In the best of worlds, we would always know this.

But of course we don't. As editorials and letters to the editor also noted, there was something decidedly tragic about the fact that it took—that it often takes—a catastrophe for people to see and feel the priority of the Other. Let's face it, some of them in effect suggested; we'll be cutting people off in traffic again in no time. Ordinarily, the priority is Job or Kitchen or Backyard. There sometimes emerge intimations of something more—seeing your wife or child get on an airplane, knowing that, in theory, you might never see her again—but they're fleeting. You know that that moment is significant and unrepeatable, just like she is, but you've got to be on your way; there are things to be done, and soon. She recedes from view quickly. She's just "there," as are lots of other people you know, on the edge of your preoccupations and worries, your aspirations and goals. Except for that brief intimation, she is anything but Other. Such is the nature of a good deal of everyday life.[3]

The Centripetal and the Centrifugal

What is the true nature of our desires and commitments? Oftentimes, they seem selfish, even petty or base. Not only can there be the usual, run-of-the-mill self-preoccupation, as above; there can be anger, even rage, particularly directed at those we love. It is not beyond us to hurt them either, if not physically then psychologically; we can be intolerant and indignant, and can pounce on their weak spots when given the opportunity. Other times, though, our desires and commitments seem much higher and better. We really *did* care for one another out there in the cold, and we really did want to do everything we possibly could for those people, those others. *That's* what's real, we might have said; everything else is clutter and noise. Which of these pictures, if either, is the true one?

That we have the *potential* to be destructive is radiantly clear. Also clear, to me at any rate, is our potential to be authentically caring and loving. That we "are" either of these by nature, however, seems much more questionable. Indeed, I don't know that we intrinsically "are" *anything* in particular—destructive or loving, aggressive or altruistic. Rather, we exist *in potentia*, moving in this direction or that as a function of the lives we lead.[4]

---

3. Following Eric Santner, in his book *On the Psychotheology of Everyday Life: Reflections on Freud and Rosenzweig* (2001), we truly enter what he terms "the midst of life" only "when we truly inhabit proximity to our neighbor, assume responsibility for the claims his or her singular and uncanny presence makes on us not only in extreme circumstances but *every day*" (p. 7). This of course suggests that much of everyday life isn't really life at all, only a too-pale facsimile. Indeed, "[e]veryday life includes possibilities of withdrawing from, defending against, its own aliveness to the world, possibilities of, as it were, not really being there, of dying to the Other's presence" (p. 9). This is precisely the aforementioned condition of "ordinary oblivion" I wish to address in this chapter.

4. See especially Geertz's chapter "The Growth of Culture and the Evolution of Mind" in *The Interpretation of Cultures* (1973). See also Lifton (1993), who suggests that situating the self in the context of social evolution "helps us redefine that elusive entity we call 'human nature'— not as a fixed set of structures or behaviors but as a mutable array of potentialities one can always draw upon" (p. 231). Whether we "can always draw upon" these potentialities is open to question; practically speaking, some may be all but shut down. Lifton's perspective on this "protean" nature of the self nevertheless does provide some hope that we can in fact change our ways and become more empathically attuned to the various plights, human and non-, we encounter. What is required is a measure of "species consciousness." Such consciousness, I would hold, is inseparable from thinking and living the priority of the Other.

At the same time, in situations like the ones I have described, there does frequently emerge the conviction that some aspect of our true nature has been disclosed, "unconcealed." We see and feel our own potential goodness coming into being *in tandem with the reality of the Other*, and we *know* it's a better way than the way we had been before: more caring, more loving, more fully *human*. Whether this is the "true" picture, therefore, is largely immaterial; the main thing is that we can, and do, quite spontaneously intuit it as a more fully realized mode of being, one that owes its very existence to the coming-into-being of the Other. That we are able to do so is noteworthy in itself and surely says *something* about our nature. We *know* that living the priority of the Other—truly *seeing* the multicolored flowers on that bicycle path, being there for my wife, recognizing and affirming my neighbors in Worcester, caring for them, serving them—is *good*, a step above where we were before, more erotically connected to the world. In true Platonic form, we may even gather the conviction that we are somehow making contact with the *Good*, with an ideal, transcendent "form" giving reality and direction to what is there, before us. There can be a deep feeling of *belonging*, too: *we are one*, living together under the magnetic pull of the Other. And we are *grateful*.[5]

But there remain questions, nagging and painful. If in fact we know, on some level, what it means to be better, why is it so difficult to realize this betterness, this *goodness*, in action, day in and day out? Is it a matter of weakness? Are there internal forces whose pressure and power are such that we simply cannot "access" our goodness? Are there external forces, societal or economic or political, that coalesce or conspire in such a way that, too often, we are either pitted against one another or "forced" to relegate one another to the status of things or ghosts? Is it a combination of the two? What else might be at work in this strange human situation?

This is another one of those issues that simply do not permit equation-like thinking. That there are internal "factors" that serve to keep us enchained, in the shadows, seems to be endemic to the human

---

5. I have no doubt that some of the language being employed in these last few sentences will make some readers uncomfortable. For one, Plato has entered the picture once again, and unfortunately, many readers mistake his perspective, in *The Republic* (2003) and elsewhere, for some sort of absolutism. A close reading, I believe, points us in a quite different direction. Perhaps more troubling still is this notion of our somehow being "grateful" in situations like the one I have described—not just for one another, but for the very gift of life itself. But grateful to whom, or what? One needn't be a believer either to experience this sort of sentiment. How might we understand it? I attempt to provide some clues in Chapter Five, "The Possibility of Transcendence."

condition. That there are external factors that can exacerbate the situation seems true as well. It is less certain, however, whether we can specify in any neat way how much is one and how much is the other. Having said this, it is clearly the case that the kind of practical effort required in order to redress the situation at hand must take place on both the internal and external fronts—that is, in terms of internal work, directed essentially toward the nature and quality of consciousness, and external work, directed toward the societal, economic, and political conditions within which we live. Of special relevance in this context is the rise of syndromes such as attention deficit disorder. Whatever reality there may be to this syndrome, there is no questioning its metaphorical significance at this particular juncture of our history. Given the kind of world we have crafted, it is no easy task to remain attentive—except, of course, to the many technological devices that now serve as virtual appendages to human being.[6]

But let me return to the messy realities of personal life. I can recall an incident some years ago when one of my daughters repeatedly asked me to help her with her homework, which I often did. We had been living in Spain for the year; she was attending a Spanish school, and she was overwhelmed by the challenges before her. At one point, when she was "bugging" me more than usual, I told her to stop, that *I* had things to do too (which was true). It was only later that the irony, and tragedy, of the situation hit me. "Can't you see," I might have told her, "that I'm busy writing an extremely important book on the *Other*?!" I have no time for *you*; I'm writing a book. *My* book! Who and what are we that we should so often keep the world from view? In a very real sense, it wasn't my *daughter* who had come to me asking for help; it was an *obstruction*, coming to interfere. Had I seen *her*, I might have been a bit more willing to rise to the occasion.[7]

Thus far in this chapter, I have been referring mainly to the interpersonal sphere, focusing especially on the ethical challenges found therein. As suggested already, however, the issues at hand go well beyond this

---

6. See especially Sherry Turkle's *Alone Together: Why We Expect More from Technology and Less from Each Other* (2011). For more general statements of some of the challenges and demands inherent in modern life, see also Gergen (1992) and Kegan (1998).

7. In my recent book *Hindsight: The Promise and Peril of Looking Backward* (2010), I spend a good deal of time addressing the issue of "moral lateness," which basically refers to a pervasive tendency to act first and think later. This "exchange" with my daughter provides a telling example of just such lateness; it was only after the fact that I could see just how silly, and wrong, my response to her had been. A significant challenge in this context—not unrelated to some of the challenges posed in this book—is to devise ways of being more morally "on time." It's not easy.

singular sphere. In some of our encounters with art or nature we may also experience intimations of a fuller, more real world than the one we ordinarily inhabit. As it is often said, these things can "take us out of ourselves," and in doing so, they can give us important clues about what the world could be, maybe even what the world *is*—if only we could attend to it. Consider for a moment what sometimes happens when we listen to a piece of music that excites us: it is as if we can *live* in it, as if we can somehow find our way into its texture of meaning. At the same time, it can feel as though it lives in *us*, "lifting" us out of our insularity.[8] This is not, of course, the only thing that can happen when we listen to such music. We can admire it for the mastery of its composition or its musicianship. We can also associate to it, straying in our thoughts and memories, thinking about this or that. In each of these latter modes, we have become distanced from the music itself, from the tapestry of sounds. *We* are admiring it or associating to it; our minds are doing something even as we are listening. In the first mode, though, "we"—qua intending, constituting egos—are largely absent from the scene, wholly immersed in the music's otherness.[9]

Moments such as these can be remarkably pleasurable in their sensuousness and beauty. They can be deeply fulfilling as well, providing both existential nourishment, as I called it earlier, and images of a wholeness or a purity of form that somehow bears upon the life we lead. Here too, it is as if something is being *realized* in the music, as if something familiar or recognizable is coming into being. And this very process of coming into being, with its forward movement—which is itself a kind of fulfillment—manages to bind us, more closely, to a fuller and more complete realm of existence than the one we often inhabit in our ordinary, everyday life.

Kathleen Higgins does well to address these issues and more in her book *The Music of Our Lives* (1991). Higgins sees music as a symbol or image

---

8. See Bollas (1992) for a discussion of this idea of "lifting." See also my consideration of the same (via Bollas) in Chapter One.

9. Here, I refer once more to Jean-Luc Marion's important idea of "the saturated phenomenon" (2002b, 2008). With specific reference to music, see also Jean-Luc Nancy's *Listening* (2007). "What does it mean," he asks, "for a being to be immersed entirely in listening, formed by listening or in listening, listening with all his being?" (p. 5). "To listen," he answers, "is to enter that spatiality by which, at the same time, I am penetrated, for it opens up in me as well as around me, and from me as well as toward me: it opens me inside me as well as outside, and it is through such a double, quadruple, or sextuple opening that a 'self' can take place. To be listening is to be *at the same time* inside and outside, to be open *from* without and *from* within, hence from one to the other and from one in the other" (p. 14). Difficult, but interesting.

of harmonious existence. In addition, in and through its very otherness, it can give us "a sense of fully 'being there,' with our faculties fully engaged" (p. 145). Moreover, one can become aware of oneself "as a being who can relate to the world nondefensively" (p. 147). One can therefore function "as a being whose powers are coordinated and harmoniously functioning" and who is also "engaged with and responsive to a larger world. Concern for something beyond oneself, a prerequisite for ethically good living," is thus "already present in the self-conception that we discover in our musical experience" (p. 149). In sum, "Music facilitates a sense of oneself as a harmonious, nonconflicted vital being and a sense of intimate connection with the larger human world, both of which characterize 'the good human being' on almost any ethical model" (p. 156).[10] In doing so, it should be noted, it can also serve to confirm our own *dis*harmony and distance from this very goodness. The kind of deep immersion into music we have been considering can thus be disturbing as well as fulfilling, and for much the same reason: the music's own harmony and wholeness, juxtaposed against one's possible dividedness and incompleteness, can serve as a potent reminder that the life one is leading may be less than it should be. So it is that people sometimes leave a terrific concert or theater performance only to find themselves let down, alienated from the gray life to which they have returned. They are back to themselves, back *in* themselves, thinking and wondering, and maybe feeling a little ill.

Notice once more the relationship between *aesthetics* and *ethics*: the beautiful otherness of art or nature can draw us into its very being, providing an intimation of not only a fuller, deeper reality but a fuller, deeper *life*, one that is more erotically charged and connected to the world. Whether one is fulfilled or disturbed, exhilarated or let down, there will have emerged a clear recognition of the priority of the Other. This time, the Other is not a person but a kind of "region," a larger, more inclusive realm outside ourselves that we somehow manage to inhabit for a while. Not unlike our experiences with persons, however—at least of the more attentive and connected sort considered earlier—there can be a profound sense that there is something more to life, or that there can be. So much of our experience is veiled, hidden behind this or that preoccupation or project. At an extreme, there can even be a kind of obsessive internality, a

---

10. Higgins is generalizing here, of course. Not all music does these wondrous things, and not all people "accept the invitation" to be there with it. Nevertheless, there is much in her reflections that is worth heeding.

perpetual turning and returning inward, to figure out what the next move is in this elaborate, and not altogether fun, game being played. But every now and then the veil lifts, the Other appears, and life's potential is disclosed.[11] To recognize the Other is, at one and the same time, to recognize the *priority* of the Other. And this very priority may provoke us to review and rethink the other "priorities" we have.

Questions abound once again: given the power and intensity and *significance* of experiences such as those being considered, why are they often not a bigger part of our lives? There are all kinds of quite concrete answers to this question. There is work to be done, there are bills to pay, leaks to fix, etc., etc., etc.; and there is just so much time grown women and men should spend spacing out on the otherness of music and other such indulgent frills and frivolities. But even acknowledging all of the Important Tasks that have to be done and all of the other reasons that there simply isn't *time* to do these more fulfilling things—the productive and consumptive structure of post-industrial capitalism, for instance—there still remain some important questions to be answered. Much of the free time people *do* have is spent doing things (watching television, ruminating, hanging around) that are not only unfulfilling but positively deadening (Csikszentmihalyi, 1990, 1994). Just so this doesn't start to seem like some moralistic how-to manual, let me be clear about this: *I* often like to watch television, ruminate, and hang around. I also like to eat and drink and go to movies and all the rest.[12] Every now and then we just need to take a *break*. The question, therefore, isn't why we are not all subscribers to the opera or the symphony, spending every free moment doing Something Significant. The question is why, given the many possible routes to significance that do exist, we elect to take so few of them.

---

11. According to Buber (1965), "Whatever has...been changed into It and frozen into a thing among things is still endowed with the meaning and the destiny to change back ever again.... The fulfillment of this meaning and this destiny is frustrated by the man who has become reconciled to the It-world as something that is to be experienced and used and who holds down what is tied into it instead of freeing it, who observes it instead of heeding it, and instead of receiving it utilizes it" (p. 90). This is another way of speaking about the "ordinary oblivion" that characterizes much of our lives. Certain people are no doubt more given to this I–It mode than others. However, none of us are exempt.

12. I do not wish to suggest that eating and drinking and going to movies are necessarily deadening. Far from it; they can be positively enlivening and enriching, and in their own way they can call forth the priority of the Other every bit as powerfully as those activities frequently considered "higher." In this instance, then, I am speaking mainly of those specific forms of these activities that are on the more superficial end of the continuum. (I like these too. There's a time and a place for everything.)

Is it laziness, or a kind of dumb inertia, that pulls us ever backward, to the television or the couch? Is it the fast-paced lives that people lead that makes them want to just "chill" during the off hours? Is it a kind of colossal culturally constituted depression, that stems from the apparent absence of those kinds of agreed-upon goods that seem to have been more available in times past? What else, I ask once more, might be at work in this strange human situation? Much of the time, for many of us, the world remains veiled—and this despite the fact that most of us know not only that it is capable of being *un*veiled, but that this state of unveiledness, wherein one beholds the Other in its otherness, is generally more fulfilling and significant. Why the seeming "reluctance" to enter this region?

Whatever the answers to these questions may be, I want to suggest that there seem to be two fundamental forces at work in us human beings. First, there is a *centripetal* force, one that moves inward, toward the ego and its myriad anxieties and preoccupations. Iris Murdoch (1970), drawing on Freud, among others, presents a somewhat extreme version of this idea:

> Freud takes a thoroughly pessimistic view of human nature. He sees the psyche as an egocentric system of quasi-mechanical energy, largely determined by its own individual history, whose natural attachments are sexual, ambiguous, and hard for the subject to understand or control. Introspection reveals only the deep tissue of ambivalent motive, and fantasy is a stronger force than reason. Objectivity and unselfishness are not natural to human beings. (p. 50)

"The problem," therefore, Murdoch continues, "is to accommodate inside moral philosophy, and suggest methods of dealing with the fact that so much of human conduct is moved by mechanical energy of an egocentric kind" (p. 51). As for the result, it is precisely the sort of oblivion, and *blindness*, described earlier. "By opening our eyes we do not necessarily see what confronts us. We are anxiety-ridden animals. Our minds are continually active, fabricating an anxious, usually self-preoccupied, often falsifying *veil* which partially conceals the world" (p. 82). This strikes me as patently true. This is the dimension of human being that operates in *centripetal* fashion.

As we have also seen, however, there are certain circumstances in which the veil is lifted, at least partially, and the world shines through. Murdoch (1970) is well aware of this *centrifugal* force:

> I am looking out of my window in an anxious and resentful state of mind, oblivious of my surroundings, brooding perhaps on some damage done to my prestige. Then suddenly I observe a hovering kestrel. In a moment everything is altered. The brooding self with its hurt vanity has disappeared. There is nothing now but kestrel. And when I return to thinking of that other matter it seems less important. And of course this is something which we may also do deliberately: give attention to nature in order to clear our minds of selfish care. (p. 82)

The priority of the Other—in this case, a kestrel—has de-prioritized the ego, with its anxieties and preoccupations; what had seemed so important and pressing has been relegated to the background, indeed to its proper place. Attention has shifted, and with it "everything is altered." The brooding is over; the ego-driven self is gone; only the Other remains. And with this shifting of attention there is a settling-down and settling-in, a restoration of order and of real priorities.[13]

Attention and Moral Life

According to Murdoch, the process of clearing our minds of selfish care via attention, which we have referred to as "unselfing," is intimately tied to moral life. For her, as we have observed, great art is the prime vehicle for doing so. In teaching us "how real things can be looked at and loved without being seized and used" (1970, p. 64), it gives us a model for regarding reality more generally, including human reality. Encountering the otherness of art, insofar as it involves unselfing, in other words, attunes us to the separateness and differentness of other people. And "[t]he more the separateness and differentness of other people is realized, and the fact seen that another man has needs and wishes as demanding as one's own, the harder it becomes to treat a person as a thing" (p. 64). Once again, therefore, Murdoch is positing

---

13. I have already referred to Mihaly Csikszentmihalyi's consideration of the "flow" experience (e.g., 1990, 1994), which is intimately related, in his view, to the phenomenology of attention. For related ideas, see also Winifred Gallagher's (2009) book *Rapt: Attention and the Focused Life*, portions of which nicely show the connection between attention and establishing real life priorities, as well as Alan Wallace's *The Attention Revolution: Unlocking the Power of the Focused Mind* (2006).

a connection between *aesthetics* and *ethics*, such that the love incited by art can lead to a greater measure of respect and care for all that is.[14]

Kathleen Higgins, from whom we heard earlier, says something similar in her reflections on music. Encountering and appreciating a (good or great) musical work "involves one's inward attitude and one's orientation toward what is outside one" and in turn "involves something like reverence for the persons one associates with it" (Higgins, 1991, p. 161). This reverence, she continues, "involves an internal state that is incompatible with a hostile or defense-prone posture. In becoming reverent, I put aside my usual opposition of self and the rest of the world; and if I kick the dog after listening to Mozart, this suggests that I have not actually made the transformation that reverence involves" (p. 162). For Higgins, therefore, the connection between attentive and reverent appreciation, as we find it in music, "transfers" more or less automatically to the ethical realm; and when it doesn't happen, we can safely assume that the reverence in question has somehow been cut short, rendered incomplete.

In keeping with what was said in the Introduction, I am less certain about the necessity of this connection. There is little doubt that being attentive to both the human and the non-human world can and sometimes does lead to a greater measure of care. Indeed, it may very well be the case that such attentiveness is required, that it is a necessary condition for care. I couldn't possibly care for those multicolored wildflowers strewn along my bicycle path until I *saw* them; before that, they were just fleeting thing-images, phantoms, without substance or depth. Once I *did* see them—once I was in a *Thou* rather than an *It* relation with them—an element of *choice* emerged: I could decide how to be with them, whether to care for them, even to "intervene" on their behalf, should they be placed under threat in some way.[15] The same may be said of the interpersonal sphere. To

---

14. I fear I am oversimplifying things here. It is clear, to me at any rate, that Murdoch is interested in positing this connection between aesthetics and ethics. The issue becomes a bit muddier when we recognize that, for Murdoch, ethics is in a certain sense *built into* aesthetics: to encounter the beautiful work of art or the beauty of nature is *already* to behold and to respect its otherness. Along these lines, one might plausibly speak of what my colleague Joanna (Jody) Ziegler called an "ethics of looking" itself. Jody was an extraordinary scholar and person. I can only hope this book preserves her memory in some small way.

15. Again, it could be that the care I am speaking of here, rather than being "brought about" by seeing, is part and parcel of such seeing, built into the process itself. For present purposes, nevertheless, it seems best to regard the two as differentiable, or at least as differentiable moments of a multidimensional process. As will become clear through the scenario about to be presented, this distinction is especially important when it comes to *behavior*, for even if the ethical is built into the process of seeing itself, there is no ensuring that this seeing will lead to ethical behavior.

truly see the face of the other person, Levinas (e.g., 1999a) has suggested, is at one and the same time to recognize one's responsibility to and for that person. None of this, however, means that one will necessarily or "automatically" go on to behave in a caring, responsible way. Levinas recognizes this as well. "The face," he tells us, "is what one cannot kill, or at least it is that whose *meaning* consists in saying: 'thou shalt not kill.' " But of course we can, and do: "Murder, it is true," he continues, "is a banal fact: one can kill the Other; the ethical exigency is not an ontological necessity" (1985, p. 87).

A chilling example of exactly this gap is found in Primo Levi's *The Drowned and the Saved* (1989), in a chapter called "The Gray Zone." Drawing on the account of one Myklos Nyiszli, a Hungarian physician who had served on the "Special Squad" in Auschwitz,[16] Levi tells the following story:

> In the gas chamber have been jammed together and murdered the components of a recently arrived convoy, and the squad is performing its horrendous everyday work, sorting out the tangle of corpses, washing them with hoses, and transporting them to the crematorium, but on the floor they find a young woman who is still alive. The event is exceptional, unique; perhaps the human bodies formed a barrier around her, sequestered a pocket of air that remained breathable. The men are perplexed. Death is their trade at all hours, death is a habit because, precisely, "one either goes mad on the first day or becomes accustomed to it," but this woman is alive. They hide her, warm her, bring her beef broth, question her: the girl is sixteen years old, she cannot orient herself in space or time, does not know where she is, has gone through without understanding it the sequence of the sealed train, the brutal preliminary selection, the stripping, the entry into the chamber from which no one had ever come out alive. She has not understood, but she has seen; therefore she must die, and the men of the squad know it just as they know that they too must die for the same reason. But these

---

[16]. The Special Squad consisted of those prisoners who had been given the "privilege" of running the crematoria in Auschwitz. Levi writes, "It was their task to maintain order among the new arrivals (often completely unaware of the destiny awaiting them) who were to be sent to the gas chambers, to extract the corpses from the chambers, to pull gold teeth from jaws, to cut women's hair, to sort and classify clothes, shoes, and the content of the luggage, to transport the bodies to the crematoria and oversee the operation of the ovens, to extract and eliminate the ashes" (p. 50). On Levi's account, there were some 700 to 1000 active members of the Special Squad in the Auschwitz camp.

slaves debased by alcohol and the daily slaughter are transformed; they no longer have before them the anonymous mass, the flood of frightened, stunned people coming off the boxcars: they have a person. (pp. 55–56)

As Levi (1989) goes on to note, "Occurrences like this astonish because they conflict with the image we have of man in harmony with himself, coherent, monolithic; and they should not astonish because that is not how man is. Compassion and brutality can exist in the same individual and in the same moment, despite all logic; and for all that, compassion itself eludes logic" (p. 56). I have never understood how compassion and brutality could exist "in the same moment"; they seem to me, still, to be so thoroughly at odds with one another as to preclude their simultaneous belonging. But Levi's main point remains: we are divided beings, living in the space between Eros and Thanatos, love and death. In true Levinasian fashion, Levi also underscores the primal significance of the face, the single and singular person: "A single Anne Frank excites more emotion than the myriads who suffered as she did but whose image has remained in the shadows." One can be, and often is, oblivious to the teeming masses of the afflicted and oppressed precisely owing to their facelessness. "Perhaps it is necessary that it can be so," Levi offers. "If we had to and were able to suffer the sufferings of everyone, we could not live" (p. 56). Perhaps, then, oblivion is something of an evolutionary necessity; and attention, in turn, something we hold in check, lest we be overwhelmed by the sheer reality of things. It may be that there are some who can take in more reality, awful though it may be. "Perhaps the dreadful gift of pity for the many is granted only to saints" (p. 56). For the rest of us, however, "there remains in the best of cases only the sporadic pity addressed to the single individual, the *Mitmensch*, the co-man: the human being of flesh and blood standing before us, within the reach of our providentially myopic senses" (p. 57). This last phrase lingers. Yes, indeed: the priority of the Other. It is quite real. But it rests on shaky ground.

What, then, about the girl? The story continues:

A doctor is called, and he revives the girl with an injection: yes, the gas has not had its effect, she will survive, but where and how? Just then Muhsfeld, one of the SS men attached to the death installations, arrives. The doctor calls him to one side and presents the case to him. Muhsfeld hesitates, then he decides. No, the girl must die. If she were older, it would be a different matter, she would have more sense, perhaps she could be convinced to keep quiet about what has happened to her. But she's only sixteen: she can't be trusted. (Levi, 1989, p. 57)

In Muhsfeld's hesitation, we encounter the aforementioned "gap" full on: captivated though he may have been by the face of the Other, it in no way translates, necessarily, into sparing her. There still remains a moment of decision, and it is in this moment that compassion is eclipsed, buried under the terrible weight of reason, logic. "And yet," Levi continues, "he does not kill her with his own hands. He calls one of his underlings to eliminate her with a blow to the nape of the neck" (p. 57).

On one level, the entire scenario being described here is a hopeful one: their oblivion interrupted by the upsurge of human reality, compassion emerges, easily and spontaneously, among the members of the Special Squad. An SS officer hesitates about killing the girl, if only momentarily, and he won't perform the evil deed himself. Let us be clear about this, however: "[T]his man Muhsfeld was not a compassionate person; his daily ration of slaughter was studded with arbitrary and capricious acts, marked by his inventions of refined cruelty. He was tried in 1947, sentenced to death and hung in Krakow and this was right, but not even he was a monolith." Levi even goes so far as to acknowledge, correctly no doubt, that "[h]ad [Muhsfeld] lived in a different environment and epoch, he probably would have behaved like any other common man" (Levi, 1989, p. 57). If there is hope in Levi's account, it is a qualified one, for in the end, whatever compassion and pity there may have been was trumped. Plus, consider what had been required in order to bring it about: an utterly unanticipated event, something "exceptional, unique." Had it not occurred, it would have been business as usual.

We therefore have at least two large problems before us. The first is this gap between attention and moral life.[17] Even if the former is required for the

---

17. Bearing this entire scenario in mind, it could be argued, still, that there is in fact a necessary connection between attentive seeing—in this case, seeing the girl—and the moral realm. Following Levi's account, seeing the girl did seem to bring about spontaneously a measure of compassion, even care. What it didn't do, however, was save her. Insofar as we regard "compassion" as ethical in itself, the possible necessity of the connection at hand remains intact. But insofar as it is "on the way" to the ethical, so to speak, but not quite there, such necessity remains open to question. One way or the other, I would still hold to the existence of this (possible) "gap." Among other reasons, it seems like a safer, more appropriately tentative way of formulating the relationship between attention and moral life.

latter, it in no way ensures it. One important challenge, therefore, is to determine whether there are ways of minimizing this gap and thereby increasing the chances that one will behave rightly. What might it have taken for Muhsfeld to have followed the lead of his own pity and compassion? Hannah Arendt explores this very issue in *Eichmann in Jerusalem* (1965):

> (J)ust as the law in civilized countries assumes that the voice of conscience tells everybody, "Thou shalt not kill," even though man's natural desires and inclinations may at times be murderous, so the law of Hitler's land demanded that the voice of conscience tell everybody: "Thou shalt kill," although the organizers of massacres knew full well that murder is against the normal desires and inclinations of most people. Evil in the Third Reich had lost the quality by which most people recognize it—the quality of temptation. Many Germans and many Nazis, probably an overwhelming majority of them, must have been tempted *not* to murder, *not* to rob, *not* to let their neighbors go off to their doom (for that the Jews were transported to their doom they knew, of course, even though many of them may not have known the gruesome details), and not to become accomplices in all these crimes by benefiting from them. But, God knows, they had learned how to resist temptation. (p. 150)

What an extraordinary, harrowing passage. Again, what might it have taken for Muhsfeld to follow the lead of his own pity and compassion? What might it take for *us* to do so? Is it even possible?

The second problem strikes me as even more vexing. Even if we were to somehow succeed in minimizing the gap at hand, there would still remain the profound, and prior, challenge of *seeing*, attending. Levi has already told us how difficult this is to do given our "providentially myopic senses." Indeed, he notes, "there are those who, faced by the crime of others or their own, turn their backs so as not to see it and not feel touched by it. This is what the majority of Germans did during the twelve Hitlerian years, deluding themselves that not seeing was a way of not knowing, and that not knowing relieved them of their share of complicity or connivance" (1989, pp. 85–86). Alongside what I have referred to as "ordinary oblivion," there is thus the "willed ignorance" about which Levi speaks, a much more purposeful, and pernicious, form of not-seeing, geared precisely toward shutting out whatever harsh realities we might encounter.[18] We have also observed that it frequently seems to take "exceptional, unique" events and circumstances—a diagnosis of leukemia, a terrible fire, a pocket of air amidst a tangle of corpses—to break the spell of oblivion and thereby allow seeing to emerge. Are there alternatives? As has already been suggested, there are practices, discrete mnemonic devices, that can move this process forward. We shall be exploring them in due time. But another kind of remembering would seem to be needed as well, one tied to our—and the *other's*—very mortality.[19] Is there a way to encounter the reality of death so that it infuses and energizes the reality of life?

We might turn to Seneca (2005) to begin to answer this question. For starters, he tells us, we can take inventory of our lives and see how much of our time is well spent. Conjuring up the possible words of "someone from the older generation," he asks us to consider the following:

> "You will find that you have fewer years than you reckon. Call to mind when you ever had a fixed purpose; how few days have passed as you planned; when you were ever at your own disposal; when your face wore its natural expression; when your mind was undisturbed; what work you have achieved in such a long life; how many have plundered your life when you were unaware of your losses; how much you have lost through groundless sorrow, foolish joy, greedy desire, the seductions of society; how little of your own life was left to you. You will realize that you are dying prematurely." (pp. 4–5)

"So," Seneca goes on to ask, "what is the reason for this?" The answer is clear:

> You are living as if destined to live for ever; your own frailty never occurs to you; you don't notice how much time has already passed,

---

18. This is a complicated issue as well. The refusal to see, it would seem, is itself predicated on what one does, on some level, see; otherwise, there would be no grounds for the refusal. Having acknowledged this, Levi's notion of "willed ignorance," the sort of purposeful not-seeing that often characterizes our relationship to suffering others, still seems all too valid.

19. Bringing these two ideas together, Christopher Dustin and Joanna Ziegler (2007) have spoken precisely of "practicing mortality," that is, taking practical measures designed, essentially, to keep mortality in view and in turn strengthen one's capacity to live fully and well. I return to some of their ideas in the final chapter, "Living Ex-centrically," in which I spell out more explicitly what might be done to live the priority of the Other. Also important in this context, once again, is Becker's *The Denial of Death* (1973), a profound exploration of both the limits and possibilities of keeping mortality in view.

but squander it as if you had a full and overflowing supply—though all the while that very day which you are devoting to somebody or something may be your last. You act like mortals in all that you fear, and like immortals in all that you desire.... How late it is to begin really to live just when life must end! How stupid to forget our mortality, and put off sensible plans to our fiftieth and sixtieth years, aiming to begin life from a point at which few have arrived! (p. 5)

Seneca thus concurs: we need to encounter the reality of death so that it infuses and energizes the reality of life.[20] And we need to do so sooner rather than later. But what exactly does this mean? And how do we translate it into how we live?

Living the Priority of the Other

Consider once more the bicycle ride I discussed at the very beginning of this chapter. The objects at hand—the wildflowers, the trees, and so on—were important; they, in fact, were part of the reason I took that particular ride to begin with. Or consider the situation with my wife. Other people, on hearing of her diagnosis, surely cared about her fate, but not, of course, in the same way I did, and for a very simple reason: she is *my* wife, not theirs! Having acknowledged this aspect of relationality, let me hasten to add that it was she, in her particularity, her uniqueness, her *face*, that called forth my care. Herein lies an important reason for my emphasis in this book on using the language of the Other rather than of relation: however much the objects before me acquire their distinctive presence and power as a function of my relationship to them, I nevertheless experience this presence and power as issuing from *them*. I don't love my relationship to my wife or kids or mother. I love *them* for who and what they palpably *are*.

Something similar may be said of aesthetic experience, religious experience, and other such potentially ecstatic modes. We are considering "a type of experience in which selves are described as merging, fusing, uniting with, or simply becoming other than themselves" (Benson, 1993, p. 2). And so, however much such aesthetic absorption "requires a conception of experience as constituted by the interactive relationship of self and

---

20. See also Heidegger's classic text *Being and Time* (1962) for a further treatment of this set of issues. For a literary version, Tolstoy's novella *The Death of Ivan Ilych* (1960 [1886]), discussed briefly in Chapter One, remains an excellent source.

object" (p. 12), this very relationship also involves what Benson refers to as the "non-deployment of I" (p. 83), such that "my 'location,' so to speak, is centred in and about the object rather than my own needs and emotions" (p. 97). "It can seem to be that of the cloud I am gazing at, or the blackbird I am listening to" (p. 99). Popular (mis)conceptions aside, experiences of this sort do not entail the wholesale dissolution of the self; as Benson notes, the condition of my absorption "in the object" is a " 'residual awareness' of myself as a spectator, listener or reader" (p. 97).[21] Indeed, without such awareness—as in certain forms of later stage dementia, for instance—there can *be* no absorption, no ecstatic union of this sort, for its very condition of possibility has been removed (see Freeman, 2008). Here too, therefore, the relational dimension of the process is operative, and relational language is certainly appropriate to employ when conceptualizing it. Phenomenologically, however, there is absorption *in the object*—that is, in the *Other*—such that the self is in abeyance, divested, even if temporarily, of its ego-driven energies.

Also relevant in this context is the aforementioned fact that the specific nature and quality of the Other—that is, the particular "object of one's attention" (Murdoch, 1970)—*matters*. While I may be in relation to an infinite number of other people or pieces of music, who and what these are is a key factor in determining the quality of my experience. Just as my wife, kids, and mother draw forth my love and care in a way that other people don't, so too do other objects in the world, both human and non-. Some will be life-giving and provide just the sort of existential nourishment I need, while others will be deadening, serving to blunt my powers of attention as well as my care. As Murdoch (1970) puts the matter, "It is...a psychological fact, and one of importance in moral philosophy, that we can all receive moral help by focusing our attention upon things which are valuable: virtuous people, great art, perhaps...the idea of goodness itself" (p. 54–55). Referring once more to Murdoch's preference for works of art, it is imperative to emphasize the importance of their "greatness." Only the great work can serve to purify and reorient my own centripetal energies, and it does this, we saw, to the degree that it is able to exist for me *as other*,

---

21. In a related vein, William Gass (1999) notes that "[w]hen we experience things as we at least sometimes should, the psychological distance between them and ourselves disappears. We are what we perceive, and what we perceive exists nowhere but in us" (p.144). At the same time, "[w]e should not imagine that such moments involve the cancellation of the self. A union is not a cancellation. What has to be left out of the self is its selfishness, but not its particular quality of mind" (p. 144).

as an object that commands my attention, that checks my own ego-driven impulses, and that allows me to get closer to the real world. Some works clearly do this much more readily than others, and we need to bear this in mind as we proceed.[22]

Now that I have underscored the idea that the specific nature of objects matters, I want to double back to the issue of my own "preparation," so to speak, for seeing them. Assuming for the time being that I can in fact speak (cautiously, of course) about the inherent properties of artistic works (among other realities), it is also patently clear that what I get out of these works also depends upon *me*—my knowledge, my quality of attention, my openness to experience, and more. But let me descend from the rarefied air of the museum to that bicycle path I have been referring to. I had approached the ride that day with a measure of attentiveness; it was a beautiful, sunny day, and I knew that some wondrous things awaited me. But for a time, you will recall, I had been oblivious to them, thinking instead about other things, including this book. At some point, my attention shifted and I remembered why I was there. A patch of flowers had caught my eye, and from that point on I could turn my attention more directly to the wonders before me. As I did so, I could not only see their beauty but feel their energy, and this in turn led to the feeling of a kind of mutual belonging, an all-of-a-piece-ness, of the sort that makes the world seem right, if only for a few moments. Even in a simple experience like this one, there are cycles of relatedness and multiple paths of influence, from me to the flowers and the flowers to me and back again. And, as just noted, there can also be the sheer fact of relation itself, self and world, being and belonging, together. When I was able to be truly *there*, attentive, so too was the Other. When I retreated into myself, the Other all but vanished.

It is much the same, I suggested, with people. Whether they emerge in their separateness and differentness (to refer back to Murdoch's terms) depends, in part, on *us*. But on what? What exactly is it that allows one to behold the Other? What is it that allows the Other to emerge, to

---

22. This way of thinking appears too universalizing. The fact is, there are many (many) different views concerning what constitutes artistic greatness—so many that some have come to question the very idea, claiming that, ultimately, there really *is* no object "in itself" and that whatever judgments we might make about it are a function of our own (socially constructed) perspectives. Important though this critique has been, it nevertheless is clear that the object matters. This is why we go to museums, concert halls, and all the rest. I return to this rather loaded issue in Chapter Four. There, I hope, my reasons for maintaining this view will become clearer.

stand forth, in priority? We have already received some plausible—if disturbing—answers: bad news, tragedies, catastrophes, and other such attention-getting and life-jolting realities. But we would hardly want to rely on these! What else, then?

"I must necessarily turn to something other than myself," Simone Weil (1997 [1952]) has written, "since it is a question of my being delivered from self" (p. 3). In this respect, she and Murdoch are of a piece: attention to the Other is a vehicle of unselfing, for being "delivered" from self. For Weil, however, this is hardly a foolproof strategy. More, therefore, needs to be done to effect this process of deliverance. How? One notable way is through a kind of killing-off of desire. "The extinction of desire (Buddhism)—or detachment—or *amor fati*—or desire for the absolute good—these all amount to the same....The reality of the world is the result of our attachment. It is the reality of the self which we transfer into things. It has nothing to do with independent reality. That is only perceptible through total detachment" (Weil, 1997 [1952], pp. 12–13).

Weil's words may sound too harsh for some. "Total detachment," the emptying of all desire, and the full-scale deliverance from self may seem entirely too severe a response to the challenge before us. As Mark Epstein argues compellingly in his book *Open to Desire: The Truth about What the Buddha Taught* (2005), "There is a drive for transcendence that is implicit in even the most sensual of desires" (p. 7). Consequently, it is best seen as an aspect of "our vitality, an essential component of our human experience, that which gives us our individuality and at the same time keeps prodding us out of ourselves....It is 'the natural,' and if it is chased away it returns with a vengeance" (p. 9). For Epstein, therefore, the question is, "How can we prevent desire from being hijacked by the divisive force of clinging?" (p. 31). Along these lines, the problem isn't desire per se but rather that corrupted form of it that, in its craving and clinging, occludes, rather than reveals, the world. Bearing this qualification in mind, there may still be something in Weil's (1997 [1952]) words worth thinking about: "When I am in any place, I disturb the silence of heaven and earth by my breathing and the beating of my heart....May I disappear in order that those things that I see may become perfect in their beauty from the very fact that they are no longer things I see." The paradoxical aim: "To see a landscape as it is when I am not there" (p. 37).

But how does one arrive at this sort of attentive, comparatively self-less place? As noted earlier, there are discrete techniques for doing so, meditative or contemplative practices geared toward sharpening one's powers of attention and thereby unselfing, divesting ourselves of excess ego. If Weil is right, however, these sorts of practices may not be quite enough. For this reason, "self-effacement"—indeed, a kind of self-*destruction*—must take place as well. Only this, she insists, will quiet the ego's appetite enough to let the world emerge. So it is that she had found in *affliction*—suffering, degradation, even humiliation—an important vehicle for launching the process at hand: she would do what she could to "lower" herself in order, ultimately, to rise. Valuable though this might have been for Weil, I am not inclined to follow her lead, and for the same reason I have stopped short of "recommending" bad news, tragedies, and catastrophes. There is enough suffering in the world already! Here too, however, Weil is clearly on to something, for what she seems to be suggesting, above all, is that without the sort of jolt to the system that affliction provides—whether self-induced or brought about by dire circumstances—we may not rise to the occasion of living the priority of the Other. As I stated near the beginning of this chapter, it can't be that these kinds of assaults are *required*—or at least I hope not. Yet without them, I also acknowledged, we often fall sorely short of being fully *there* for the Other. Now, if Weil is right in maintaining that attention alone (and the practices needed for sharpening it) may not suffice to perform the difficult work of unselfing, and if we would rather not rely on catastrophes and the like to do so, what else might be done in service of the task? Can there be *non*-catastrophic jolts to the system that would somehow do the work that affliction and catastrophe do? I certainly hope so, and as I suggest in Chapter Six, we would do well to seek them out.

Following Weil's and Murdoch's respective leads, there are two fundamental fronts from which to live the priority of the Other, one through attention and the other through intentional unselfing, through purposefully divesting ourselves of self-interest; and although these surely overlap—attention to the Other can lead to unselfing, and vice versa—they remain distinctive inroads into the project of living the priority of the Other, the former being more oriented toward objects outside the self and the latter toward one's own internal processes.[23] Somehow, therefore, both of these fronts will need to be mobilized in service of the task at hand. The task is a daunting one. With our e-mail and our cell phones and the vast array of

---

23. As David Tracy notes in an interesting piece, "Iris Murdoch and the Many Faces of Platonism" (1996), Murdoch's way of speaking about spiritual practices, especially her reference to detachment and attention, call forth what he terms "a new kind of Platonized Buddhism" (p. 73). This does indeed sound like an apt description of what her, and Weil's, work is about.

techno-gadgets that are increasingly flooding the marketplace, our attention is frequently scattered and dispersed. It can be difficult to pause, to reflect, to truly be where we are; there is always something else to do, somewhere else to be. I am not suggesting that this problem is completely unprecedented. Inattention and misconceived priorities are hardly newcomers on the human scene. At the same time, to be attentive to the world in the way I have suggested has surely been made more difficult in our era.[24] To break the spell of oblivion may therefore require an extra effort on our part.

As for the challenge of divesting ourselves of self-interest, it is, and will no doubt remain, a massive one. While the "fat relentless ego" of which Murdoch speaks may have grown fatter still in recent times, it too is hardly a newcomer on the human scene. We need not decide whether this longstanding condition is definitive of "who we are." Indeed, as I argued earlier, we cannot do so, for there is no separating who we are from the particular lives we lead. But there is no mistaking this appetitive dimension of the human condition and the challenges it poses to living well.

Let me close this chapter with two interrelated ideas. In what has been said thus far, I have used such terms as "unselfing" and have even referred to (metaphorical) self-destruction. Some of these words appear in the pages to follow as well, and for good reason: insofar as the self is dominated by the hungry desires of the ego, it needs to be taken down to size. But this reduction of the appetitive ego may also be seen as the very condition for regaining a more capacious mode of being, one that has been nourished and made more whole and real by the presence of the Other. We therefore return to an important—and, on the face of it, paradoxical—implication: *experiencing the priority of the Other is the requisite condition for realizing the Self.* By "Self," I refer not to the preoccupied, narcissistically invested ego but to that ecstatic mode of being—both personal and supra-personal—that is "given back," as I put it earlier, by experiences of the sort we have been considering in this chapter. We are *enlarged* by them and become in closer touch with deeper dimensions, dimensions that are at once "ours" and beyond us.[25]

---

24. See, e.g., Sven Birkerts's *The Gutenberg Elegies: The Fate of Reading in an Electronic Age* (2006); see also Bill McKibben's *Enough: Staying Human in an Engineered Age* (2004).

25. It may be that "Self" isn't the right term for what is being described here. By using it, in fact, I run the risk of conveying the impression that, ultimately, this book isn't about the Other at all. Why use it, then? In part, it is to underscore the fact that there are different ways entirely of conceiving the idea. More substantively, it is to underscore what I have referred to elsewhere (Freeman, 2004b) as the "secondarity" of the self, the notion that is not only sustained but brought into its very being by the Other.

We have also encountered words like "detachment," which, in the eyes of some, is a kind of co-requisite of attention: we need to un-clutter our relation to the Other, separate ourselves from the objects of our attention so as to let them be. I find myself ambivalent about this word, and further on in this book I explain why this is so. Here too, however, there is good reason for its having been employed: given that my very presence cannot help but "intrude" on the otherness of the Other, I should do what I can to "keep away." This language can appear cold and objectifying, even isolating. But there is a paradox of sorts at work in this context as well. In a distinct sense, *detachment is the requisite condition for connection*, for my belonging in and to the world, my ability to receive its energy and warmth. It is this energy and warmth, as it issues from the Other, that allows us to flourish and to grow. With this growth, there frequently emerges renewed reverence and care for the Other, such that the cycle of attentive being can be sustained.

NOW THAT WE have made some preliminary contact with the profound challenges entailed in living the priority of the Other, it is time to return to the various spheres of otherness—that of other people, the non-human world, and the mystery of being—identified by Buber. For Buber, along with Levinas, the human Other would seem to be the sphere of spheres. It should be noted that for both, albeit in different ways, there is no separating this sphere from God. The *ultimate* source of our regard for people, in other words, can only issue from "on high," as it were. Others, of course, see the issue differently and are perfectly willing to accord priority to the human Other without invoking an ultimate source. Whichever path we choose, there is no questioning the importance of people in both thinking and living the priority of the Other. It is time now to see how and why this is so. In the process, we will also have opportunity to question this putative priority among priorities and determine where exactly we humans might stand in the vast realm of otherness of which we are a part.

3
For the Other

The Possibility of Humanity

The Worcester Cold Storage and Warehouse Co. fire brought home in the most direct and unequivocal way the importance of people. I recall turning on the television the morning after the disaster only to find the anguished faces of several of our neighbors, relatives of one of the lost firefighters, on the scene of the fire. I saw one of them, a son, face to face the next day. Soon after, I would see more—other children, his wife, his father and mother, his brother. We really didn't know them very well; they were just neighbors, good people, coming and going, mowing their lawns and tending their flowers. But they emerged that grim week with a vividness and a humanness that was striking. Normally, they, like so many others, were part of the setting, part of the backdrop through which we moved, occasionally coming into view for a few quick words or a wave hello but then receding, fading from view once more. For a long while after the fire, though, everything was different.

There were also those people we came to know in the form of images on a television screen or photos from the local newspaper. These proved to be remarkably powerful in their own right. Especially powerful were images of the fallen firefighters themselves. A group of fellow firefighters had elected to miss the memorial service for their fallen brothers in order to continue sifting through the rubble of the building in search of remains. A monitor had been installed on the scene so they could stay connected. "It's tough," one of them was quoted as saying (in our local newspaper, the *Worcester Telegram & Gazette*), "but then you look over at those jumbo TV screens that tell you why you're there.... Every time you see a picture of them, it makes you want to find them that much more" (1999a, p. A8). There had also been buttons made displaying the faces of the dead, and posters and placards. Their faces quickly became emblazoned in memory.

And then there were those people we didn't get to know at all—passers-by, visitors, strangers. What was so curious was that they had all become neighbors in a way. Not unlike the people across the street, they had become more vivid and human. Far from being a mere part of the setting, they emerged as living beings, with names and faces and histories. Countless letters were sent to the *Worcester Telegram & Gazette* in the aftermath of the tragedy. "It is almost impossible to find words to describe the sorrow and grief I feel since the loss of the six gallant firefighters," wrote one man who had spent 47 years in the fire service. "During this long period of grief and sorrow I pray that God will be with the family members, survivors, officers and members of the fire department to ease their pain and suffering...[and] grant eternal rest to the members who gave up their lives" (1999a, p. A9). Another letter, written by a captain from a nearby fire department, speaks to the notion that the deceased firefighters might have died in vain: "It would have been wrong not to allow the firefighters to search the building and do their jobs and also wrong not to send them in to help their brothers in trouble.... Every firefighter in Worcester, if they had the chance to make a deal with God to give their life to bring back our six brothers," he continued, "would do it without hesitation because a firefighter's only flaw is also his greatest attribute, which is they put others before themselves. And when a brother firefighter is in trouble, they will walk into the fires of hell to help" (1999a, p. A9).

There was much to be learned from the entire train of events. Indeed, added another letter-writer, "The courageous work of Worcester's firefighters offers a profound lesson on living for us all." The fact is, "The firefighters who rushed into Friday night's blaze gave their lives to the possibility that other lives might be preserved. Their colleagues will tell you that such an effort is part of their job," that "living in constant readiness to place one's life on the line for the protection and preservation of any human life is the very essence of the firefighter's selfless work." As for the lesson that was offered, it was a simple one: "We are connected. In a time when many of us feel our society dividing against itself, one human being from another, the firefighter speaks to the essential lifeline that is our deepest bond" (1999a, p. A9).

Other letters and editorials repeatedly called attention to the fact that the fallen firefighters had given their lives to the homeless. There were proclamations that "every life is as valuable as every other" and an insistence on "service to the poorest among us." There had actually been some fear of backlash against the homeless; in some people's eyes, they had been the ultimate "cause" of the entire tragedy. But the backlash never materialized. In one letter, written by someone from the Massachusetts Housing and Shelter Alliance, it was even suggested that a homeless shelter be dedicated to the memory of the firefighters: "In making the sacrifice to save the lives of homeless people, the Worcester firefighters exemplified the spiritual legacy of selflessness so often lacking in our society. In doing their duty, they reached out to the poorest of the poor, placing themselves at risk to save the lives of those chronically at risk. Truly, they personified the definition of love found in the Scriptures: 'What greater love hath any person than this, that they would lay down their life for others.'" (1999a, p. A9). Another letter urged families and friends of the fallen firefighters to "take immense comfort in knowing that your neighbors as well as those from the farthest reaches of the globe, feel your heartbreak, your pain and your sense of loss" and also asked that "this generosity of love respectfully extend to the homeless persons arrested for this event, as well as for their families and friends" (1999a, p. A9).

Uplifting though many of these thoughts were, there was also some anger expressed regarding the stature of firefighters, particularly in comparison to the wealthy. "In a society where prima donna athletes make millions of dollars entertaining us, while these men along with their counterparts in the Police Department earn enough for nothing more than a modest existence, something is wrong." At the same time, this letter continues, "Witness to the consideration displayed by the people of this great community leads one to believe that the norms of society can change for the better." Echoing a theme we encountered in the previous chapter, some came to wonder about the "necessity" of such tragedies as wake-up calls for a misdirected humanity: "Perhaps an event as tragic as this is the only thing that can redirect the public's attention to the fact that these men and women, as well as men and women like them throughout the country, are America's true heroes" (1999a, p. A8).

In a related vein, a number of other letters addressed the theme of our "forgetfulness," both about the community of Worcester and about our humanity itself. One man noted that [t]he tragedy has informed me again with a profound understanding of the nobility and honor of a life spent in public service.... [It also] reminded me of something I have forgotten too often, namely, the character of warmth of Worcester and the people who call it home. I have been stirred by the sense of caring, community and collective loss expressed throughout the last week by all people, including the youngest schoolchildren. In an age of supposed cynicism and lost faith, Worcester's example in this sad time reminds us all of the decency of human beings and the goodness in men's hearts" (1999b, p. A23).

A woman from a neighboring town was more pointed in her reflections about forgetfulness: "Why do people come together so tremendously for tragedies?" she asked. "Why don't we show this compassion on a daily basis? Take current road rage.... The person we cut off in traffic, those we say vulgarities to or send unfriendly hand signals could be the same person we stood next to on Central Street as we both cried when the procession went by." For this woman, the event was indeed a profound wakeup call. The fact is, "No one knows when they will not see tomorrow. More attention should be paid to how we live our lives." Surely, "[e]veryone reading this has the power within themselves to honor those gone," but also, she adds, "to honor those remaining. There are countless ways for us to extend ourselves every day to each other, to strangers. Do it now, in support of those who so painfully need our healing and loving encouragement. Honor them all today and every day" (1999b, p. A23).

What was it, finally, that had been learned from Worcester's tragic fire and the events that followed in its wake? First, something was learned about the depth of "sorrow and grief" we are capable of feeling for complete strangers. Ordinarily, these emotions are reserved for those we know, especially those near to us. As such, they seem to be linked to our own concerns, perhaps to the life we will be leading in their absence. This, in turn, has led some to suppose that even emotions such as these are essentially egoistic, that their primary reference is to the self and its losses. In the present case, however, there appeared to be little egoistic investment involved. Indeed, by all indications there was little "processing" involved, in the sense of deliberative thought, consciousness, reason. People's response was direct and immediate—that is to say, largely unmediated by their own concerns and preoccupations.

Something was also learned about the possibility of human sympathy and compassion, about the desire "to ease [the] pain and suffering" of the afflicted. All throughout the city, there had been acts of remarkable kindness and generosity. People wanted to help, to soothe; they would do whatever it took to be there for those in need. It could be that some kind of rapid-fire calculation had taken place: "If that ever happened to me, I'd sure want to be helped too." Judging by what went on, however, there was, again, something much more direct and immediate about this desire to alleviate others' suffering. All one needed to see was the face of the Other. It was this, above all else, that proclaimed priority.

This notion of the Other's priority was also found in people's reflections about the actions of the firefighters. Initially, some had questioned the wisdom of the firefighters' entering the burning building on a mere hunch that there might be people inside. Some had also questioned the wisdom of having additional firefighters enter later on. Two had been lost already; what sense was there in sending in more? But as many insisted in the wake of such "second-guessing," to have done anything other than what had in fact been done would simply have been "wrong." Indeed, as one man had insisted in his letter, there had been no choice involved at all; like every other firefighter he knew, he would do absolutely anything, including give up his own life, to bring back one of his brothers. As was pointed out in another letter, efforts of this sort were simply "part of [the] job," the "readiness to place one's life on the line" in order to help others being the essence of the firefighter's work. As the author of that letter hastened to add, this should not be construed merely in terms of job requirements and the like. Something much more profound had been learned: "We are connected," he said. And given the kind of society we have come to inhabit, we ought to remember it. "The firefighter," he added, "speaks to the essential lifeline that is our deepest bond." *This* is what is real and primary; how tragic it is that we have fashioned a world in which it so easy to imagine otherwise.

This "lesson" is a complicated one. In keeping with what was said earlier on, that we are *potentially* connected seems unarguable; there are surely times when we rise to the occasion of being with and being for others. Whether we *are* so connected, as a matter of course and necessity, is a tougher question to answer. Was something about our essential lifeline to one another "realized" through the event of the fire? Was it "there," unacknowledged, all along? I spoke earlier of our neighbors and of the many people who had, in effect, *become* our neighbors; to think that all of them had been there too, all along. But in what sense had they been there? It could be that all of this fellow-feeling was *created* rather than *discovered*. But it could not be created with such power and passion, I would argue, without there having already been an inclination, a prior state of preparedness, readiness.

As for the question of whether tragedies of this sort are in fact required in order to bring such readiness into being, the most honest thing to be said is, I don't know for sure, but I certainly hope not; there must be other ways. I wish I could be more unequivocally hopeful here. I have no doubts whatsoever about the sincerity and authenticity of the sentiments expressed in the last few pages. The priority of the Other had surely come into view, spontaneously and with the kind of urgency that bespeaks something real, something enduringly significant. In view of this, it might be argued that, yes, being there for the other in this way is part of our nature—a part, perhaps, that has been buried, covered over by the ugly exigencies, or ostensible exigencies, of a narcissistic, crudely competitive, and at times positively violent culture. This seems to be the view set forth by Mary Midgley (2010), whose work we considered in the Introduction. Drawing especially on Darwin's *The Descent of Man* (2010 [1872]), she notes that, "among social species, 'the fittest' are not necessarily the strongest, nor indeed the cleverest, but the most sociable: those whose temperament most inclines them to friendly cooperation" (p. 49). The reason this tendency has gone so woefully under-recognized is that it does not jibe with the reigning ideology of competitive, even solipsistic, individualism. This is emphatically not to deny our capacity for aggression and violence; human history provides ample evidence. But there has been a too-ready tendency to posit this capacity as part of the immovable furniture of human nature, the Hobbesian "war of all against all" thus being seen as primary.[1] As Tzvetan Todorov (1996) has added, it could very well be that "the popular version of Hobbes's doctrine is wrong" and that "human beings are prompted...to communicate with one another, to help one another, and to distinguish good from evil." Rather than seeing morality as "but a superficial convention jettisoned at the first opportunity," therefore, we should recognize that "moral reactions are spontaneous, omnipresent, and eradicable only with the greatest violence. Plants

---

[1]. Marilyn Robinson (2010), whom we also heard from, expresses a similar view. The "parascientific" literature, rooted in this ideologically driven ethos of (genetically founded) individualism, generally places the idea of altruism "in a context that questions whether [it] is possible or desirable, or whether apparent instances are real, or what survival benefit might be conferred by that would account for its undeniable persistence among insect colonies" (p. 42). This is a strange, troubling, and dangerous state of affairs, not least because it relegates whatever goodness we might observe in human affairs to the status of an epiphenomenon, if not an outright illusion.

can be forced to grow horizontally, Rousseau says, but unconstrained they will nevertheless grow upward" (p. 39).[2]

Is this true? I'm afraid I need to offer much the same sort of answer I offered in the previous paragraph: I don't know. My own inclination, voiced earlier, is to resist speaking of human nature as either this or that—altruistic or selfish, good or bad. This doesn't mean that we *have* no nature, only that our nature exists *in potentia*, in the form of "readinesses," there to be activated and realized as a function of our circumstances, the ins and outs of our lives.[3] Are we *more* one than the other? Is one set of such readinesses more primary or dominant than the other? You guessed it: I don't know! I suppose I could offer a hope here—that we are primarily, maybe even essentially, good. But even this more qualified version essentializes our nature and renders us more "monolithic," as Levi puts it, than we seem to be. As I noted earlier, however much I might question whether we "are" anything (in particular) by nature, there is no questioning our basic intuitions about goodness (and badness): generally speaking, we *know* better and worse ways of being. This is precisely why so many of the people of Worcester were at once heartened by the goodness they saw and saddened by it. The situation is reminiscent of what was said in Chapter Two about the rapture and subsequent discomfort that may issue from our experience of great music: juxtaposed against the more mundane forms of being characteristic of much of everyday life, these higher forms can emerge as beautiful, painful reminders of what life could be.

For the time being, then, let us try to move beyond skepticism and extract what more we can of the possible lessons learned in the aftermath of the fire. As one man had noted after some time had passed, the incident had "reminded" him of something he had "forgotten too often."

---

[2]. See also Alfie Kohn's *The Brighter Side of Human Nature: Altruism and Empathy in Everyday Life* (1990) for related ideas, as well as Post et al.'s edited volume *Altruism and Altruistic Love: Science, Philosophy, and Religion in Dialogue* (2002). For an important evolutionarily based treatment, see also Eliott Sober and David Sloan Wilson's *Unto Others: The Evolution and Psychology of Unselfish Behavior* (1998).

[3]. According to Buber (1965), likewise, "man generally is not 'radically' this or that. It is not radicality that characterizes man as separated by a primal abyss from all that is merely animal, but it is his potentiality" (p. 77). As such, "Man is not good, man is not evil; he is, in a pre-eminent sense, good and evil together.... Good and evil, then, cannot be a pair of opposites like right and left or above and beneath. 'Good' is the movement in the direction of home, 'evil' is the aimless whirl of human potentialities without which nothing can be achieved and by which, if they take no direction but remain trapped in themselves, everything goes awry" (p. 78).

Concretely, he had forgotten "the character of warmth of Worcester and the people who call it home." He had been "stirred," he said, "by the sense of caring, community," and it was good to be reminded of these things once more, whatever the circumstances. More than this, however, he had been reminded "of the decency of human beings and the goodness in men's hearts." This was especially important, he had noted, in our current age "of supposed cynicism and lost faith." Not only would people the world over learn something about the city and its citizens, they might learn something about themselves and their possibilities as human beings. As another person had added, it had been "overwhelming to see the immense response from people around the city, the United States and the world." Indeed it had.

But that person had also been puzzled, and troubled, about why people "come together so" in the face of tragedies and why they—we—seem unable to show this compassion more regularly. Somehow, she went on to imply, we need to internalize the reality of death. "No one knows when they will not see tomorrow," she reminded us. For this very reason, "more attention should be paid to how we live our lives." As another woman had added, there were "countless" ways to do so, and we should "do it now, in support of those who painfully need our healing and loving encouragement." Yes, indeed: we should "honor them all day and every day." But how?

The Human Other

The priority of the Other is perhaps most readily recognized in the form of our care for other people. This is not so much a "decision" we make or the outgrowth of some "principle" we hold; it is a directly revealed, unassailable reality, issuing from the Other's very presence. We need not look to fires and other such dramatic events to see that this is so. We can look to our wives and husbands and children, our lovers and friends, our colleagues, our acquaintances, our neighbors. There are many things in the world that can have an impact on us. As Buber noted, in fact, there are many things, from trees to horses, that can serve as our partners in dialogue; they can be the "You" with which "I" am in relation. But there is no dialogue quite like the one we can have with another human being, and there is no "You" quite like the one that assumes the form of the living, breathing person, standing before us. Without wishing to sound anthropocentric—the Other, I have insisted, is not to be considered in human terms alone—human beings do seem to have a certain priority over the many other beings, inanimate as well as animate, we might encounter.[4]

For Buber, there are some straightforward reasons for this condition of priority. For one, others talk back to us in a way that is patently unparalleled. Buber's horse did seem to have a good deal to "say," and so does the world of nature more generally. For that matter, so do many other worlds—like that of art, for instance. Broadly speaking, we are in dialogue with them all. One might even hold that some of the beings encountered in these non-human worlds can "speak to me" like nothing else, humans included. But none of this detracts from the fleshy specificity that is found in the encounter with a human "You," particularly one we know and love—or *hate*: "Before we are thinkers," Midgley (2010) writes, "we are lovers and haters, creatures deeply aware of those around us and fully integrated into their life" (p. 130).[5]

The capacity to "talk back," as I have put it, is but one way of framing the situation of human-to-human dialogue. Buber also speaks of *reciprocity*, of the essential symmetry of the human-to-human relationship. In an important sense, the other human being, with whom I am in dialogue, is a being like me. As such, we can relate to one another with a knowledge and sensibility regarding our respective worlds that simply cannot be had in our relationships with other beings. This is not to claim that the other person is *just* like me. Nor is it to claim that our knowledge about others is complete or adequate or even very good. Indeed, the very notion of "knowledge" of another person, in the sense of comprehending, "grasping," may be suspect at its very core (Buber, 1970; Marcel, 1950). In a deep sense, the Other, qua person, cannot help but elude me; there is both an *indefiniteness* and an *infiniteness* about the very existence of the other person (Levinas, 1969, 1985). But none of these "qualifications," Buber implies,

---

4. Admittedly, it is difficult to set forth this idea without sounding anthropocentric. And by way of providing something of a reminder, for Buber (as well as Levinas) the importance of people is not to be separated from God, the "eternal You" that gives meaning and form to any and all of our relationships. I sincerely thank a reviewer for highlighting this important point. In most "secular psychology," as he put it, Buber's theistic commitments tended to be minimized, if not effaced. Given the nature of contemporary academic culture, in psychology especially, this is understandable. But the fact is, the I–Thou relation, both human and non-, is, for Buber, of a piece with the I–Thou relation to God.

5. See, again, Marion's *The Erotic Phenomenon* (2007), which we considered briefly in the Introduction. He would certainly concur with the "lovers" portion of Midgley's statement: *ego amans* is more primary than *ego cogitans*. Whether he would accept the "haters" portion is more questionable.

take away from the condition of reciprocity that is part and parcel of our dialogue with others. Indeed, these qualifications serve as testimony to the fact that the human-to-human relationship is a unique and special one, perhaps the very model of any that might obtain between an "I" and a "You." So it is that he speaks of the "mystery of reciprocity" (1970, p. 64).

As Buber goes on to note, "The I of the basic word I-You is different from that of the basic word I-It. The I of the basic word I-It appears as an ego and becomes conscious of itself as a subject (of experience and use). The I of the basic word I-You appears as a person and becomes conscious of itself as subjectivity.... Egos appear by setting themselves apart from other egos. Persons appear by entering into relation to other persons" (1970, pp. 111–112). This is yet another way of speaking about the primacy of dialogue and the mystery of reciprocity: our very entry into personhood, Buber tells us, is contingent upon our relatedness to others. It is also another way of underscoring the aforementioned idea that recognizing and experiencing the priority of the Other is the requisite condition for the realization of Self.

Buber offers an important qualification to what has been said in this context. "No human being is pure person, and none is pure ego.... Each lives in a twofold I. But some men are so person-oriented that one may call them persons, while others are so ego-oriented that one may call them egos. Between these and those," he maintains, "true history takes place" (1970, pp. 114–115). Bearing these terms in mind, it might plausibly be said that during the course of recent history especially, the balance between a person-orientation and an ego-orientation has shifted, in favor of the latter. As I have suggested already, I do not mean this only in terms of the familiar categories of narcissism and individualism, relevant though they remain. I mean it in a more thoroughgoing, fundamental sense. The epoch of the ego, we might say, has tended to occlude *persons* from view. Too often, they, *we*, have become It-like entities, circumscribed by bodies, treated in the manner of things. Academic psychology is especially guilty of such mistreatment. Indeed, "Thou" has largely been eclipsed by "It," the prevailing supposition being that, in the end, we must regard ourselves as we would any and all other thing-like beings, able to be objectified, encapsulated, contained.[6] Let us not forget the wide world beyond academic psychology either, the one found in psychiatric wards and asylums, in

---

6. For a comprehensive treatment of the ideas of persons and personhood, see especially *Persons: Understanding Psychological Selfhood and Agency* (2009) by Jack Martin, Jeff H. Sugarman, and Sarah Hickinbottom.

eugenics programs and concentration camps, in racism and sexism and the many other isms that insist on turning persons into mere instances of this or that crude category of phenomena.[7]

We may live in a "twofold I," as Buber puts it, but much of what surrounds us pulls us backward, centripetally, toward the pole of the ego. We have therefore deprived ourselves of that element of personhood—and Selfhood—that accrues from true relationship, true dialogue, with other persons. Following Dupré's (1976) ideas, which were introduced in Chapter One, we have thus in some sense managed to become "less" than what we actually are.[8]

In part, the key to our being able to move more fully into personhood may be found in the quality of our relationships with others. Buber (1965) writes,

> This person is other, essentially other than myself, and this otherness of his is what I mean, because I mean him; I confirm it; I wish his otherness to exist, because I wish his particular being to exist.... That the men with whom I am bound up in the body politic and with whom I have directly or indirectly to do, are essentially other than myself, that this one or that one does not have merely a different mind, or way of thinking or feeling, or a different conviction or attitude, but has also a different perception of the world, a different recognition and order of meaning, a different touch from the regions of existence, a different faith, a different soil: to affirm all this, to affirm it in the way of a creature, in the midst of the hard situations of conflict, without relaxing their real seriousness, is the way by which we may officiate as helpers in this wide realm entrusted to us as well, and from which alone we are from time to time permitted to touch in our doubts, in humility and upright investigation, on the other's "truth" or "untruth," "justice" or "injustice." (pp. 61–62)

---

7. Interestingly enough, Suzanne Kirschner (2012) refers to this process as "othering"—more specifically, the "othering of difference." But this very process, in its reductive circumscription of other persons, is at one and the same time a denial and negation of the other's very otherness. The person becomes an example, an instance, anything but who she is.

8. Speaking in this way might seem to essentialize and bring us back to that sort of "robust" conception of human nature I have been questioning. Referring to what we "are" in this context, however, is not about human nature per se—for instance, whether we are fundamentally altruistic or egoistic. Rather, it is about personhood and what it might conceivably mean for us to be "fully formed." Dupré's main concern in the (1976) book we considered is the transcendent dimension of selfhood, a dimension, he believes, that has been severely diminished, owing especially to the secularizing movement of modern culture.

On this account, we must somehow deepen our attention to and regard for the other in his or her otherness, his or her differentness—not, I hasten to emphasize, as the Alien, the feared and dreaded Other, but as the unique being he or she is. We must in fact "affirm all this," take it to heart. Recognition is not enough; there needs to be care as well. More to the point still, and by way of harking back to a term we encountered earlier, there needs to be a measure of *devotion* to other persons, predicated upon their dignity and worth as human beings. Notice in this passage that Buber seems to have moved beyond the discourse of reciprocity and dialogue. There is talk instead of what is "essentially other than myself," of what is inexorably "different." As we shall see shortly, through considering the work of Emmanuel Levinas, this apparent shift in language is potentially significant, for it may be that reciprocity and dialogue, important though they are, do not suffice to convey the essential nature of our relationship to others. The Other, Levinas argues, must take priority.

But we have not left Buber behind quite yet. Interested as he is in relationships between persons, between "I" and "Thou," he also wants to consider the "*We*." The "We" is to be distinguished from mere community: "Only men [and women] who are capable of truly saying *Thou* to one another can truly say *We* with one another" (1965, p. 176). True community, therefore—that is, community taken as a quality of relationship rather than as a mere condition of affiliation—depends on how caring and devoted we are to the others in our midst. If in fact we are able to regard these others as persons, we are that much more likely not only to "have" community, but to *be in* community. If, however, we regard the others in our midst as mere egos (just like us), then the possibility of community diminishes in turn. Community is not a state of mere agglomeration or affiliation; it is a state of *relationship* between persons, writ large. Given the kinds of egos we seem to have formed in recent times, it is little wonder that community has suffered. Communities cannot be built with ego bricks alone; the mortar of human relationship is required as well. "We," together, must be there.

In addition to the more constant forms of the We just considered, there are, Buber (1965) notes, transient forms.

> Among these is to be reckoned, for example, the closer union which is formed for a few days among the genuine disciples and fellow-workers of a movement when an important leader dies. All impediments and difficulties are set aside, and a strange fruitfulness, or

at all events incandescence, of their life with one another is established. Another transient form is seen when in face of a catastrophe which appears inevitable the really heroic element of a community gathers together within itself, withdraws from all idle talk and fuss, but in it each is open to the others and they anticipate, in a brief common life, the binding power of a common death. (p. 176)

The "really heroic element of a community" of which Buber speaks had been abundantly present during the Worcester fire. All that had been dispersed, throughout the ordinary course of things, had been bound, "gathered together within itself," the vortex of the catastrophe serving to draw people near to one another, nearer perhaps than ever before. Moreover, not only had there been a pronounced withdrawal from all "idle talk and fuss," there had been a movement into the very depths of discourse. This was about life and death, and about the possibility of love even amidst the ashes of anguish and sorrow. It was also about the possibility of our truly being *neighbors*, engaged in a relationship wherein "each is open to the others."

There was another dimension operative in the community's response to the fire as well. In the "brief common life" people had lived together, there had been for many a glimpse of unadulterated *good*. Somehow, there had been more than the coming together of a community. Through the formation of an unparalleled "We-bond," there had been the revelation of a common identity, a common spirit, beyond the disparateness of people's lives. Indeed, far from representing the *denial* of difference, this common spirit served to affirm it and, in this affirmation, transcend it. "We are connected," one man had said—and, he might have added, the connection is good. In accordance with the perspective I have offered thus far, whether we *are* connected remains an open question. But we certainly *were*, and wondrously so. That we can *become* so, therefore—that it exists as a realizable possibility—is perfectly clear and surely reveals something vitally important about who and what We might be. For some, however, the revelation at hand seemed to go even further: in this intimation of connectedness and goodness, there had also been an intimation of *God*. "Extended," Buber (1965) writes, "the lines of relationships intersect in the eternal You. Every single You is a glimpse of that. Through every single You the basic word addresses the eternal You" (p. 123).

As Buber (1965) emphasizes, this glimpse of the eternal You does not emerge *apart* from the stuff of human relations but *through* these relations. Moreover, it "does not involve ignoring everything but seeing everything in the You, not renouncing the world but placing it upon its proper ground. Looking away from the world is no help toward God; staring at the world is no help either; but whoever beholds the world in him stands in his presence" (p. 127). On one level, Buber clarifies, God is "the wholly other" (see also Otto, 1958 [1923]). On another level, however, God is "the wholly same: the wholly present. Of course he is the *mysterium tremendum* that appears and overwhelms; but he is also the mystery of the obvious that is closer to me than my own I" (Buber, 1965, p. 127). This mystery is not to be considered an "inference," in the sense of something extrapolated from life, from the ongoing reality of things. "It's not as if something else were 'given' and this were then deduced from it" (p. 129). Rather, the mystery is present in what is there, immanent in the ordinary course of events.

From this perspective, the formation of a "We-bond," the revelation of a community's identity, such as that which took place in the aftermath of the Worcester fire, is to be understood through the relationship to the Other. The Other has given rise to the "Self" of the community through its priority, its primacy. Whatever good may have been glimpsed in and through the bond formed thus owes its existence to the Other. It is not to be "found" in us except as a *gift*, received from without.[9] Even as we may wish to take pride in our seemingly essential goodness, we should remain cognizant of the fact that this goodness cannot be "ours" at the source. "Real good," Simone Weil (1997 [1952]) reminds us, "can only come from outside ourselves, never from our own effort. We cannot under any circumstances manufacture something which is better than ourselves" (p. 41). This "outside"—this outside that is at once inside, this transcendence that is at once immanence—for many goes by the name of God.

Some readers, I realize, will not want to move in this direction. There is no need to, they might be argue. Indeed, there may not be any need to talk about "good" either, especially if it is taken to refer to some (putatively) ethereal Platonic form outside the messy stuff of human life. In the face of catastrophe and hardship, people set aside their usual preoccupations and behaved in a way that is conventionally regarded as good, largely, perhaps, because behavior of this sort tends to lead to the formation of more

---

9. This notion of the gift is dealt with extensively in Marion's *Being Given: Toward a Phenomenology of Givenness* (2002a). See also his chapter entitled "Sketch of a Phenomenological Concept of the Gift" in *The Visible and the Revealed* (2008).

civil, peaceful societies than would otherwise be the case. Why bother with "God" and "good"? Why, for that matter, bother speaking of the priority of the Other in this context? Buber was certainly right to point out the dialogical quality of our relationships with one another. He was also right to show how these relationships could be strengthened and deepened in the face of catastrophe; this is nothing more than an empirical fact. But on what basis can it be said that "something more" had gone on? Is the priority of the Other finally to be considered a matter of faith?

The answer to this last question, I believe, is a qualified "yes." Let me try to explain why I believe the "yes" is qualified. If what we mean by "a matter of faith" is an a priori conviction in the priority of the Other, perhaps held out of some institutionally codified system of belief, then my answer to the question posed would be a firm "no." That is to say, the priority of the Other has not been posited out of some preexisting belief system or structure of moral sentiments (consonant though it may be with these). Nor, again, has it been posited out of a conviction in the goodness of human nature—that is, the conviction that we are, at bottom, altruistic. To the greatest extent possible, I have tried to remain faithful to experience. It is exactly here, in this faithfulness, that the qualified "yes" emerges: to assume that what is *felt* to be the priority of the Other actually *is* the priority of the Other itself requires a kind of faith, one that abandons skepticism and cynicism, for a while at any rate, and trusts that what is there is real. I should admit that I also hold the belief that we *ought* to uphold the priority of the Other more than we do. I in fact argue as much in the final chapter. Even there, however, "ought" has two quite different senses. The first is moral and ethical: we should try to be better people—kinder, more compassionate, more loving. The second is rather more (how shall I put it?) "existential" in its meaning: given the kinds of people we are capable of becoming, we really ought to be doing a bit better. This latter meaning, it should be emphasized, bears within it the radically empirical nature of the Other's priority. We don't merely *believe* we can be better; we *know* it. And we know it directly and spontaneously whenever the Other's priority goes "without question."

Murdoch (1993) offers an interesting comment in this context in her treatment of the notion of perfection:

> We *experience* both the reality of perfection and its distance away, and this leads us to place our idea of it outside the world of existent being as something of a different unique and special sort.

> Such experience of the reality of the good is not like an arbitrary and assertive resort to our own will; it is a discovery of something independent of us, where that independence is essential. If we read these images aright they are not only enlightening and profound but amount to a statement of a belief which most people unreflectively hold. Non-philosophical people do not think that they invent good. They may invent their own activities, but good is somewhere else as an independent judge of these. Good is also something clearly seen and indubitably discovered in our ordinary unmysterious experience of transcendence, the progressive illuminating and inspiring discovery of *other*, the positive *experience* of truth, which comes to us all the time in a weak form and comes to most of us sometimes in a strong form (in art or love or work or looking at nature) and which remains with us as a standard or vision, an *orientation*, a *proof*, of what is possible and a vista of what might be. (p. 508)

This is not theology, Murdoch insists; she is talking about ordinary experience, and what is revealed in it, to anyone willing and able to give himself or herself over to its otherness. When I look into the face of a suffering person and am myself called into question by her infinite presence, does it really make sense to doubt her priority? Can I even do so except as a strange intellectual maneuver, an afterthought that flies in the face of what palpably *is*?

Some time ago, I was at a local hospital, and in the parking lot I saw a woman in a car, weeping. I have no idea over what; I imagined that she might have just received some bad news. There wasn't a whole lot I could do in this context. Had I knocked on the window of her car door to offer some soothing words, she probably would have called security. But I did wish I could have been there for her, somehow. The Other comes before me. And there are times when I know this as indubitably as I know anything at all.

Dissymmetry and Priority

Yet this "knowing" of which I just spoke is not a knowledge of the usual sort. As suggested earlier, ordinarily, when we speak of "knowledge," we speak of grasping or comprehending. Knowing is something *I* do. Knowledge is something *I* acquire. But in the kind of knowing that we

For the Other 93

have just considered, "I" am doing nothing at all. I am called out of myself, toward that other person, suffering, in need. I know her misery by the directness and immediacy with which I am disrupted and displaced, ejected from "my" world into hers. I also know that, in a profound and abiding way, I am responsible to her and for her.[10]

Emmanuel Levinas (1999a) uses the language of "summons" to convey the dynamic thrust of this movement toward the Other. He also uses the language of the "neighbor." "It is precisely in that recalling of me to my responsibility by the face that summons me, that demands me, that requires me—it is in that calling into question—that the other is my neighbor" (p. 25).[11] As Levinas goes on to suggest, the "knowledge" that is operative here does not derive from some "store," some reservoir of information, that I had beforehand. Nor is it the other person's similarity to me, which I somehow recognize, that calls me toward her. "Does not that summons to responsibility destroy the forms of generality in which my store of knowledge, my knowledge of the other man, represents the latter to me as similar to me, designating me instead in the face of the other as responsible with no possible denial, and thus, as the unique and chosen one?" (p. 27).

On Levinas's (1999a) account, it is precisely in the directness and immediateness of this summons to responsibility that we encounter in full force the priority of the Other: "There arises, awakened before the face of the other, a responsibility for the other to whom I was committed before any committing, *before* being present to myself or coming back to self" (pp. 30–31). The encounter with a stranger underscores this point. But "[w]hat does this *before* mean?" Levinas asks.

> Is it the before of an *a priori*? But would it not in that case come down to the priority of an idea that in the "deep past" of innateness was already a present correlative to the *I think*, and that—retained,

---

10. Particularly relevant here is the aforementioned distinction in Marcel (1950) between "object" and "presence." Whereas grasping an object is something I do, a presence, he told us, "can only be gathered to oneself or shut out from oneself, be welcomed or rebuffed" (p. 255). In the case at hand, I surely wasn't "comprehending" this woman in the sense of deriving some bit of conceptual knowledge from her situation (however much I might have speculated about its origin). Rather, and again, I was "called out of myself" by her, her very presence having acquired priority.

11. See also Jeffrey Bloechl's *Liturgy of the Neighbor: Emmanuel Levinas and the Religion of Responsibility* (2000) for a helpful discussion of related issues.

> conserved, or resuscitated in the duration of time, in temporality taken as the flow of instants—would be, by memory, re-presented? (p. 31)

In other words, must there not be some prior state of cognitive preparedness that somehow resurfaces in instances like these? Levinas's answer is "no."

> Here I am, in that responsibility cast back toward something that was never my fault, never my doing, toward something that was never in my power, nor my freedom—toward something that does not come to me from memory.... The responsibility for the other is not reducible to a thought going back to an idea given in the past to the "I think" and rediscovered by it. (p. 32)

As he clarifies further, "it is not a question of receiving an order by first perceiving it and then obeying it in a decision, an act of the will. The subjection to obedience precedes, in this proximity to the face, the hearing of the order" (p. 33).[12] In sum,

> Thinking the other person is a part of the irreducible concern for the other. Love is not consciousness. It is because there is a vigilance before the awakening that the *cogito* is possible, so that ethics is before ontology. Behind the arrival of the human there is already vigilance for the other. The transcendental *I* in its nakedness comes from the awakening by and for the other. (p. 98)

Let me try to unpack some of this dense material. Following Levinas, the priority of the Other—with priority in this context referring to what is "before"—derives from the fact that my commitment to the person in need is a spontaneous one. I was not *already* committed to this person; as was the case with the woman I encountered in the hospital parking lot

---

12. This brings us back to our earlier discussions of both the relationship between attention and moral life and the idea of obedience. From Levinas's perspective, the kind of spontaneous response I had to that suffering stranger was already ethical; that is, it was "built in," as I put it earlier. This seems right. At the same time, I would hold, there still remains some sense in which my compassion was a function of my being able to *see* her; for the fact is, I might not have let myself do so. The main point here, in any case—that my response to the Other is "summoned," elicited, directly and immediately—remains.

(and the many people I encountered in the wake of the Worcester fire), I may never have seen her before in my life. It therefore cannot be from "memory" that I find myself committed. The "before" in question cannot be one of chronology, of an earlier taking-place. When Levinas speaks of the "before," he means something different, something beyond chronology and indeed beyond thought. Thinking is ordinarily something that takes place in time, and again, it is something "I" do. But "thinking the other person" is a part of my "irreducible concern" for that person. The ethical relation is primary: ethics is before ontology, before "being." Indeed, "I" am "awakened," as Levinas puts it, "by and for the other."[13]

Here, as elsewhere, Levinas seeks to take us beyond dialogue, beyond the condition of reciprocity of which Buber has spoken. There is "proximity" between persons, but the movement at hand is "toward the Other where he is truly other," to "that place from which, for an insufficiently mature soul, hatred flows naturally or is deduced with infallible logic" (Levinas, 1999a, p. 88). As Levinas explains, the concept of reciprocity had bothered him "because the moment one is generous in hopes of reciprocity, that relation no longer involves generosity but the commercial relation, the exchange of good behavior. In the relation to the other, the other appears to me as one to whom I owe something, toward whom I have a responsibility" (p. 101). He thus insists on the "gratuitousness" of the "for-the-other," the idea again being that I am responsible to and for the other before any commitment has been established, before there has come to be a pact of "exchange" between me and the other person: "In the alterity of the face, the for-the-other commands the *I*" (p. 103).

Levinas (1996b) even draws upon some of Buber's language to articulate his own position regarding the I–Thou relation:

> The *I-Thou* relation consists in placing oneself before an outside being, i.e., one who is radically *other*, and in recognizing that being as such. This recognition of alterity does not consist in forming an idea of alterity. Having an idea of something belongs to the realm of

---

13. Although Levinas's main focus is the ethical relation, he is also interested in the more general problem of representation and "the exclusive privilege that Western culture has conferred on consciousness" (1999a, p. 125). In emphasizing directness, the non-mediated, in the ethical relation and beyond, he is considering the possibility of "a *meaningfulness* prior to representation, in which transcendental philosophy situated the origin of thought" (p. 130). Along these lines, he is very much urging us to "think Otherwise" about some long-standing philosophical concerns.

I-It. It is not a question of thinking the other person, or of thinking him or her as other—but of addressing that person as a *Thou*. The adequate access to the alterity of the other is not a perception, but this saying of *Thou*. There is immediate contact in this invocation, without there being an object... The I-Thou relation, then, appears from the outset to escape the gravitational field of the I-It in which the alleged exteriority of the object remains held. (p. 22)

But as Levinas goes on to suggest, the I–Thou relation, as Buber has framed it, does not create an adequate space for the *priority* of the Other, with priority in this case referring not so much to the "before" as to firstness, primacy. "How," he asks, "can we maintain the specificity of the interhuman *I–Thou* without bringing out the strictly ethical meaning of responsibility, and how can we bring out the ethical meaning without questioning the reciprocity on which Buber always insists? Doesn't the ethical begin when the *I* perceives the *Thou* as higher than itself?" (p. 32).

Buber, along with Marcel, had indeed managed to break away from an "ontology of the object and of substance," as Levinas (1994) puts it; the very distinction between the I–Thou relation and the I–It relation reflects this break, as does the aforementioned distinction between "presence" and "object." If Levinas is correct, however, both Buber and Marcel continue to characterize the I–Thou relation in terms of *being* and therefore remain locked within that sort of ontological discourse which retains a privileged place for the "I," who considers the presence of the other person and acts accordingly.

> The statement that others do not appear to me as objects does not just mean that I do not take the other person as a thing under my power, a "something." It also asserts that the very relation originally established between myself and others, between myself and someone, cannot properly be said to reside in an act of knowledge that, as such, is seizure and comprehension, the besiegement of objects. (p. 30)

Levinas, contra Buber, thus wants to speak not of reciprocity or symmetry but rather of "the dissymmetry of intersubjective space" (p. 45).

It is not clear to me whether Levinas has been entirely fair to Buber. Buber does use the language of reciprocity and, in the very positing of the I–Thou relation, implies a certain "equidistance" between one person and another. But he also speaks of that which is "essentially other than myself," of the person whose very differentness from me may even provide a glimpse of the "eternal You" that is God. Bearing this in mind, there are aspects of Buber's own reflections on the I–Thou relation that go beyond reciprocity and symmetry and that therefore appear to carve a space for the Other's priority. Whether this space is ultimately one of "being," thus remaining within ontology, will be for others to decide. What is most important for present purposes is the idea that my encounter with the human Other—whether it is the Worcester firefighter, steadfast in his aim of bringing his lost brothers home, the suffering stranger weeping in her car, or any one of countless others—is one in which his or her priority is spontaneously and immediately called forth. I don't rely on some previous store of knowledge I have. I don't "think" about what's going on and then care, and I don't "decide" to feel their presence. In fact, following Levinas, there is a very real sense in which "I" am utterly secondary. The priority here is the priority of the Other, the "I" and the "I think"—Descartes's *ego cogito*—having been unseated through this very priority.[14]

Receiving the Summons

Of particular importance in the present discussion is the aforementioned idea that our engagement with the Other, in the form of the other person especially, is, for Buber, Marcel, and Levinas alike, a dimension of human experience, human *life*, that has become diminished and deformed by virtue of our seemingly unquenchable desire for control and mastery, for turning our relations with people, along with everything else, into I–It relations. Oftentimes, that person over there is someone I can use, for my advancement or my pleasure or my ego. She is a some-one who is a some-thing. She is a tool, an instrument, a means to my own ends, whatever they may be. I can even kill this person if need be, perhaps in the name of some allegedly "just cause," but perhaps not. Dostoevsky's Raskolnikov comes to mind in this context; so too does Tolstoy's Ivan

---

14. Levinas's discussion of the other person's "cry" is most fitting here. "My responsibility in spite of myself—which is the manner by which the other is incumbent upon me, or how he disturbs me, that is, the way in which he is close to me—is a hearing or an understanding of this cry. It is awakening.... This is immediacy. Responsibility does not come from fraternity, it is fraternity that gives responsibility for the other its name, prior to my freedom" (1999b, p. 72)—indeed, prior to *me*.

Ilych, who had, up until the very last moments of his life, relegated the world of human beings, including those he "loved," to the world of things, with which he could decorate his abysmal life.

Levinas, you may recall, argues that we are "commanded" not to kill the other person whose face comes before us: "This face of the other, without recourse, without security, exposed to my look and in its weakness and its mortality is also the one that orders me: 'Thou shalt not kill' " (1999a, p. 44). As he explains elsewhere (1985),

> The face is signification, and signification without context. I mean that the Other, in the rectitude of his face, is not a character within a context. Ordinarily one is a "character": a professor at the Sorbonne, a Supreme Court justice, son of so-and-so, everything that is in one's passport, the manner of dressing, of presenting oneself. And all signification in the usual sense of the term is relative to such a context: the meaning of something is in its relation to another thing. Here, to the contrary, the face is meaning all by itself. You are you. In this sense one can say that the face is "seen." It is what cannot become a content, which your thought would embrace; it is uncontainable, it leads you beyond.... The face is what one cannot kill, or at least it is that whose *meaning* consists in saying: "thou shalt not kill." (pp. 86–87)

None of this, again, means that one cannot kill. But the commandment *not* to do so remains "the first word of the face" (p. 89).

For Levinas, this commandment—recall once more the notion of obedience discussed by Simone Weil and Iris Murdoch—is a matter of necessity. "It is an order. There is a commandment in the appearance of the face, as if a master spoke to me." At the same time, "the face of the Other is destitute; it is the poor for whom I can do all and to whom I owe all. And me, whoever I may be, but as a 'first person,' I am he who finds the resources to respond to the call" (Levinas, 1985, p. 89). It is precisely these "resources," mobilized in response to the *emergency* of the call, that characterize our orientation in the face of catastrophes, like fires, that swallow up the lives of the innocent. And it is precisely in virtue of these resources that Levinas wants to consider "responsibility as the essential, primary and fundamental structure of subjectivity" (p. 95). Alongside the commandment not to kill is the call to help, to serve "the poor for whom I can do all and to whom I owe all." Fragile pleas thus supplement firm orders. "So what distinguishes the face from all known objects," Levinas writes, "comes from its contradictory nature. It is all weakness and all authority" (1999a, pp. 104–105). In both cases, he insists, "[t]he face is the locus of the word of God" (p. 104). For Levinas, therefore, not unlike for Buber, the human You signifies the eternal You. The priority of the Other is nothing less than the priority of God, who comes *well* before us.

We thus come full circle, returning to the idea of the "summons," with which we began our discussion of Levinas. There is, he writes,

> [a] turning on the basis of the face of the other, in which, at the very heart of the phenomenon, in its very light, a surplus of significance is signified that could be designated as glory. It demands me, requires me, summons me. Should we not call this demand or this interpellation or this summons to responsibility the word of God? Does not God come to the mind precisely in that summons, rather than in the thematization of the thinkable, rather even than in some invitation to dialogue? (1999a, pp. 26–27)

Moving still farther in this direction, Levinas maintains that "[i]n that relation with the face, in a direct relation with the death of the other, you probably discover that the death of the other has priority over yours, and over your life" (p. 164). There is something decidedly noble about this kind of discovery: "Man is the being who recognizes saintliness and the forgetting of self." Indeed, man is the being who recognizes justice and even, perhaps, its ultimate source: "We live in a state in which the idea of justice is superimposed on that of individual charity, but it is in that initial charity that the human resides; justice itself can be traced back to it" (p. 180). Justice itself, in other words, is a direct outgrowth of our "initial charity." The priority of the Other thus lies at the very source of whatever "thematizable" formulations we might fashion regarding goodness and its maintenance.

There is a kind of hopefulness running throughout Levinas's thought. In a distinct sense, his work is about the spontaneity and primacy of goodness itself. "The concreteness of the Good," he maintains, "is the worth of the other man. It is only to some formalization that the ambivalence of worth appears, as undecidable, at equal distances between Good and Evil. In the worth of the other man, the Good is more ancient" (1999b,

p. 147).¹⁵ Responsibility, in turn, is to be understood as preservation, summoned forth out of the indubitability of the Other's worth: "Responsibility here is not a cold juridical agency. It is all the gravity of the love of the neighbor" (p. 163). For Levinas, therefore, *the priority of the Other is the priority of the Good,* and this dual priority is signified by the very spontaneity of our care, compassion, and *love* in the face-to-face situation. Again, as he himself recognizes all too clearly—the horrors of the Holocaust loom large throughout his thinking—the spontaneity of our care does not in any way ensure that we will enact it in our behavior. The fact is, there is a great deal of hate in the world, and a great deal of violence and cruelty. We not only *can* kill, we *do*. Given the alleged priority of the Other, how are we to come to terms with this all too clear fact? Isn't this what some of the letter-writers from whom we heard earlier had asked?

There seemed to be some genuine confusion on their part, and for good reason. They had beheld the face of Goodness in and through the face of the Other. For them, as for Levinas, there was nary a shred of doubt about who and what had priority. Moreover, they weren't just caught up in the moment; there had been lessons learned about what truly mattered. Tragedy had thus brought redemption in its wake. And yet, as they well knew, it was the tragedy itself that had brought them their realizations and their passions, and it was difficult to say what might have transpired in its absence. What did this say about the ordinary course of things?

There was also the fact that giving to others, and being there for them, felt natural and right and good. It wasn't a burden to reach out to people. Nor, it seemed, were they doing so out of some hoped-for exchange. It was something they wanted and needed to do, *for the Other*. One could of course claim in this context that, ultimately, they needed to do this for themselves, and on some level this may be so. But this "for themselves," I would argue, had its source in the priority of the Other.¹⁶ How else could

---

15. I am not quite sure what to make of this statement. For one, it isn't clear where exactly he is locating this "Good." For another, there is some ambiguity, to me at any rate, to the word "ancient." This uncertainty and ambiguity notwithstanding, I take his statement here to be a positive and hopeful one, one that seeks to restore the Good to its proper place, as it were, in ethical and moral life.

16. In this respect, the present account is vastly different from the kind of account offered by sociobiologists and other such ethical and moral skeptics. From a sociobiological perspective, whatever care we might extend toward others is likely to be seen as an "investment," one that is ultimately in the service of perpetuating our genes. No matter how real such care may be, therefore, it is secondary, subservient to our own interests. The priority at hand thus remains rooted in the self, not the Other.

there emerge such profound desire? This brings us back to the brief account I gave of some of my students in the introductory chapter. Many of them are involved in community service; they work as volunteers in shelters and soup kitchens, hospitals and schools. When asked about why they do so, they sometimes say that these kinds of activities make them feel good. But why should there be such good feeling? Why should being there for the Other be as significant as it is? Why should we feel most *human*, most fully realized in our humanity, in these kinds of situations?

There are, of course, thoroughly mundane answers to these kinds of questions. Some might suggest that people feel good when serving others because they are doing what they are supposed to be doing; they are doing something that society values. Those who are more cynical might even claim that these avid helpers are merely stocking their resumés with activities that will look good to those future employers or graduate programs who are seeking responsible, civic-minded people. Less severely, it could simply be the case that we feel most human in situations of service and care because these are the kinds of situations that customarily define being "most human." It could be, in other words, that our feelings are finally a matter of convention, a function of the standard portrait of "the caring person." Along these lines, perhaps I feel most human holding my child or caring for my ailing mother, perhaps I feel *love*, because I love the image of myself as one who holds and cares: "I'm so nurturant." Perhaps there *is* some measure of self-gratification entailed in our caring postures; rarely are our motives wholly and unequivocally pure. Nevertheless, it takes a great and cynical effort to explain away the sympathy and fellow-feeling, the devotion and love, we often feel for others, especially those in need.

Tvetan Todorov's chapter "Caring," from his book *Facing the Extreme: Moral Life in the Concentration Camps* (1996), disentangles the relevant issues well. The brutality found in the camps—on the part of guards and prisoners alike—is well known. Less well known, unfortunately, is the fact that "there is not a single prisoner, male or female, who does not remember being cared for, counseled, or protected at least once by someone else—the person in the next bed, perhaps, or another laborer" (p. 72). As Todorov goes on to suggest, "The giver of care...is also a beneficiary"—even, perhaps, in terms of one's very survival; "[a]part from any future reward, that person profits simply from the accomplishment of the act." Indeed, he insists, "[t]he testimony is unanimous on this point. 'Probably this is the best way to retain one's humanity in the camps,' Irini

Ratushinskaya has remarked, 'to care more about another's pain than about your own' " (p. 88).[17]

Why might this be? There are a number of possible answers. Not unlike some of those service-oriented students I referred to, "[p]erhaps by caring about others, one experiences a recovery of one's own dignity and self-respect because one is doing something recognized as morally laudable" (Todorov, 1996, p. 88). And perhaps "that feeling of dignity, in itself, strengthens one's ability to stay alive" (p. 88). This account is reminiscent of Viktor Frankl's account in *Man's Search for Meaning* (1960), Frankl's own argument being that finding some measure of meaning amidst the horrors of camp life—possibly, though not exclusively, by caring for others—was critical for survival. "It has also been observed," Todorov (1996) continues, "that individuals find much more strength within them when looking after someone than when they are taking care of themselves alone." As one prisoner had put the matter, "In order to hang on, each one of us has to get out of himself, he's got to feel responsible for everybody."[18] This statement is a difficult one, for, seen from one angle, it implies that one's responsibility to and for the other was for the sake of oneself, "in order to" ensure one's own survival. Was this a calculation one made, a purposeful, ultimately self-interested, mode of being and acting? It is possible. More likely is that the responsibility referred to was primary and somehow provided the motive fuel the prisoners needed in order to hang on. "The reward," Todorov insists again, "lies in the act itself: in caring for another, one continues to care for oneself as well. Here, the one who spends the most is also the richest" (p. 89). Todorov, unlike Levinas, seems most interested in providing evidence in support of the primacy of altruism, his foremost aim in this work being to upend the Hobbesian "war of all against all" account of human nature (or at least the popularized version of it). Put in simple terms, we are better than we have tended to assume. Todorov's concerns are thus more ontological than Levinas's, the putative goodness within us leading to the care we display. For both, however, this care is brought forth *by* the other and is fundamentally *for* the other, and whatever benefits might accrue to the carer are secondary.

Thus far in this chapter I have focused mainly on the ethical dimension of the priority of the Other, with special reference to the issue of care.

---

17. This remark, cited in Todorov's text, is from Ratushinskaya's *Grey is the Color of Hope* (1988, p. 238).

18. This remark is from Robert Antelme's *Human Race* (1992, p. 196).

Alongside this ethical dimension is the dimension of existential nourishment that has also been focal in this book. I refer here especially to the fact that many of life's most wondrous and transformative moments are with other people. Some of these moments are monumental: births, weddings, baptisms, confirmations, bar and bat mitzvahs, birthdays, anniversaries, and all the rest. There are also less formal monumental moments: first kisses, falling in love. Then, of course, there are those routine moments that come our way, unannounced, like gifts: playing catch or swimming together in the ocean, through the waves, with our children. Others can also be a profound source of energy and life when one is in the depths of despair. Primo Levi, having been through the horrors of concentration camp life, considers just this kind of situation in *The Periodic Table* (1984) when he recounts his encounter with his wife-to-be. There was

> the encounter with a woman, young and made of flesh and blood, warm against my side through our overcoats, gay in the humid mist of the avenues, patient, wise and sure as we were walking down streets still bordered with ruins. In a few hours we knew that we belonged to each other, not for one meeting but for life, as has in fact been the case. In a few hours I felt reborn and replete with new powers, washed clean and cured of a long sickness, finally ready to enter life with joy and vigor; equally cured was suddenly the world around me. (p. 153)

The Other, in this case, had been nothing short of life-giving. She had been the vehicle of Levi's resurrection, his movement back into the realm of the living.

Things can work in the opposite direction as well. In the face of the Other's departure, or death, one can feel as if one's lifeblood has been drained; the "joy and vigor" of which Levi speaks is gone, as if never to return. Even as the presence of the Other can be a profound source of energy and life, the absence of the Other can be an equally profound source of anguish and suffering. Most of us can recount our own experiences of each. But the importance of people goes well beyond such "experiences." In a distinct sense, the Other's presence, or absence, is at the very heart of our own humanness. Can this possibly be denied?

But then there is the ever-present "and yet": and yet, there is all that hate, and violence, and cruelty, "the person we cut off in traffic, those we say vulgarities to, send unfriendly hand signals." That person, this woman had written (in her letter following the Worcester fire), "could be the same person we stood next to on Central Street as we both cried when the procession went by." And the people we love the most are the very same people we often ignore and shut out, thereby depriving ourselves of exactly that nourishment which sustains us. I ask again: what is this about? The Other would seem to have priority, both ethically and existentially, but oftentimes, this priority doesn't quite *become* a priority: the "before" only comes "after."[19] How shall we make sense of this?

Divided Selves

At this point, we must interrogate Levinas—as well as ourselves—and see whether in fact the priority of the Other, as he conceives it, holds up under our scrutiny. In doing so, I focus once more on the ethical dimension. It is important again to emphasize that Levinas's most basic intellectual project is not so much to fashion a different, more Other-directed image of humanity. This would be to commit himself to ontology, to the dimension of *being*. It is precisely this commitment, enshrined throughout the history of philosophy, that he wants to cast into question and, ultimately, supersede. Ethics comes *before* ontology, Levinas has insisted. It is "first philosophy" and is thus *prior* to anything we might wish to say about who and what the human being *is*. This is a truly radical reorientation of perspective, with profound consequences for how we think about the human condition, the self, the juridical and political realms, and much more. It is that much more important, therefore, that we determine as best we can its validity and value.

Although I am not sure whether Levinas would want to put it this way (or whether he would want *me* to put it this way), his philosophy is at base about the importance of *people*. It is not only about this. It is about ethics and metaphysics. It is also about transcendence and the infinite, about the Absolute and God. To say that his philosophy is essentially about the importance of people might therefore seem like a reduction, or a watering-down, of what his work is all about. Nevertheless, there is no escaping this most basic commitment to people, to the Other that is human. The face is that of the human person; it is this aspect of the Other

---

19. Here, I refer once more to my (2010) book *Hindsight: The Promise and Peril of Looking Backward*, in which, among other things, I consider the fact that we are frequently "late" in our understandings of things and that this is especially so in the moral domain, where there is a special tendency to act first and think later.

that most draws me out of myself, that summons me most urgently. It is this human face that exists on high, uttering the word of God.

Levinas (1996d) addresses precisely this dimension of "height" by noting that "[t]he epiphany of the Absolutely Other is a face by which the Other challenges and commands me through his nakedness, through his destitution. He challenges me from his humility and from his height." It is shortly after this passage that Levinas explicitly states that

> "[t]he Absolutely Other is the human Other. And the putting into question of the Same by the Other is a summons to respond. The I is not simply conscious of this necessity to respond, as if it were a matter of an obligation or a duty about which a decision could be made; rather the I is, by its *very position*, responsibility through and through. And the structure of this responsibility will show how the Other, in the face, challenges us from the greatest depth and highest height—by opening the very dimension of elevation" (p. 17).

These passages demonstrate clearly the main thrust of Levinas's intellectual project. Contra Buber (or at least Levinas's reading of Buber), the Other, rather than being equal to me, a partner in a reciprocal exchange, is *above* me. And even as this very state of being-above bears within it intimations of the infinite, indeed of God, "[t]he Absolutely Other," Levinas insists, "is the human Other." As for my own response to the Other, he goes on to say, it is not to be considered a product of my deliberation, but is, again, a matter of "necessity," not unlike the necessity—and obedience—of which Weil and Murdoch had spoken. This dimension of necessity is of critical important for Levinas. To *truly* see the face of the Other, he has insisted, is to be *unable* to kill: we cannot do that which we are *commanded* not to do. The priority of the human Other is thus the ultimate source not only of "responsibility" but of peace and justice.

Bringing together the notions of height and necessity, Levinas (1996d) goes on to suggest that "[t]he one for whom I am responsible is also the one to whom I have to respond. The 'for whom...' and the 'to whom...' coincide. It is this double movement of responsibility which designates the dimension of height" (p. 19). God is thoroughly present in this dimension. But it is not to be defined, as such, through God. As Levinas explains,

> I do not want to define anything through God because it is the human that I know. It is God that I can define through human relations and not the inverse. The notion of God—God knows, I'm not

opposed to it! But when I have to say something about God, it is always beginning from human relations.... I do not start from the existence of a very great and all-powerful being. Everything I wish to say comes from this situation of responsibility which is religious insofar as the I cannot elude it.... You find yourself before a responsibility from which you cannot escape. You find yourself before a responsibility from which you cannot steal away. (p. 29)

This passage is an especially strong statement of Levinas's convictions regarding the priority of the Other. Even God is "defined" through the human, and the responsibility that we in turn confront is beyond escape.

Against the backdrop of this portrayal, I want to raise two fundamental questions, the first about the issue of priority and the second about the issue of the Other. Is the priority of which Levinas speaks as "inescapable"—spontaneous, immediate, necessary—as he maintains? And is it only the *human* Other that warrants this priority? Without in any way seeking to minimize the importance of people, could it be that his vision of the priority of the Other qua human overstates the case?

In an important essay entitled "Substitution," written back in 1968, Levinas (1996c) addresses the notion of priority by inquiring into the precarious status of the ego. "The ego," he writes, "is *in itself* not like matter is in itself, which, perfectly wedded to its form, is what it is. The ego is in itself like one is in one's skin, that is to say, cramped, ill at ease." As he goes on to explain, "The ego is not merely a being endowed with certain so-called moral qualities, qualities which it would bear as attributes." In a sense, it is always in the process "of being emptied of its being, of being turned inside out." Moreover, "The ego is not a being which is capable of expiating for others; it is this original expiation which is involuntary because prior to the initiative of the will" (p. 86). Alongside the "inescapability" of responsibility, therefore, is the "involuntary" quality of our responding, prior to will, prior to freedom. Later on in the essay, Levinas employs the metaphor of the "hostage" to convey this sense of imprisonment by the Other: "It is through the condition of being a hostage that there can be pity, compassion, pardon, and proximity in the world—even the little there is, even the simple 'after you sir' " (p. 91). Indeed, it is through this condition of being a hostage that there can be a *self*.[20] "It is this responsibility for the creature that constitutes the 'self.'

---

20. Or, as I would prefer to put it, *Self*.

Responsibility for the creature, for that which the ego had not been the author. To be a 'self' is to be responsible before having done anything. It is in this sense to substitute oneself for others" (p. 94). (Hence the essay's title.)

What is at stake in the notion of substitution is nothing less than a revisioning of subjectivity, selfhood, freedom, and philosophy itself.

> To say that subjectivity begins in the person, that the person begins in freedom, that freedom is the primary causality, is to blind oneself to the secret of the self and its relation to the past. This relation does not amount to placing oneself at the beginning of this past so as to be responsible within the strict limits of intention, nor to being the simple result of the past.... The notion of hostage overturns the position that starts from presence (of the ego to the self) as a beginning of philosophy. I am not merely the origin of myself, but I am disturbed by the Other. (Levinas, 1996c, p. 94)

Elsewhere, Levinas (1996a) writes, "My responsibility in spite of myself—which is the way the other's charge falls upon me or disturbs me, that is, is close to me—is the hearing or understanding of this cry. It is awakening. The proximity of a neighbor is my responsibility for him; to approach is to be one's brother's keeper; to be one's brother's keeper is to be his hostage" (p. 143).

But are we in fact "hostages" to the Other? In situations such as a catastrophic fire that has left human devastation in its wake, the answer is, perhaps, yes. We find ourselves "captivated" by the situation; we are held fast by the grip of the Other's need; we are "awakened," as Levinas puts it, from our ordinary slumber. But what about this slumber? We are "disturbed" by the Other daily. On some level, we may even be "awakened." But oftentimes we go right back to sleep. Would that we were always the hostages of which Levinas speaks. Would that the Other always took priority! It could be that I am over-translating Levinas's perspective into psychological terms, testing it, so to speak, against the empirical world, the world of experience. It could be, for instance, that the "necessity" about which he speaks is not a matter of experience at all; given that he is formulating an ethics and not an ontology (and certainly not a psychology), such testing may be beside the point. In my view, however, there is no escaping the fact that Levinas is, at times, making claims about experience—in this case, about the idea that my way of being for the Other, on the plane of subjectivity, is much more hostage-like than we have ordinarily assumed, thereby leading to an entirely different sense of selfhood, freedom, and moral life. I do not wish to condemn Levinas's efforts in this context; they are nothing short of valiant. But if the world of experience—the world of difficult life—is any clue, our responsiveness to and responsibility for others may not be a matter of unadulterated necessity. As captivated as I might be by the face of the Other, as spontaneous and direct as my response might be, I must still exercise my freedom, my will to responsibility; I must *consent* to the call. This is surely one reason that I sometimes do *not* heed the call of the Other—why, despite my being captivated by her, disrupted and moved, she remains untouched, my responsibility having been directed elsewhere. Furthermore, this captivation itself is not without competition, from other Others as well as from the ego, which frequently issues its own "commands." Put another way, my response to the Other is never entirely pure and unalloyed, but is always, to a greater or lesser extent, a complex composite of the multiple strands of my existence.

Levinas surely knows this. In addition, he would likely insist that I *am* responsible for the Other no matter *what* my response—that, indeed, responsibility bespeaks the very existence of the "I am." He might also want to argue that in those circumstances in which I do not heed the call of the Other, I have simply managed to ignore, bury, or somehow "override" my immediate response. In these situations, moreover, perhaps I am not *seeing* the face of the Other but only *looking*. If we truly see, Levinas has told us, we cannot kill. Whenever there has been killing, there has therefore been un-seeing; it cannot be otherwise. But is this true?

There is no way of knowing. It could also be that the question I have just posed is the wrong one, that in raising the issue of truth in this manner I have retreated from ethics back to ontology, to the project of discerning qualities of being. But is there not an implicit ontology in the very ethics Levinas wishes to promote? Is there not an implicit image of what, fundamentally, human beings *are*—or at least would be, if only they, if only *we*, could see? My aim in raising these issues is not to reinstate the priority of freedom over responsibility. Indeed, one implication of Levinas's work is that we need to rethink the very order of this relationship. While we often think of responsibility as issuing from freedom—as in "I am free; therefore I am responsible"—we would do well to reverse this order and see this very freedom as issuing from responsibility.[21] Nor is my aim to detract from proclaiming the Other's priority. The Other, I have repeatedly said, comes before me. But this is not only to be construed as an empirical verity, an indubitable "fact" around which to fashion an ethics. What is still required is an element of consent and, again, of *devotion*. The fact is, upholding the priority of the Other often takes work. Life is too difficult, our motives too muddled and impure, for the situation to be wholly otherwise. This is not pessimism; it is realism. And it is only through such realism that the Other has a fighting chance to win our affections during the ordinary course of things. As several of the letter-writers from whom we heard earlier argued, we need to *make* the Other a priority. We cannot wait for catastrophes to awaken us. "Everyone reading this," one woman had written, "has the power within themselves to honor those gone, to honor those remaining" and to do so "today and every day."

There remains a gap, a space, still to be filled with our care; we have to locate the "power" within ourselves and mobilize it so as to "honor" the Other, whether neighbor or stranger. At the same time, it is important to ask: Where does this apparent need to make the Other a priority arise? Why should there *be* a call to locate the power within ourselves to honor the Other? Even if my response to the Other falls short of Levinasian necessity, and even if this response is less unalloyed than the idea of necessity would seem to suggest, there still exists an *awareness* of the Other's priority and a *desire* to make this awareness—and the *love* with which it is bound—a greater part of our lives. How could there be such awareness and desire, how could there be such love, if the Other didn't call them forth? I don't know whether I am a "hostage." I don't know whether I am unable to kill the person whose face I truly see. But I am quite sure that my desire to be there for the Other, too often dormant, too often sadly in need of the kind of alarm a catastrophic fire brings, still signals priority. What a challenge it is to remain awake! What a challenge it is to *remember*.

---

21. See Williams (2002) for a discussion of the Levinasian conception of freedom in relation to psychology. Coming from a different, but not unrelated, perspective is Murdoch (1970): "Freedom is not the sudden jumping of the isolated will in and out of an impersonal logical complex, it is a function of the progressive attempt to see a particular object clearly" (p. 23) and to thereby allow the object to exert its own presence and power. Also relevant in this context is Viktor's Frankl's (1960) work. Although Frankl emphasizes the primacy of "spiritual freedom," he also acknowledges that this very freedom is itself a function of one's responsibility to the Other, whether human or non-. In this respect, Frankl's conceptualization is sometimes belied by the realities at hand. See Chapter Six for related comments.

In some ways, it is surprising it isn't easier. Recall for a moment the remarkable correlation I spoke about toward the end of Chapter One: the more humble and Other-directed we are, I said, the more meaningful, gratifying, and fulfilling our lives seem to be. This isn't to say, I immediately emphasized, that we ought to think of being Other-directed merely as a means to our fulfillment. That wouldn't be Other-directedness at all; it would be self-directedness, plain and simple. But the correlation nevertheless holds. And what it means in the present context is that the more caring, giving, and loving we are with others, the more caring, giving, and loving they are likely to be in return. What's more, our own lives will more likely be characterized by a sense of fulfillment and self-realization—indeed, a sense that our own place in the world has *mattered,* that it has brought something of value to our fellow human beings. Given the great rewards of being good to people, for them as well as for ourselves, it is surprising we aren't better. We really ought to be.

I want to be sure I am being clear about this issue. The last thing I hope a reader takes away from this discussion is the notion that being good to others—making it a priority, in fact—is simply an investment, a deposit that is bound to produce solid returns. On some level, I suppose, operating in this way would still be better than not—it's better to be good with people than bad, whatever one's motives—but the "goodness" that is being manifested in this case is a superficial one, a mere display. What is being manifested is good-*seeming* behavior, not goodness itself, which in this context, I argue, can only mean acting in a way that is truly *for the Other.* One might even provide something of a warning here to those with utilitarian inclinations: behaving in a good-seeming way, though it might yield some respectable short-term returns, does not and cannot work over the long haul. That is to say, it cannot provide the kind of meaning, gratification, and fulfillment we have considered. Only being good can. Being good and living well, I proposed earlier, entail remaining cognizant of the priority of the Other, which in turn is contingent on our capacity both to attend to the Other and to divest ourselves of self-interest. There is no shortcut, and the path is not an easy one.

What a challenge it is to preserve a sense of who and what has priority! Who and what: we have spoken mainly about the "who" in this chapter; the "what" is explored in the chapter to come. But this very attempt to explore the "what" under the rubric of the priority of the Other would seem to run counter to many of the ideas we have been considering. As

Levinas repeatedly insists, it is the *human* Other that has priority: ethics is first philosophy. Is he right? Or, to put the matter more subtly, in what ways is he right, and in what ways not?

It almost seems sacrilegious to be critical of a perspective that is so thoroughly humane and Other-directed. Levinas is a philosopher who wants to talk not only about the priority of the human Other but about the priority of peace and justice and love. These come before knowledge, before truth, before the dignity and the rights of persons; they are the source and substance of our humanity itself. Maybe we should just believe him and live his ideas and ideals as best we can! Much of what he says is also undoubtedly right. Is there anything—any "thing"—that has more value than a human person? I would give up every last thing I possess, and I would be willing to live without all of those things I do not possess—the sun and stars, the wind, the trees—to preserve my children. And I think I would be willing to do all of this for *your* children too (though I have no illusions about the fact that it would be difficult). I am even willing to die in the name of the Other's priority. This is exactly what those firefighters did. What else would we be willing to die for?

And yet, the human Other is not the only being that draws me out of myself. There *are* the sun and stars, the wind, the trees. There are poems and paintings, churches and synagogues and mosques. There is the way a road winds through the mountains as if it belonged there, thrilling in its way. And there is all that food and drink! At the time I initially penned these words, I was living with my family in Spain, and not too long after my writing day had passed, we would head out to some wonderful little restaurant or *bodega*, where we would have another feast and be grateful for the world's bounty. We would probably be sitting outside amidst the sun and orange trees. Every day felt like an incredible gift.

None of this quite compares to my child or to yours. None of this comes before the possibility of there being homeless people in a burning building. About this, Levinas is surely right. But it is not only the human Other that has priority. The Other, as I described it earlier, is that which calls us out of ourselves with a compelling, magnetic, and sometimes mysterious power. It is precisely this power that suggests the Other's priority. Can there be any doubt but that there are a great many things besides human beings that have this wondrous power? Let's not forget Buber's horse! The "Thou" is not only human. In Buber's terms, it is whatever truly speaks to me, whatever I can engage, through my care, in a relationship of reciprocity. I would formulate the matter somewhat differently. The Thou is the Other, and the Other—here I follow Levinas—is what exists *before* me, what has priority over me, what calls forth my devotion. Now that we have underscored the importance of people, we can turn our attention toward the Other that is not human. As I have suggested already, there is much to be explored.

4

Beyond the Human

Nearness and Otherness

"See you later, puppy." Those were the last words I uttered today when I left the house for work. My dog is not a puppy, though; she's just about eleven years old, she's diabetic, she's blind in one eye (going on two), and one of her hind legs recently stopped working completely. It hurts to leave her behind each day, just lying there, panting a little (it's been hot), spaced out (I imagine), and just…vulnerable. Her face carries a great deal of meaning. How much does it have in relation to my daughters' faces (for instance)? It's impossible to say; meaning can't be quantified in this way. Her face means *differently*, to be sure, and calls forth different regions of care and responsibility than the faces of my daughters. I also don't know that I would die on her behalf. But when I left this morning, she was a commanding presence in her own right.[1]

Several times in the preceding chapters I have insisted that the Other is not to be understood in human terms alone. Insofar as the Other is that which draws us out of ourselves, takes us somewhere beyond our customary preoccupations and concerns, *moves* us, it may be human or non-human, animate or inanimate. Along the lines being drawn here, it is not so much the *object* that defines what is Other as the *process*. Far from implying that the specific nature of the object is irrelevant—I have already argued that the nature and quality of a given object are extremely relevant—all that is being said is that the object in question becomes an Other only when it exercises its magnetic power and draws the self outward, beyond itself. The priority of the Other, therefore, is a function neither of

---

[1]. Tawny has passed on since this passage was written. May she rest.

the object alone nor of the subject alone but, as we also noted earlier, of the relationship between them. What kind of a relationship is it?

At a most fundamental level, it is one of attention and absorption. Upon witnessing the smoldering ruins of the warehouse that had taken the lives of six firefighters, I found myself utterly transfixed by the spectacle before me; there was a kind of ghastly, ghostly presence, magnetic in its way, pulling me forward and thereby lifting me from the condition of dispersion—being neither quite here nor quite there—that characterizes much of everyday life. But there was more to the experience as well. There was a spontaneous intimation of fragility and mortality, the building itself signifying, in what felt like a wholly unmediated way, the very suffering and loss that had been buried within it.

Analytically speaking, there had surely been an element of mediation entailed in the experience: my encounter with the building had been conditioned by my knowledge of what had gone on there, my ability to see, in the broken bricks, the remnants of death and destruction. This underscores once more the relational dimension of our encounter with the Other, whoever or whatever it might be. We do not confront neutral objects set wholly apart from our knowledge, interests, and values; we encounter meaningful ones, that emerge as they do, in part, by virtue of what we bring to them. Phenomenologically speaking, however, the *building itself* had become the primary locus of my attention and care. Unlike the many buildings around it, as well as the cars and trees and trash cans populating the periphery, it had become an *Other*, a terrible figure amidst debris-strewn ground. Whatever I might have brought to the encounter, *it* stood forth, captivating me, indeed *transforming* me through its very captivatingness.[2]

Something similar may occur in our experience of nature. I can recall, for instance, a trip to a local nature preserve with my family. It is of course true that certain expectations are set up when one goes to places like nature preserves. The aim is to attend and appreciate, to heighten one's awareness of nature's beauty and bounty. On this particular occasion, we

---

2. I address a similar issue in a piece called "Charting the Narrative Unconscious: Cultural Memory and the Challenge of Autobiography" (2002). On my initial encounter with the city of Berlin, I found myself feeling that death was in the air and that the horrors and atrocities of times past had somehow been emblazoned on the faces of buildings and other sites. What I was perceiving and feeling, I surmised, surely had been mediated by my knowledge of what had gone on there. Phenomenologically, however, it was the sites themselves that had so captivated me. We shall return to this rather perplexing state of affairs shortly.

found ourselves in exactly this mode for some time, walking, looking, exploring, taking a break from the usual sights, the usual routines. This mode is valuable in itself; when one purposefully abandons the structures and strictures of everyday life, there is the opportunity to move into different regions of being, ones that are more carefree, more in touch with the world. It was all very "relaxing" and "pleasant," just as we hoped it would be. But at one point, as we were sitting near a little pond in the middle of a meadow, silent and still, everything suddenly changed, acquiring a kind undulating electricity, filled with energy and eerily calm at the same time. The contours of the hills suddenly seemed perfect somehow, as did the rustle of wind through the flowers and weeds and the placement of human things, here and there—a fence, stones, a house in the distance, cars. I wouldn't call it "beautiful." Rather, it was as if everything *belonged*, as if it were part of the same world, even in its difference; it was all part of a deeper, more real reality. I felt lucky to be there.

Upon thinking about this experience, I was initially inclined to say that everything that had theretofore been "far" had suddenly come "near." On one level, this still seems right: that which had experientially been distant (even if in the midst of being "appreciated") had come forward, emerged out of its ordinariness, its quality of being an array of pleasant-to-behold things, decorating my perception. On another level, though, it might also be said that that which had been experientially near, in the sense of its normalcy and everydayness, had suddenly become something else altogether, something strange and different, something *Other*.[3] One need not choose between these two renditions of the experience. Indeed, it could be that this dialectic of nearness and otherness itself signals the Other's priority.

But what does this actually mean? And how are we to reconcile the apparent paradox at hand? Let us turn to another, perhaps more familiar, example. Much of the time we spend with our lovers (including husbands and wives) is in the mode of ordinary everydayness. We pass them on the way to the bathroom, make breakfast together, go shopping, talk about how to pay the bills, and so on. There may certainly be some measure of

---

3. See Santner (2001) for related comments. Also relevant are Gadamer's and Heidegger's reflections on the work of art. On one level, there is generally an aspect of recognition, a being-made-familiar, "knowing something as that with which we are already acquainted" (Gadamer, 1986, p. 47) and finding a deeper, more authentic truth within it. In addition, however, "[t]he setting-into-work of truth," as we encounter it in the work of art, "thrusts up the unfamiliar and extraordinary and at the same time thrusts down the ordinary and what we believe to be such" (Heidegger, 1971, p. 75).

pleasantness to these facets of the relationship, and there may be some unique and special qualities that emerge in the course of these everyday occurrences: there is no one quite like her. All the same, these very lovers of ours can, and often do, become part of the "furniture" of things—more alive and lovable than the new coffee table, but in certain respects not vastly different. (We're glad they're both here.) But there are also times when this mode of everydayness suddenly shifts. Perhaps she has burned her hand, or taken ill. Or, less eventfully, perhaps she just looks a certain way as she reads her book or speaks to one of the kids. She is suddenly lifted out of the fabric of everyday roles and routines and becomes radiant in her otherness, her existence as a being-apart, possessed of her own style and special qualities. She has become, at once, unfamiliar—different from all that furniture out there—and much, much closer. She is close enough to be seen, and loved.

As with the experience at the nature preserve, there has been a dual movement. This person, just moments ago part of the ordinary landscape of my world, has emerged in her extra-ordinariness and incomparability; from being part of the fabric of the Same, she has emerged as Other, and it is this very condition of her emergence into otherness that creates the possibility of my being drawn near. Notice that the example I have employed in order to explicate further what I called "the dialectic of nearness and otherness" comes from the human realm. This is not because human relations provide the only model for understanding our relations to the non-human world. Nor is it to suggest that the non-human Other is a secondary concern, or that our attraction to it represents a displacement or sublimation of more basic impulses. What is being suggested once again is that the priority of the Other, whether located in the human or the non-human realm, has as a necessary correlate the mobilization of *eros*, broadly conceived—following Plato and Freud, among others—as that sort of outward-moving life energy that serves to bind us both to one another and to the larger world. It's not for nothing that in addition to speaking of romantic love or love of neighbor, people speak of love of nature or music or painting. Our relationship to all of these is erotic through and through: the Other, in and through its magnetic presence, incites my desire and draws me near.

Wendy Farley's (1996) reflections on "eros for the other" may be helpful in this context. In speaking of eros, she refers to "those modes of thought and relationships whose movement runs...outward, toward others, toward the world" (p. 67). Not unlike Benson (1993), from whom we heard earlier (see Chapter Two), she is interested in the process of "passionate detachment" by which we become absorbed in "exteriority," drawn outward by the beauty and vulnerability of people and things. "Idolatrous egocentrism is razed by detachment," Farley notes, "but selfhood itself is not destroyed; it is, rather, reoriented from itself to others, to the world" (p. 84). The process is at one and the same time one of "self-emptying" and "self-fulfillment," with "fulfillment" here referring not so much to pleasurable gratification as to a sense of fully being there, in the world, with one's heart and soul. It is also, Farley argues, one of moving toward *reality*: in and through one's passionate detachment, the otherness of the Other may emerge.[4]

Following Weil and Murdoch, Farley (1996) also goes on to consider the centrality of attention in the process of encountering the Other, focusing especially on the dimension of truth-seeking that is part and parcel of the movement toward reality. "The struggle toward truth," she writes, "requires a practice or practices that order one toward others in their unique beauty and suffering, practices that permit the exteriority of reality to be acknowledged." Indeed, "[t]his refocusing of attention is the essential dynamic of any practice—scholarship, mothering, gardening, cabinet making, social work, political activism, meditation—that orients one toward reality" (pp. 190–191). According to Farley, attention "rightly implies a kind of effort; it is a practice, a moral discipline. It is a disposition toward the world" (p. 191). In line with what was said earlier, I would characterize this disposition as a *devotional* one as well, in which one actively "gives oneself over" to the Other. Devotion, as I have tried to frame it, might be seen as a kind of compound of attention and care, the cognitive and the ethical. Standing before the smoking ruins of that warehouse, I found myself doing more than attending. I had assumed a stance in which my own sense of responsibility had been called forth. I had thereby devoted myself to the cause of seeing and feeling and remembering. I had also devoted myself, then and there, to a particular way of life, one that could somehow match in its realness and presence the spectacle before me, awful though it was. In the face of the Other, whether suffering person or burning building, nature preserve or poem, one often takes a kind of

---

4. I have already noted (in Chapter Two) that some readers may find this notion of detachment troubling insofar as it connotes being separated off from the external world. As I quickly suggested, however, detachment, as Farley (along with Weil and Murdoch) conceives of it, is to be equated not with separation so much as with a kind of self-divestiture, a process of what Paul Ricoeur (1981a) refers to as "distanciation," whereby the Other—his main concern at the time was the literary text—can emerge in its otherness.

pledge or vow to live differently, to live better, more thoroughly in accord with what is real.[5]

The idea of devotion thus entails more-than-momentary attention and care, made manifest in the form of the life one lives. In addition, and perhaps more important, the idea of devotion serves to underscore the primacy—and priority—of the Other. Attention is a kind of pointed but abstract energy, directed to this or that by me; I have some measure of control of this energy, some ability to focus it, "home in," *pay*, whatever the object might be. Devotion, in contrast, always has a specific object in mind, and it is this object, this Other, that is the very source of the devotion it inspires. It should be emphasized that this object need not be a "thing" at all; it can be an activity or a process, even an idea (following Murdoch, for instance, the idea of goodness). Indeed, given what has been said here, the Other is constituted and defined essentially by its power over me, its capacity to call forth my attention and desire. It is distant and draws me nearer. The result can be ecstatic exhilaration as well as deep existential and spiritual nourishment. It can also be unswerving moral commitment. And, not least, it can be self-annihilation. In the case of Simone Weil, it is all three. Her case also does particularly well to take us "beyond the human" and thus serves as a valuable site for examining some of the complexities of our relationship to the non-human world. It may therefore be useful to explore her life and work in some detail.

In Service of the Real

In a distinct sense, Weil's own life project was to become wholly Other—"to see a landscape," as she had put it (see Chapter Two), "as it is when I am not there" (1997 [1952], p. 37). She would therefore work toward her own self-erasure, absence, the "I" inevitably being an intrusion on reality. Consider in this context her thoughts on writing, which are conveyed in a letter to her good friend and confidant Gustav Thibon:

> In the operation of writing, the hand which holds the pen, and the body and soul which are attached to it, with all their social

---

5. See, again, Bonnefoy (1989), who earlier spoke of the pledge the (attentive) reader of poetry makes "to the author, his brother, that he too will remain in intensity" and will "go and live out the promise" (p. 162). Gadamer (1976) conveys a similar idea when he writes, "The intimacy with which the work of art touches us is at the same time, in enigmatic fashion, a shattering and a demolition of the familiar. It is not only the 'This art thou!' disclosed in a joyous and frightening shock; it also says to us, 'Thou must alter thy life!' " (p. 104).

environment, are things of infinitesimal importance for those who love the truth. They are infinitely small in the order of nothingness. That at any rate is the measure of importance I attach in this operation not only to my own personality but to yours and to that of any other writer I respect. Only the personality of those whom I more or less despise matters to me in such a domain. (1997 [1952], p. xiii)

As for Weil personally: "[M]y greatest desire is to lose not only all will but all personal being" (1973 [1951], p. 59). The "virtuoso" or "genius"—religious, artistic, philosophical, whatever—is one who has succeeded in *effacing* his or her personality to such a degree that reality can shine through. In addition, he or she will be rooted, to the greatest extent possible, in the present. "If we consider what we are at a definite moment—the present moment, cut off from the past and the future—we are innocent. We cannot at that instant be anything but what we are" (Weil, 1997 [1951], p. 32). We are emptied of those imaginings and fantasies and illusions that mire us in the personal, the subjective.

Weil could be wrong about all of this. It could be that virtuosity or genius *requires* the personality, the distinctive signature of this particular person, this particular self. It could also be that one brings this signature, with its own unique history, to any and all encounters with reality, and that cutting oneself off from the past and the future—would that we could even do it—would undermine, rather than support, the efforts in question. There is also a good deal of evidence to suggest that despite her very loud protests against the ego, her fervent wish to lose her personal being, Weil herself remained ego-invested in her own self-effacement in a big way (Thibon, 1953a, 1953b). As Thibon (1953b) has noted,

> On the one hand there was a longing for absolute self-effacement, an unlimited opening to reality even under its harshest forms, and, on the other, a terrible self-will at the very heart of the self-stripping; the inflexible desire that this stripping should be her own work and should be accomplished in her own way, the consuming temptation to verify everything from within, to test everything and experience everything for herself. (p. 114)

But that is not all. "[S]he, who when her pleasure or her needs were involved would not have allowed anyone to make the slightest sacrifice on her behalf, did not seem to realize the complications and even sufferings she caused in the lives of others as soon as there was a question of her vocation to self-effacement" (p. 117). Thibon goes on to speak of a "transcendental egoism" in this context:

> This soul, who wanted to be flexible to every movement of the divine will, could not bear the course of events or the kindness of her friends to change by one inch the position of the stakes with which her own will had marked her path of immolation. Though utterly and entirely detached from her tastes and needs, she was not detached from her detachment. And the way she mounted guard around her emptiness still showed a terrible preoccupation with herself. In the great book of the universe spread often before her, her *ego* was, as it were, a word which she may perhaps have succeeded in *effacing*, but which was still *underlined*. (p. 119)

Thibon, it should be noted, is not particularly troubled by Weil's egoism. "The saints are not given us for the sake of comfort, and I do not entirely reproach her for this uncomfortable side of her nature. Moreover there were some delightful moments when she let herself go and relaxed. Yet she lacked that supreme peace of mind, that sweetness and all-embracing indulgence which [are] the signs of God's maturity in man" (1953b, p. 120). So it is that he speaks of the "green immaturity" of Weil's spiritual life, the fact that she "had not yet reached the reversed summit of supreme humility, that point where height and depth correspond, that divine abasement which counterbalances man's baseness, that final simplicity in which the saint no longer judges anything but bathes all in the unity of love" (p. 126), the presumption being that, had she lived longer (she died at 34) and continued to develop spiritually, she might have succeeded in achieving the full-scale self-immolation she so desired. "Simone Weil," Thibon writes, "was complete truth and, at a certain level, complete love; she was not yet complete welcome . . . In a sense, she remained all her life the inflexible child who sat down in the snow and refused to go on because her parents had given the heaviest baggage to her brother to carry" (p. 126). The priority of the Other, personified!

One might ask at this point, how did she come to be the person she did? Among other things, she was a philosopher, a political activist, and a mystic who at age six swore off sugar in order to send her share to French soldiers fighting at the front (Perrin, 1953), at age 10 had become involved in labor union demonstrations, and by age 14 had developed what some have considered an "almost pathological receptiveness to the suffering of others" as well as "a strong tendency to cultivate her own" (du Plessix Gray, 2001, p. 15). There had also been extraordinarily painful migraines and, as time wore on, a seemingly obsessive preoccupation with eating issues—to the extent that some (e.g., du Plessix Gray, 2001) have become convinced of her anorectic status. Then there were her multiple attempts to immerse herself in the experiential world of the afflicted, particularly through hard factory labor, her ostensible goal in these endeavors being nothing less than reaching rock bottom, such that misery would somehow pass over into the clearest and most profound testimony to God's presence. There is little doubt but that she died in such a state of misery as well, at least one of the known causes being self-starvation—which, not unlike her swearing off sugar as a six-year-old, was apparently another act of solidarity with the afflicted. In the end, Robert Coles (2001) has written,

> Simone Weil seemed to have no interest in survival, at least the human survival most of us want. A discussion continues among many who knew her or admire her as to whether she did or did not take her own life, whether she was anorectic, a masochist, irrational, or psychotic at the end of her life. Her doctors were confused, frustrated, and enraged by her behavior. Here was a young woman as bright as any human being could want to be, educated and refined, not poor or without friends, who yet had no interest in cooperating with her doctors and nurses. Ultimately they tried tube feeding in a futile effort to save her. She died alone, on August 24, a thirty-four-year-old woman mourned by only a handful of London friends. (p. 18)

Given this profile, it should come as no surprise that chroniclers of Weil's life and work should turn to her early life, her childhood in particular, and "maybe find reasons to be concerned" (Coles, 2001, p. 7). Especially curious were her efforts at hard labor, whether they bespeak "silly romanticism or self-righteousness masked as idealism or a decent person's hard struggle to find out how to live and work and in a morally useful way, and by doing so, to learn something precious" (p. 10). There was also a serious, if complicated, strain of anti-Semitism on Weil's part—and this despite the fact (or because of the fact) of her Jewishness. Consider too Weil's physical presence as well as her own relation to her bodily/sexual being. "The beauty of her porcelain skin, of her delicate features," du Plessix

Gray (2001) writes, "continued to be all but hidden by her huge glasses, her grubby clothes, her awkward gait. And those who saw through to her beauty wondered why she had chosen to make herself so ugly" (p. 25). Some of her philosophy students, du Plessix Gray notes, had initially been "amused by her awkwardness, her clumsy way of holding the chalk, the total anarchy of her clothes." In due time, "they came to admire her deeply and tried to protect her from her own clumsiness, helping her to change her sweaters, for instance, which she often put on inside out." There was something about her "halo of voluntary poverty" and "the ascetic disarray of her life" that "touched them deeply" (p. 53) and that seemed, through it all, authentic and real. But there was no getting around the sheer strangeness of her presence. As Thibon (1953b) puts the matter, "she was not ugly, as has been said, but prematurely bent and old-looking through asceticism and illness." It was only her "magnificent eyes" that "triumphed in this shipwreck of beauty" (p. 116).

Weil also was "averse to physical contact,...shunning even the most casual of hugs or comradely linking of elbows," and demonstrated a positive "dread of sexuality" (du Plessix Gray, 2001, p. 25). As for her manner, du Plessix Gray continues, "she retained the argumentative, eccentric style she had evolved in her mid-teens, and which had become even more intransigent" (p. 25) over the course of time. There were times, in fact, when she was nothing short of "ruthless" in the way "she could cut off friends who in some small way displeased her" (p. 42). Du Plessix Gray also calls attention to Weil's "impulse to extreme domination, which is now recognized as another frequent symptom of anorexia" (p. 29), as well as her hyperactivity. "Such hyperactivity, fueled by the constant rationale of urgent causes, is a symptom that very frequently attends eating disorders" (p. 60). It was these urgent causes that would lead to Weil's "growing interest in the redemptive value of suffering" (p. 98) and, eventually, the birth of her spiritual consciousness. "The day-to-day struggles of trade unionism," Fiedler (1951) adds, "unemployment, the Civil War in Spain, the role of the Soviet Union, anarchism, and pacifism"—filtered, as above, through Weil's own distinctive character and manner—"these are the determinants of her ideas, the unforeseen roads that led to her sanctity. Though she passed finally beyond politics," therefore, "her thought bears to the end the mark of her early interests, as the teaching of St. Paul is influenced by his rabbinical schooling, or that of St. Augustine by his training in rhetoric" (p. 4). Much of her thought, in short, can be accounted for, at least in part, by looking toward her history, her past. But as we shall see shortly, there nevertheless remain fundamental aspects of her thought that owe their existence to the Other—that is, those particular objects of attention and devotion that beckoned her forward.

The Other That Is Not Human

"In a profound sense," Fiedler (1951) maintains, "[Weil's] life is her chief work, and without some notion of her biography it is impossible to know her total meaning" (p. 12). On one level, indeed, Simone Weil's life and work lend themselves readily—too readily, perhaps—to biographical analysis. Du Plessix Gray's (2001) portrait of Weil, in particular, provides a great deal of compelling biographical detail, and there are many places in her account that seem essentially to proclaim that, yes, finally, these biographical data are the surest means we have to get hold of Weil's life and work. And yet, there is a refusal in virtually all of them to go the biographical route exclusively:

> The severe secularist might trace Simone's religious emergence to the myriad disenchantments she'd experienced in the social and political sphere: Passionate young woman lives through a series of traumatic disillusionments; turns away from Marxism, Revolutionary Syndicalism, trade unionism, the Spanish Republican cause; is successively shaken by her experience as a factory worker, by her disappointment at the fate of France's Popular Front, by the growing evidence of her country's moral malaise; and throughout remains ambivalent—just as her father had been all along—about her Jewish origins. (p. 129)

But there are aspects of Weil's profile, du Plessix Gray maintains—particularly the nature of her mystical experiences—that resist this purely secularist account, or that at least underscore its limits. Perhaps more important for present purposes, there are aspects of her profile that serve to underscore the extraordinary power the non-human Other can have over us, even resulting in the most radical self-transformation. Weil's own convictions notwithstanding, it may be that some measure of personal "preparation" is required in order for this power to emerge. Indeed, paradoxically, it may be that such preparation is in fact of a piece with precisely that sort of self-effacement she sought. How can this be?

Let us turn briefly to Weil's own account of these transformative experiences in her "spiritual autobiography" (1973 [1951]), written to her friend Fr. Perrin in 1942. Weil begins by writing, "[N]ever at any moment in my life have I 'sought for God.'...As soon as I reached adolescence, I saw the problem of God as a problem the data of which could not be obtained here below, and I decided that the only way of being sure not to reach a wrong solution, which seemed to me the greatest possible evil, was to leave it alone. So I left it alone. I neither affirmed nor denied anything" (p. 62). Strictly speaking, therefore, her earlier life was largely devoid of explicit religious commitment or belief. If there was preparation, it hadn't come from this.

Looking backward, Weil can nevertheless see some important precursors, if not determinants, of her spiritual vocation. At the age of 14, for instance,

> I fell into one of those fits of bottomless despair that come with adolescence, and I seriously thought of dying because of the mediocrity of my natural faculties. The exceptional gifts of my brother, who had a childhood and youth comparable to those of Pascal, brought my own inferiority home to me. I did not mind having no visible successes, but what did grieve me was the idea of being excluded from that transcendent kingdom to which only the truly great have access and wherein truth abides. I preferred to die rather than live without that truth. After months of inward darkness, I suddenly had the everlasting conviction that any human being, even though practically devoid of natural faculties, can penetrate to the kingdom of truth reserved for genius, if only he longs for truth and perpetually concentrates all his attention on its attainment. He thus becomes a genius too, even though for lack of talent his genius cannot be visible from the outside. (1973 [1951], p. 64)

As early as her adolescence, therefore, Weil had gained intimations of the "transcendent kingdom" to which she would ultimately devote herself and the possibility of her own "genius." She also recalls an experience at age 16 when the idea of purity "took possession" of her. "This idea came to me when I was contemplating a mountain landscape and little by little it was imposed upon me in an irresistible manner" (p. 65). These formative experiences aside, Weil is quick to emphasize that none of these are to be equated with her entry into the Church. By her own account, there was little reason to add "dogma" to her own conception of life, and the institutional dimension of the Church, in her view, could only detract from authentic religious experience. This is why she would never be baptized. True religion, she believed, could only be had outside the gates of religious institutions, with their inevitably collectivistic codes and strictures.

In view of the account provided thus far, the story Weil is telling brings forth a variety of experiences that are preparatory to her mystical experiences—at least as judged in retrospect—but not causative in any obvious way. Not surprisingly, particularly in light of her own emphasis on the idea of "obedience" and her suggestion that "the most beautiful life possible [is] the one where everything is determined, either by the pressure of circumstances or by impulses...and where there is never any room for choice" (1973 [1951], p. 63), there is also little talk of intention. This narrative strategy may, of course, be purposeful on Weil's part. In line with her philosophy, there would be little room in such an account for purely personal decisions.

Continuing with her story, Weil (1973 [1951]) acknowledges that she "had three contacts with Catholicism"—or, perhaps more accurately, three contacts with objects that would serve to establish and solidify her connection to Catholicism—"that really counted." After a year of brutal factory labor, in which, coupled with her own "prolonged and first-hand experience" of affliction, the affliction of others had "entered into my flesh and my soul," she had accompanied her parents to Portugal, where she had visited a little village. "I was, as it were, in pieces, soul and body, [the] contact with affliction [having] killed my youth" (p. 66). Weil continues as follows:

> In this state of mind, then, and in a wretched condition physically, I entered the little Portuguese village, which, alas, was very wretched too, on the very day of the festival of its patron saint. I was alone. It was the evening and there was a full moon over the sea. The wives of the fishermen were, in procession, making a tour of all the ships, carrying candles and singing what must certainly be very ancient hymns of a heart-rending sadness. Nothing can give any idea of it. I have never heard anything so poignant unless it were the song of the boatmen on the Volga. There the conviction was suddenly borne in upon me that Christianity is pre-eminently the religion of slaves, that slaves cannot help belonging to it, and I among others. (p. 67)

It is difficult to know which (language of) "enslavement" came first, the factory experience or the encounter with the fishermen's wives—or whether, perhaps more likely, it came after the fact of both, during the course of autobiographical reflection and writing. Weil's narrative at any rate establishes a connection between the two: the factory experience was the condition without which there would have been no being "borne in" upon her the idea of Christianity as "the religion of slaves." In this context, again, there is no questioning the relevance of Weil's biography, even by Weil herself. In her (retrospective) view, the earlier experience had, at the least, "set the stage" for the latter. At the same time, this first recounted mystical experience and the "conviction" it brought in its wake would, of necessity, work *against* the intentional, the biographical, the *personal*. The very idea of enslavement, not unrelated to the aforementioned idea of obedience, says as much. She was a captive—of affliction, of beauty, and, she would soon see, of Christ.[6]

In the second of her three experiences, in 1937, Weil would venture to Assisi. "There, alone in the little twelfth-century Romanesque chapel of Santa Maria degli Angeli, an incomparable marvel of purity where Saint Francis often used to pray, something stronger than I was compelled me for the first time in my life to go down on my knees" (1973 [1951], pp. 67–68). Unlike the first experience, for which she establishes a precursor of sorts, this second experience seems devoid of one. She does acknowledge at one point in her autobiography that she "fell in love with Saint Francis of Assisi as soon as I came to know about him," and she also acknowledges that she "always believed and hoped that one day Fate would force upon me the condition of a vagabond and a beggar which he embraced freely. Actually," she adds, in true Weilian form, "I felt the same way about prison" (p. 65). (The more affliction, the better!) But, in her own rendition of things, there was simply no denying that "something stronger than I was," strong enough indeed to force her to her knees, had descended upon her. This "something," in its powerful otherness, would not only serve to provide some much-needed existential and spiritual nourishment to Weil's existence; it would serve to call forth

---

6. Levinas's language of the "hostage" (1996c; see also Chapter Three) is surely relevant here. For Levinas, you may recall, we are hostage to the human Other, the other person, who holds us captive, commands us, insists on our care. Weil would no doubt have some trouble with this formulation, not least because of its very insistence on the centrality of the human. Nevertheless, she would likely be of a piece with Levinas in other aspects of his views, particularly regarding the idea of necessity.

her own devotion, her own sustained commitment to including such otherness in her life.

The final experience would happen a year later:

> In 1938 I spent ten days at Solesmes, from Palm Sunday to Easter Tuesday, following all the liturgical services. I was suffering from splitting headaches; each sound hurt me like a blow; by an extreme effort of concentration I was able to rise above this wretched flesh, to leave it to suffer by itself, heaped up in a corner, and to find a pure and perfect joy in the unimaginable beauty of the chanting and the words. This experience enabled me by analogy to get a better understanding of the possibility of loving divine love in the midst of affliction. It goes without saying that in the course of these services the thought of the Passion of Christ entered my being once and for all. (Weil, 1973 [1951], p. 68)

But there is more. In the course of this experience, she had also encountered a "young English Catholic" from whom she would gain her

> first idea of the supernatural power of the sacraments because of the truly angelic radiance with which he seemed to be clothed after going to communion. Chance—for I always prefer saying chance rather than Providence—made of him a messenger to me. For he told me of those English poets of the seventeenth century who are named metaphysical. In reading them later on, I discovered the poem...called "Love." I learned it by heart. Often, at the culminating point of a violent headache, I make myself say it over, concentrating all my attention upon it and clinging with all my soul to the tenderness it enshrines. I used to think I was merely reciting it as a beautiful poem, but without my knowing it the recitation had the virtue of a prayer. It was during one of these recitations that...Christ himself came down and took possession of me. (1973 [1951], pp. 68–69)[7]

---

7. As Diane Ackerman has suggested in her reflections on "deep play," "There is a way of beholding that is a form of prayer" (1999, p. 23). Whether such play-full beholding makes religion "inevitable," as she puts it, is open to question. In Weil's case, however, it surely served to intensify her religious commitments.

This visitation was apparently a shock to Weil. "In my arguments about the insolubility of God," she writes, "I had never foreseen the possibility of that, of a contact, person to person, here below, between a human being and God. I had vaguely heard tell of things of this kind, but I had never believed in them." In fact, she continues, "accounts of apparitions rather put me off if anything, like the miracles in the gospel." She apparently didn't have any familiarity with mystical works either. "I had never read any mystical works because I had never felt any call to read them.... God in his mercy had prevented me from reading the mystics, so that it should be evident to me that I had not invented this absolutely unexpected contact." Indeed, "[i]n this sudden possession of me by Christ, neither my senses nor my imagination had any part; I only felt in the midst of my suffering the presence of a love, like that which one can read in the smile on a beloved face" (p. 69).[8]

Weil's skepticism had apparently met its match. Given that she was vehemently "anti-apparition," and given as well that she apparently knew precious little about the mystics, she could only assume that neither her senses nor her imagination had played a role. What had descended upon her was wholly *Other*. That, at least, was her own view on the matter. But what are the possibilities here? One is straightforwardly theological and in strict keeping with Weil's own view: Christ possessed her! Case closed. One could also go the Jamesian (1982 [1902]) route and essentially suspend the question. In other words, one could say that these experiences were binding and valid for Weil herself, but that they certainly need not be considered so by anyone else: if *she* says that neither her senses nor her imagination had entered the scene, then so be it. With all due respect to James, most psychologists would likely move in a different direction. After all, it was *Christ* who had possessed her, not the Buddha or Mohammed or any other putatively divine being or force. Maybe if she had never *heard* of Christ, we could more easily assume that there was no imaginative work going on. But clearly she had, and it stands to reason that *some* of what she knew had found its way into these ostensibly unanticipated and, in the last case, "absolutely unexpected" encounters.

In some recent work (e.g., Freeman, 2002, 2010), I have spoken of the "narrative unconscious," which, I have suggested, refers not to what

---

8. This strikes me as an interesting twist on the Levinasian notion, discussed in the previous chapter, that the human face is the very "locus of the word of God" (1999a, p. 104). For Weil, it would seem, the human face is not so much a "locus" as a metaphorical site for signifying much the same sensuous presence and palpability she would find in Christ.

has been dynamically repressed but to that which has been lived through but remains largely unthought and thus untold—which is to say, to those aspects of one's *history* that have not yet become part of one's *story*.[9] Bearing this idea in mind, it could be that Weil had internalized—from her reading, from the people she met, and from the cultural surround more generally—much more than she (consciously) knew and that, somehow, she brought this knowledge with her to Portugal, Assisi, Solesmes, and countless other places, infusing the quite real features of the world (such as those extraordinarily moving Portuguese songs) with her memory and imagination, covertly at work. But this sort of account, valid though it may be within its own sphere, isn't entirely satisfactory either, for in the end it does a kind of violence to Weil's own story, essentially relegating her visitations from without to the internal machinations of her mind and the particularities of her life history. In doing so, it diminishes the *otherness* of the Other. This would seem to be true of virtually any explanatory account of this sort, however hermeneutically sensitive it might be.

This leads us to an important question, relevant not only to Weil's case but to the larger case I have been trying to make throughout this book. It has already been acknowledged (in Chapter One, especially) that the Other is always part of a relationship. This doesn't mean that we cannot ever talk about the self-evident properties of certain objects of attention or devotion, what these objects are "in themselves"; in some instances, we surely can. But in other instances—such as the present one—it becomes decidedly more difficult, not least because it is patently clear how important Weil's own hermeneutical (and perhaps characterological) preparation was. In this case, therefore, the various objects that have come her way, indeed taken her by storm, have been circumscribed by her own previous experiences as well as her own beliefs, needs, and wishes. Without this preparatory constellation, these objects could not have had the power they did. As we shall see in the next chapter, this is true of putatively "transcendent" experience more generally. Powerful though such experience may be, and unassailable though its objects are to those who have been captivated by them, it is frequently the case that the objects in question would not, and could not, affect others—particularly those from distant times or places—in the same way. Because they bring a different *world* to these objects, a historically and culturally saturated world that circumscribes the objects'

---

9. See also Footnote 2, toward the beginning of this chapter.

possible meanings, they will not be able to "get out of them" what the locals can. Does this mean that the Other really isn't so other after all, that it is so thoroughly suffused with the experiencing subject's world that it is ultimately a kind of projection, emanating from the self? Let me frame this more positively, bringing us back to Weil: is there a way to preserve the otherness of the Other while also acknowledging the preparatory role played by the distinctive history she had brought to her various encounters?

Biography and Beyond

For du Plessix Gray (2001), who offers a more purely psychological account of Weil's life and work than most others, Weil's testimony bears within it "all the earmarks of a true mystical experience: the severe physical and emotional suffering that preceded it robbed her of all self-will; the experience came unexpectedly—she had no premonition of it; the feelings of submission, joy, and particularly of a Pascalian *certitude* brought her by her epiphany (a presence 'more certain and more real') were unrelated to any emotions she'd known thus far" (p. 129).

Fiedler (1951), while also comfortable enumerating "the determinants of her ideas," concurs. Given the prominence of her political commitments, there were many who were shocked upon learning about Weil's posthumous meditations on spiritual and religious life. "Surely," he writes, "no 'friend of God' in all history, had moved more unwillingly toward the mystic encounter. There is in her earlier work no sense of a groping toward the divine, no promise of holiness, no pursuit of a purity beyond this world—only a conventionally left-wing concern with the problems of industrialization, rendered in a tone at once extraordinarily inflexible and wonderfully sensitive" (p. 4). What is so compelling about Weil's testimony is, again, "the feeling that her role as a mystic was so unintended, one for which she had not in any sense prepared." Indeed, "an undertone of incredulity persists beneath her astonishing honesty: quite suddenly God had taken her, radical, agnostic, contemptuous of religious life and practice as she had observed it" (pp. 4–5).

My interest in this chapter, I should emphasize, is less the religion-specific aspect of Weil's transformation (important though it is) than the *object*-specific aspect—that is, the fact of her having had three notable, object-laden experiences that serve to highlight the potential power of the non-human Other to effect radical personal change, in this case her spiritual awakening. One could, of course, see this awakening as little more than reaction-formation. One could also return to Weil's ostensibly pathological characteristics and trace them back, one by one, to this or that dimension of her history. But most agree that there remains a marked gap in her case between any and all wholly secular determinants and the sheer depth of her spiritual vocation. Anna Freud has commented that, even though Weil undoubtedly had some significant eating issues, and even though these issues point in the direction of a form of narcissism, hers "is a narcissism that is not pathologically 'fixed' on her own appearance and weight and her appetite and her potential obesity" (cited in Coles, 2001, p. 39). Indeed, Freud maintains, despite the severity of her various commitments, it isn't at all clear whether any sort of "clinical emphasis" is warranted in Weil's case. Coles picks up on this line of thinking in his own rendition of the matter:

> Her hunger was for God, not a slim waistline. She was not the first mystic to be a picky eater. She wanted the quickest possible life consistent with her own tenaciously held ideas.... She wanted to live, so she could die in the most honorable manner.... One feels sure that this brave and yet scatterbrained person, as shrewdly sane as could be and as wacky as could be, had a central dream: her moment of release, her giddy ascent, His welcome. Her intense moral imagination simply couldn't stop doing its work, couldn't stop distracting her from the routines the rest of us take for granted, including our meals. She refused the food offered her while awaiting the big feast she often mentioned, the one given the symbolic form of the Holy Communion. She yearned to have her appetite appeased, not for a day or for a week, Sunday to Sunday, but forever. (p. 41)

"Once Simone Weil met Christ," Coles continues, "her life began anew, a slave, now, to a particular master." For Coles, it is not stretching things to say that Weil "fell in love with Jesus; that he became her beloved; that she kept him on her mind and in her heart." The last five years of her life would be spent "thinking about Jesus, writing about him, praying to him, fitting him into her social and economic and political scheme of things. She was a nun of sorts, following her vocation alone. She was an ambitious, dedicated follower, anxious to meet him—maybe become one of his saints" (p. 119). Again, then, how shall we deal with her case, in particular her writing, which at once grows out of her distinctive biography and yet, somehow, moves beyond it? "One does best...to accept her writing for what it was, a gift of the gods who resided in her, inspired sparks that had not yet come together as a single flame" (p. 19).

This is a familiar refrain in the lore about Weil. Gabriel Marcel, for instance, "warned" against any and all attempts to situate Weil's thought within extant categories or, for that matter, to analyze her life and work. Whatever is said about her cannot help but distort her (cited in Miles, 1986). As Finch (2001) adds, "Psychology and sociology and even philosophy will not help us with Simone Weil. Her messages are messages of grace, received by those who wait and not by those who grasp." It is because "the very premises of psychology and sociology and philosophy are grasping willed knowledge," Finch maintains, that they cannot rise to the challenge at hand. "We are used to people who impose interpretations on the world, not those who wait and let it come to them." But again, it is precisely such "waiting" that "puts the world into a new context, a sacred human one," and that underscores "the recognition that everything that matters most to us comes to us as a gift" (p. 112), derived from without. According to Finch, one of the most important lessons learned from Weil concerns the distinction between the psychological and the spiritual (or what Jung [1933] calls the "visionary"). It is a "delusion of our age," as Finch puts it,

> that it is possible to "explain" the spiritual psychologically (Freud, Jung, Reich, and the rest). We have myths that have the appearance, but not the reality, of science. They have to be taken on faith, "believed in," like pseudo-religions....Simone Weil herself has been the victim of such psychological "explanations," which in effect ignore her philosophy and try instead to fit it into categories of masochism or anorexia or self-hatred, in the way that psychologists have attempted to explain Leonardo da Vinci's art as a mother-fixation or Dostoevsky's as parricide. In the case of Simone Weil, such "theories" may fulfill a useful purpose by forming a protective shell around her that guarantees that only those who are seriously interested will be able to see through it. This will prevent her from being turned into a cult. Those who cannot recognize her genius had best stay away. Thus, her intellectual and moral and spiritual

integrity will remain protected until such reductive psychology has disappeared and we are able to meet her truly. (p. 115)

But what does it mean to "meet her truly"? What exactly is Finch calling for here?

Weil's friend Thibon (1953a) raises concerns similar to Finch's in his discussion of the challenge of dealing biographically with the likes of Weil. "Who could conceive a biography of the sun?" Baudelaire had written. "From the time when the flaming ball gave its first sign of life the story is one of monotony, light and greatness." "And indeed," Thibon writes,

> one can no more write the story of the sun than the story of God. What a condemnation of all that side of history which appeals to the depraved appetite of the crowd!...The deep reality is too eternal to be "actual," too intimate and too continuous to be sensational....The true greatness of Simone Weil was of such an order. Depths of silence have to be traversed in order to grasp the authentic meaning of her words. Moreover, it is no longer she who pronounces those words; it is the Spirit from above, into whose submissive instrument her body and soul are transformed; at those times of supreme inspiration the hand which writes and the mind which thinks have become nothing but a "link between mortal and immortal," an impersonal intermediary through which the "the Creator and the creature exchange their secrets." (p. 3)

Not unlike Marcel, Thibon continues, "it is better not to speak [of Weil]; her message absorbs her personality; her life, her character, her actions become as she herself expresses it 'infinitesimal to the nth degree'—particles of change in the bosom of an ocean of necessity. Biography can only deal with what is contingent, the absolute and universal provide no handle for narrative" (pp. 3–4).

After this rather romantic rendition of things, Thibon (1953a) seems to catch himself. Her "greatness" notwithstanding,

> Simone Weil,...like every created being, was not constantly and completely under the influence of supreme inspiration. Side by side with her deep originality...and her purity which was invisible to the outward eye, she was gifted with another kind of originality which was not only visible but striking, provocative, almost

aggressive. And these two sides of her nature were not only juxtaposed, but were very closely interconnected.... Like most of those who are marked by a transcendental vocation, she was at the same time above and below the level of normal activities, and the picturesque singularity of her person was at once the consequence and the antithesis of the self-effacement and transparency of her personality. (pp. 4–5)

As Thibon (1953a) goes on to note, there is a twofold tendency in accounts of Weil's life and work. First, there is the tendency for her message to be considered "as a kind of infallible revelation of universal import," set essentially apart from her imperfections and weaknesses, from the messy details of her life. The result of such an enterprise is generally

a deplorably flat picture of the being or the work unduly adored ... for, in refusing the see the limitations of a human being, one is bound to miss his deep reality which is marked and as it were moulded in its very foundations by these same limitations. One substitutes a perfection, the frozen immutability of a mummy for the warmth and movement of a finite human body. Much could be written about the sterilizing process of idolatry. (p. 5)

The second tendency is "to stress everything which might be considered as exaggerated or illusory in the thought of Simone Weil in order to question, not only the deep value, but even the authenticity of her spiritual testimony" (p. 5). Thibon goes on to speak of "these totalitarian, and for that reason, mutilating, interpretations." We are therefore left with the following idea: "The finite and infinite, which paradoxically coexist in all men, in her case form contrasts so great and of such violence as to confound the judgment. Attracted by that in her which is infinite, one is tempted to forget her limitations, or else, shocked by her limitations, one is in danger of misunderstanding that which is infinite." The challenge, therefore, is "to avoid this double pitfall" (p. 6).

We will save the issue of the infinite for the next chapter. For now, the much more terrestrial challenge is to somehow try to square the idea of the priority of the Other—in this case, the non-human Other, as Weil encountered it through the transformative experiences she recounts—with the aforementioned preparation required for its emergence. Let us turn to it.

Personalized Depersonalization

Thibon, along with Finch, has presented us with a difficult task. For Thibon, it is necessary to preserve the tension between the biographical and that which, on some level, transcends it—to recognize and embrace the "limitations," the "warmth," and the "movement of [the] finite human body" that shape the deepest realities of being and, at the same time, to convey both the "authenticity" and "value" of the spiritual testimony in question. Only then will we avoid a "deplorably flat picture" or a "totalitarian, mutilating" one. We must therefore recognize and avow the importance of biography without lapsing into reductionism. Our own challenge is a similar one: we must recognize and avow the relational and hermeneutical dimension of Weil's profound encounters with Other without draining and emptying their autonomous power. Is it possible?

This challenge is particularly significant in the context of lives like Weil's, in which the Other is not only "not human" but, ostensibly, not of the earthly world. Can there be a biographical perspective on lives like Weil's (not that there are many) that avoids the sort of mutilating violence about which Thibon speaks? As for Finch's rendition of things, one can ask a related question: can there be a different kind of *psychology* than the one he refers to, one that avoids the (al)lure of reductionism and is able to deal appropriately with the spiritual as such—that is, that truly acknowledges the Other qua Other? Or is this simply a contradictory and ultimately untenable project?

While these questions have a special urgency when it comes to spiritual and religious matters, they are readily applied to other domains—the arts, especially—as well. Insofar as creativity is itself an act of transcendence of a sort, a going beyond the determinants of the past in the service of creating something new, its existence poses similar questions and problems. So it is that Jung (1933), for instance, insists that "the creative aspect of life which finds its clearest expression in art baffles all attempts at rational formulation" and "will for ever elude the human understanding" (p. 153). None of what is being said, he clarifies, means that biographical data are irrelevant. "No objection can be raised if is admitted that this approach"—which Jung associates with Freud—"amounts to nothing more than the elucidation of those personal determinants without which a work of art is unthinkable. But should the claim be made that such an analysis accounts for the work of art itself, then a categorical denial is called for." Jung's next sentences might have been spoken by Simone Weil herself: "The personal idiosyncrasies that creep into a work of art are not essential; in fact, the more we have to cope with these peculiarities, the less it is a work of art. What is essential in a work of art is that it should rise far above the personal life and speak from the spirit and heart of the poet as man to the spirit and heart of mankind. The personal aspect is a limitation—and even a sin—in the work of art" (p. 168). As Jung goes on to suggest, "Art is a kind of innate drive that seizes a human being and makes him its instrument. The artist," in turn, "is one who allows art to realize its purposes through him" (p. 169). Put another way, he or she must hear the voice of the Other, serving as a vessel or conduit for its energies.[10]

Something similar may be said in regard to aesthetic experience. As Clifford Geertz (1983) notes, "The chief problem presented by the sheer phenomenon of aesthetic force, in whatever form and as a result of whatever skill it may come, is how to place it within the other modes of social activity, how to incorporate it into the texture of a particular pattern of life" (p. 97). For the fact is, "[a]rt and the equipment to grasp it are made in the same shop" (p. 118). What I take Geertz to mean by this is that certain works *acquire* their aesthetic force precisely owing to their embodying a particular mode of life, to which they have given new meaning and new form. Such works, therefore, far from being untethered to the world, derive their very lifeblood from it and, in turn, create the conditions of possibility for others to feel their force.

Stephen Crites (1971) gives a particularly nice rendition of these issues in the context of music. "People take such satisfaction in music," he writes,

> because it answers to a powerful if seldom noticed aspect of everything they do, of every gesture, every footstep, every utterance; answers to it and gives it a purified expression. Courtship, worship, even violent conflict, call forth musical expressions in order to give these activities a certain ideality, a specific ideality rooted in the activities themselves. That is why the music of a culture or subculture has such a vital connection, so revealing yet so hard to define, with its whole style of life. The music of a people, or even a cohesive

---

10. Along these lines, Jung goes on to say, "It is not Goethe who creates Faust, but Faust which creates Goethe" (pp. 170–71). Heidegger (1971), similarly, writes, "The artist is the origin of the work. The work is the origin of the artist.... As necessarily as the artist is the origin of the work in a different way than the work is the origin of the artist, so it is equally certain that, in a still different way, art is the origin of both artist and work" (p. 17). For both Jung and Heidegger, therefore, the artist, rather than being seen as the sole and primary source of creation, is instead partly secondary, constituted by his or her art. This perspective is very much in keeping with what I earlier referred to as the "secondarity" of the self.

group, is peculiarly its own. It is the particular musical style that permits a group's life style, its incipient musicality, to express itself in full dance and song. (pp. 294–295)

Along these lines, Crites adds, "There is a beautiful paradox in the peculiar intensity with which a person responds to music which is 'his own': Even if he has not heard it before it is familiar, as though something is sounding in it that he has always felt in his bones; and yet it is really new. It is his own style, revealed to him at an otherwise unimaginable level of clarity and intensity" (p. 295). Why this movement of recognition should be as ecstatically transporting as it sometimes is remains something of a mystery.[11]

Returning to Weil and the broader question of the relationship between what one brings to the world and what one is able to derive from it, is there a way of conceptualizing the process at hand such that the personal becomes transformed into the *im*personal? Whether the object in question is religious or aesthetic, what we seem to be considering is a kind of psycho-spiritual alchemy, a process of transmutation, wherein one's own hermeneutical preparation, rooted in the particularities of one's history, is somehow raised to a higher, more suprapersonal level. Recall in this context Weil's own "everlasting conviction" that "any human being...can penetrate to the kingdom of truth reserved for genius, if only he longs for truth and perpetually concentrates all his attention on its attainment" (1973 [1951], p. 64). Here, it would seem, we have a preliminary, if somewhat rudimentary, clue about this transmutative process. Not surprisingly, attention is key. But this attention, it would seem, cannot be a wholly empty one, stripped of one's history. Rather, it must make use of this history, draw on it; otherwise, the very grounds of experience and relatedness to the Other are lost. With this in mind, let us turn to Weil herself once more, focusing especially on her thoughts regarding attention.

In *Gravity and Grace* (1997 [1952]), Weil speaks of the necessity, first, of adopting an "attitude of supplication." "Grace," she writes, "fills empty spaces but it can only enter where there is a void to receive it, and it is grace itself which makes this void" (p. 10). Somehow, therefore, the self needs to be emptied, made void. As we saw earlier, the experience of affliction

---

[11]. I explore this set of issues in significantly greater detail in the next chapter, focusing especially on the idea of transcendence. Perhaps we will gain some headway then.

is one significant way for this self-emptying to occur. "To strip ourselves of the imaginary royalty of the world" (p. 12), through suffering, degradation, even humiliation, serves to carve out the necessary space. Indeed, "[r]elentless necessity, wretchedness, distress, the crushing burden of poverty and of labour which wears us out, cruelty, torture, violent death, constraint, disease—all these constitute divine love" insofar as they pave the way to the operation of grace. This is Weil's notion of "decreation": "It is God who in love withdraws from us so that we can love him. For if we were exposed to the direct radiance of his love, without the protection of space, of time and of matter, we should be evaporated like water in the sun" (p. 28).

Following this line of thinking, Weil (1997 [1952]) maintains that we, as individual selves, need to "withdraw" in much the same way. "He emptied himself of his divinity. We should empty ourselves of the false divinity with which we were born. Once we have understood we are nothing, the object of all our efforts is to become nothing." Weil goes on to suggest that there is a deep connection, even a "resemblance," as she puts it, between the "lower" and the "higher." "Hence slavery is an image of obedience to God, humiliation an image of humility, physical necessity an image of the irresistible pressure of grace." The implication? "On this account it is necessary to seek out what is lowest." And so, "[m]ay that which is low in us go downwards so that what is high can go upwards" (p. 30). The preliminary aim, therefore, is nothing short of disappearance—"in order that those things that I see become perfect in their beauty from the very fact that they are no longer things I see." Again, this is patently impossible; whenever she is present, she cannot help but "disturb the silence of heaven and earth by my breathing and the beating of my heart" (p. 37).[12] But the aim remains: to see the world for what it is, in its difference, apart from the self and its baggage.

What Weil has presented thus far, however, is only part of the equation. Alongside the process of self-emptying, there needs to be attention directed outward, to the *other*-than-self; for "attention, taken to its highest degree, is the same thing as prayer" (Weil, 1997 [1952], p. 105). In line with Weil's idea regarding the attainability of genius by all, here too she is convinced that "if we turn our mind towards the good, it is impossible that little by little the whole soul will not be attracted thereto in spite of

---

12. See also the discussion toward the conclusion of Chapter Two.

itself." Ultimately, she argues, "[e]xtreme attention is what constitutes the creative faculty in man and the only extreme attention is religious." As such, "[t]he amount of creative genius in any period is strictly in proportion to the amount of extreme attention and thus of authentic religion at that period" (p. 106). Weil makes an interesting move at this point by noting that not only is the dissolution of the self a prerequisite for the work of attention, but attention is instrumental in the dissolution of the self: "Attention alone—that attention which is so full that the 'I' disappears—is required of me" (p. 107). It is this dialectic of decreation and attention that is constitutive of the "creative faculty" in art and religion alike. It is tempting to fashion a model of sorts with this last idea in mind. In order to draw nearer to reality, a certain measure of detachment may be required. Following Weil, discrete practices may be needed in order for such detachment to occur. Insofar as this detachment results in drawing one nearer to reality, it creates the possibility that this reality will provide a greater measure of meaning and nourishment than it had before, which in turn "unselfs" one that much more. This latter moment of unselfing, however, is also a *re*-selfing, as I called it earlier, such that a larger, more capacious mode of being—a Self—emerges.[13]

In another interesting move, Weil seems to offer a correction of sorts to the earlier notion of self-emptying. In one sense, "[a]ttention consists in suspending our thought, leaving it detached, empty, and ready to be penetrated by the object." But it also means

> holding in our minds, within reach of this thought, but on a lower level and not in contact with it, the diverse knowledge we have acquired which we are forced to make use of. Our thought should be in relation to all particular and already formulated thoughts, as a man on a mountain who, as he looks forward, sees also below him, without actually looking at them, a great many forests and plains. Above all our thoughts should be empty, waiting, not seeking anything, but ready to receive in its naked truth the object that is to penetrate it. (1973 [1951], pp. 111–112)

---

13. I don't know that Weil would be pleased with the last sentence of this paragraph. As we have already seen, she is not one to speak too readily about "larger, more capacious" modes of being. At the same time, there is a very real sense in which this larger mode, infused by the energy of the Other, retains a certain humility and vulnerability. "We only become truly large," I suggested earlier, "when we are willing to embrace our own real smallness in the total scheme of what is real." With the idea formulated in these terms, Weil might well be willing to sign on.

Rather than seeing virtuosic achievement, whether in art or religion, either as a full-scale visitation from without or as a product of some special faculty or personal characteristic, therefore, Weil, not unlike Jung, sees *depersonalization* as the requisite condition. When personality dominates in the process of creation, wonderful achievements remain possible. "But above this level, far above, separated by an abyss, is the level where the things are achieved," and these are "essentially anonymous" (Weil, 1986, p. 55). It is for this reason that "every time that a man rises to a degree of excellence...we are aware of something impersonal and anonymous about him. His voice is enveloped in silence. This is evident in all the great works of art or thought, in the great deeds of saints and in their words" (Weil, 1997 [1952], p. 179). Weil has also told us, however, that the kind of attention that is requisite for the emergence of these impersonal and anonymous dimensions must itself *pass through* one's history, including all the "diverse knowledge" that has been acquired. Her formulation is a provocative one. In a distinct sense, Weil is calling for a kind of "personalized depersonalization," a process that draws upon the energy and movement of one's own unique history even as one seeks to purge oneself of it.

The situation is a complicated and paradoxical one. Only by self-emptying does there exist the possibility of experiencing what is authentically *other*; short of this, the Other in question is bound to be veiled by one's own anxieties, projections, fears, and wishes. This veil must be removed in order for the world to be unconcealed (see Heidegger, 1971). At the same time, what we have seen through our exploration of Weil is that the preparedness one brings to the encounter with the Other may well be the requisite condition for the occurrence of this unconcealing. Indeed—and this is the core of the paradox—the very autonomous power that is generated by the Other is frequently dependent upon the hermeneutical readiness of the self. As such, *whatever* Weil had brought to those mystical encounters, it was the objects themselves—the wives of the Portuguese fisherman, the chapel of Santa Maria degli Angeli, the "unimaginable beauty" of chant, the metaphysical poem "Love"—that had captivated her.

Acknowledging the importance of one's readiness, as above, and acknowledging as well the relativity of taste and in turn the great variability of our interest in and responsiveness to particular objects, what these objects are, *in themselves*, is thus a vitally important determinant of our experience. This is so for both "inferior" and "superior" objects, including, especially, works of art. "The chief enemy of excellence in morality (and also in art)," Murdoch (1970) writes, "is personal fantasy: the tissue of self-aggrandizing and consoling wishes and dreams which prevents one from seeing what is there outside one.... We can see in mediocre art, where perhaps it is even more clearly seen than in mediocre conduct, the intrusion of fantasy, the assertion of self, the dimming of any reflection of the real world" (pp. 57–58). The fact is, "[a]rt presents the most comprehensible examples of the almost irresistible human tendency to seek consolation in fantasy and also of the effort to resist this and the vision of reality which comes with success." Success is rare and difficult. "To silence and expel self, to contemplate and delineate nature with a clear eye, is not easy and demands a moral discipline" (pp. 62–63). What's more, whether consciously or unconsciously, artists are bound to bring their own "issues" to bear upon their practices. "Of course great artist are 'personalities' and have special styles," Murdoch acknowledges.

> But the greatest art is "impersonal" because it shows us the world, our world and not another one, with a clarity which startles and delights us simply because we are not used to looking at the real world at all.... Consider what we learn from contemplating the characters of Shakespeare or Tolstoy or the paintings of Velasquez or Titian. What is learnt here is something about the real quality of human nature, when it is envisaged, in the artist's just and compassionate vision, with a clarity which does not belong to the self-centred rush of ordinary life. (pp. 63–64)

Weil, Jung, and Murdoch are thus of a piece on this issue. However important the personal dimension may be in giving rise to the art in question, its *artistry* is dependent on what I have here called depersonalization, a going-beyond one's own personal "peculiarities" (Jung's term) and a raising-to a higher level, one that through its impersonality can come to acquire *trans*-personal, even *supra*-personal, value.

For Murdoch, you may recall, such artistry is seen to have moral consequences as well, both for the (great) artist and for the audience. For the artist, the capacity to raise his or her art to a higher level entails a kind of selflessness, an ability to "check" purely personal considerations and concerns. Something similar may be said of the process of appreciation; it too entails "the checking of selfishness in the interest of seeing the real" (1970, p. 63). By encountering great art objects, therefore, Murdoch maintains, we cannot help but receive a measure of "moral help." I have already confessed some uncertainty about this equation. Among other reasons, it is simply not clear that the process of unselfing, as it is seen to transpire in the context of art, automatically strengthens moral life; there still has to be "transfer," as I have called it, from one domain to another, and there still has to be a measure of *consent* on the part of the experiencing person. The same may be said of great science, great mathematics, and any and all other such vehicles of unselfing.[14] Openness to the whole of reality *may* lead to care and compassion, but it also may not.

In what sense, then, do these great and wondrous things *matter?* Great art, Murdoch (1970) tells us, can present the world with a clarity that delights us "because we are not used to looking at the real world at all" (p. 63). The very otherness of the work of art commands not only attention, however, but respect and care. More to the point still, art, along with nature, can display "a perfection of form which invites unpossessive contemplation and resists absorption into the selfish dream life of the consciousness" (p. 83). It can thus put us in our proper place, as it were, serving as a vehicle of both our humility and our awareness of that which exists apart from us, that which has its own independent being. Along these lines, Murdoch insists, there is a moral dimension, of a sort, to attentive appreciation itself.

Within a given domain of experience—let us stay with the appreciation of art or nature—this appreciation may well translate, directly, into care. The more I appreciate works of art or the wonders of nature, the more likely I am to want to preserve and protect them; they are beings in their own right, "Thous," and I want to ensure their independent existence and survival. There is thus a smooth and unbroken transfer here between the aesthetic and the ethical. Indeed, Murdoch might argue that there isn't really transfer here at all, that the very appreciation I have is

---

14. Weil would appear to be closer to Murdoch's camp about the matter. She writes, "If we concentrate our attention on trying to solve a problem of geometry, and if at the end of an hour we are not nearer to doing so than at the beginning, we have nevertheless been making progress each minute of that hour in another more mysterious dimension. Without our knowing or feeling it, this apparently barren effort has brought more light into the soul. The result will one day be discovered in prayer. Moreover," she continues, "it may very likely be felt in some department of the intelligence in no way connected with mathematics. Perhaps he who made the unsuccessful effort will one day be able to grasp the beauty of a line of Racine more vividly on account of it. But it is certain that this effort will bear its fruit in prayer. There is no doubt whatever about that" (1973 [1951], pp. 106–107). As I state above, I am not at all sure whether there is *no* doubt about the matter at hand. Her idea nevertheless remains a fascinating and important one, providing a deeper rationale for studying mathematics and the sciences than is sometimes provided.

at once aesthetic *and* ethical.[15] Where the question of transfer emerges more forcefully is in the movement from one domain to another and in the movement from the particular to the universal. Does my appreciation and care for nature translate into my appreciation and care for human beings? Does it make me a more caring person more generally, giving me a more capacious and inclusive sense of things? In Chapter Two, I tried to provide a tentative answer to these questions: yes, I said, sometimes; but no, not necessarily. This still strikes me as the right answer. Why? There are people with a deep and abiding devotion to art (for instance) who have carried out horrific crimes against humanity, and there are people who rally on behalf of the natural world who seem to care far less about the human world (and vice versa). But the general point stands: attention and devotion to the Other, whatever it may be, can and often does lead to a greater measure of care, and this care can and often does extend to other objects, other people and things, inspiring a kind of good will in regard to the wider world, perhaps even a commitment to justice. But there is something else still that great art, in particular, can do: it "pierces the veil and gives sense to the notion of a reality which lies beyond appearance" (Murdoch, 1970, p. 86). It provides intimations of an ur-reality, a *beyond*, a transcendent realm of some sort. But of what sort? Let us continue our exploration of the priority of the Other by turning to this important, and difficult, question.

---

15. See Chapter Two for a related discussion.

5

The Possibility of Transcendence

"True Transcendence"?

"The sun," Socrates says in *The Republic* (Plato, 2003), "not only makes the things we see visible, but causes the processes of generation, growth and nourishment, without itself being such a process." The "form of the good" functions in much the same way, and "may be said to be the source not only of intelligibility of the objects of knowledge but also of their being and reality; yet it is not itself that reality, but is beyond it, and superior to it in dignity and power." There is but one conclusion to be drawn: " 'It really must be miraculously transcendent,' remarked Glaucon to the general amusement" (p. 234). It is difficult to know what to make of Glaucon's response, particularly in regard to the "amusement" generated by it. It is also difficult to know what to make of the idea of transcendence itself. It is against the backdrop of this difficulty that Iris Murdoch (1970) asks, "Are you speaking of a transcendent authority or a psychological device?" Her question is an important one. "As with so many of these large elusive ideas," she notes, "it readily takes on forms which are false ones." People latch on to these false forms with alarming frequency, seeking just that sort of comfort and consolation that illusions so readily provide. Again, therefore, "[i]s there...any true transcendence, or is this idea always a consoling dream projected by human need onto an empty sky?" (p. 57).

For Murdoch, the idea of transcendence may be related to two other ideas, "certainty" and "perfection." "Are we not certain," she goes on to ask, "that there is a 'true direction' toward better conduct, that goodness 'really matters,' and does not that certainty about a standard suggest an idea of permanence which cannot be reduced to psychological or any other set of empirical terms?" Certain though we may be, there does remain a problem, one that we have encountered several times throughout this book. "How is one to connect the realism which must involve a clear-eyed contemplation of the misery and evil of the world with a sense of an uncorrupted good without the latter idea becoming the merest consolatory dream?" (Murdoch, 1970, p. 59). If something like a transcendent form of the good exists, why aren't things better? Why aren't *we* better? And yet, there still remains this "certainty," the conviction, held by many, that there does indeed exist a "true direction" toward better conduct—that, through it all, and for all the complexities involved, meaningful distinctions can in fact be made, sometimes, between "worse" and "better," evil and good.

As for how the idea of perfection enters the picture, Murdoch (1970) asks the following:

> [I]s it important to measure and compare things and know just how good they are? In any field which interests or concerns us I think we would say yes. A deep understanding of any field of human activity (painting, for instance) involves an increasing revelation of degrees of excellence and often a revelation of there being in fact little that is very good and nothing that is perfect. Increasing understanding of human conduct operates in a similar way. We come to perceive scales, distances, standards, and my incline to see as less than excellent what previously we were prepared to "let by." (p. 60)

None of what has been said thus far constitutes definitive evidence on behalf of the idea of transcendence. Indeed, as Murdoch realizes, there can *be* no such evidence—not, at least, of the definitive sort that many seek. It is difficult enough to posit the priority of the Other when it is right there before us. It is that much more difficult when the Other is considered to be a "form," tied to an idea of "the Good" that not only can never be met with face to face but seems to run counter to the *not*-good way the world frequently works. These difficulties aside for the time being, for Murdoch, the idea of transcendence is intimately connected to what she calls the "sovereignty" of Good (in her [1970] book by that title)—which is to say, its existence *as* Other, especially as a source of both existential nourishment and virtue.

Does the idea of transcendence warrant our entertaining it as a possibility? It's a serious stretch, and as we have already seen, there is some compelling evidence against it. What might be the evidence *for* it? We have observed that for Murdoch (1970), great art is the most compelling evidence of its reality, providing just that sort of "tiny spark," as she had put it, "which automatically suggests that 'there is more than this' "—and that this "more" is *good*. As she is quick to add, it is imperative that this conviction does not become "corrupted by some sort of quasi-theological finality" (p. 71), for that, in her view, would spoil the whole thing, returning us to exactly that condition of fantasy and illusion she wishes to move beyond. Art, however, is not the only evidence to be adduced. Indeed, "[i]f one is going to speak of great art as 'evidence,' is not ordinary human love an even more striking evidence of a transcendent principle of good?" (p. 73). Then there are mystical experiences of the sort we considered via the case of Simone Weil, which, in terms of sheer ecstatic transport, may well provide the most compelling evidence of all. But let us begin our examination of these issues closer to home. This way, we may be able to see more clearly that the kinds of (ostensibly) transcendent experiences that Weil and others have talked about are not so far afield as they initially appear.

Mystery, Musical and Otherwise

In the very first page of Chapter One, I recounted the experience of driving into Cambridge to do some bicycling just after the semester had ended. The stereo was on and I felt good. But I was also preoccupied and scattered, sifting through the remains of the year gone by. Then a song came on and took hold of me, utterly washing everything away, if only for a little while. Music is remarkable for its capacity to do this: if I can be there with it and let it work its ways, "I"—the preoccupied self, lost in thought, anxious, perhaps—will be (all but) left behind, replaced by the music.[1] This basic process is not limited to music; I might just have easily been dis-placed and re-placed by a newsflash or by some scene on the side of the road. What is different about music is that what is most integral to it—namely, the meaningful movement of sound itself—is not to be "comprehended" in the same way as the newsflash or the roadside scene. Rather than calling forth my own conceptualization or schematization, it comes over me,

---

1. See my reference to Jean-Luc Nancy's *Listening* (2007) in Chapter Two, especially his idea that "[t]o be listening is to be *at the same time* inside and outside, to be open *from* without and *from* within, hence from one to the other and from one in the other" (p. 14). Along these lines, while the "you" being referred to is indeed replaced by the music, this very replacement simultaneously awakens the You—the larger Self—within. "Inside" and "outside" are thus of a piece.

shapes me, forms me anew.² In addition, certain musical works somehow manage to speak the *truth*—that is, it presents a tapestry of sounds that discloses something significant about experience, articulates it.³

But "What," Hans-Georg Gadamer (1986) asks, "is the importance and significance of this particular experience which claims truth for itself, thereby denying that the universality expressed by the mathematical formulation of the laws of nature is the only kind of truth?" (pp. 16–17). What *is* this truth? "Certainly not the truth or universality to which we apply the conceptual universality of the understanding. Despite this, [however,] the kind of truth that we encounter in the experience of the beautiful does unambiguously make a claim to more than subjective validity" (p. 18). This doesn't mean that it is thought-less, purely sensual; "there is always some reflective and intellectual accomplishment involved" (p. 28). But the musical work, and the work of art more generally, "does not simply point toward a meaning" that we might recover and translate into conceptual terms; rather, "it allows that meaning to present itself" (p. 34). This hardly solves the problem, for now we must ask, what *is* this meaning? "What is it about a piece of music that allows us to say that it is rather shallow or, in the case of a late Beethoven quartet, that it is truly great and profound?...What accounts for the sense of quality here? Not a determinate relation to anything that we could identify in terms of a meaning" (p. 38); but, as Gadamer has just told us, a meaning, of a sort, is nevertheless "presented" in the very course of its unfolding.

Peter Kivy finds himself facing a similar set of questions in his book *Music Alone* (1990). His questions begin when he considers "the genuine,

---

2. "In this sense," Murdoch (1993) writes, "art also *creates* its client; it inspires intuitions of ideal formal and symbolic unity which enable us to co-operate with the artist and to be, as we enjoy the work, artists ourselves" (p. 8). The composer Karlheinz Stockhausen conveys a similar idea when he speaks of being "modulated by a specific piece of music in a specific way," even that "we become this music up to a certain point, and we will never be the same again once we have heard that music" (cited in Harvey, 1999, p. 22).

3. For a different point of view (I think), see Robert Jourain's *Music, the Brain, and Ecstasy* (1997). Listening to music, he writes, "makes us larger than we really are, and the world more orderly than it really is." In this sense, music is a domain of *illusion*. And yet, "[a]s our brains are thrown into overdrive, we feel our very existence expand and realize that we can be more than we normally are, and the world is more than it seems" (p. 331). In realizing that we *can* be more, I would argue, we *are* more at that very moment, and so too is the world. Perhaps we, and the world we inhabit, are not quite so "small" as Jourain's first statement implies.

if insoluble, mystery of why we have 'pure' music at all, and why, since we do, we don't have 'music' for other sense modalities" (p. 12). Not unlike Gadamer, Kivy is ambivalent about the issue of meaning. From his perspective, music does have expressive properties; that much is clear. But it doesn't really "say" anything meaningful about the world—not if by "meaningful" we are referring to the kind of "determinate relation" Gadamer speaks of. For this reason, he advocates musical "purism," essentially insisting that we need to take music strictly on its own autonomous terms and leave aside our own need for interpreting it, making sense of it, linking it up with the extra-musical world.[4] But then there is the proverbial "and yet." Some music, Kivy avows, is plainly and palpably profound and touches "the vital center of our moral and metaphysical concerns" (p. 216). Again, how might we understand this? Is there any "rational justification" at all for positing this clear and obvious profundity? Kivy's answer is wonderfully refreshing: no! The fact is, "I find myself at present, then, unable to refrain from thinking that some musical works are profound yet unable, as well, to provide any rational grounds for my thinking it" (p. 218). Claude Levi-Strauss would seem to concur: "Since music is the only language with the contradictory attributes of being at once intelligible and untranslatable," he writes, "the musical creator is a being comparable to the gods, and music itself the supreme mystery of the science of man" (1970, p. 18).

That is not all. "At some deep level of perception and analysis," the composer Jonathan Harvey (1999) writes, "every idea is simultaneously every other idea. Axioms of conceptual reasoning aim to exclude such ambiguity" (p. 24). Music, Harvey maintains, "contradicts these precepts," thereby allowing us to witness the "ever-changing flux" (p. 24) of reality itself. In addition to revealing this ambiguity and flux, however, music "reconciles it in harmony, contains it" (p. 25).[5] So it is that when one moves through certain pieces of music, "one tastes the delicious flavor of unity (if

---

4. The great "non-objective" painter and theorist Wassily Kandinksy held to a similar view about painting—or least what painting ought to aspire to. Indeed, for Kandinsky, music is "the best teacher," and the painter "cannot but envy the ease with which music, the most non-material of the arts today, achieves [the] end [of expressing inner life]" (1977 [1914], p. 18). This project is, finally, about the "spiritual," about the possibility of tapping into those energies that transcend this or that specific time or place. More on this shortly.

5. See also Anton Ehrenzweig's extraordinary book *The Hidden Order of Art: A Study in the Psychology of Artistic Imagination* (1971), which brings a rich, complex psychoanalytic perspective to works of art, focusing especially on modern painting and music.

the piece encourages it); one is moving and moved, yet also still, part of a promised harmony. At the end, the profound satisfaction of a mysterious insight possesses one. It seems as if the answer has been found" (p. 32).[6] Such "sudden perceptions of unity," which seem to "answer," reconcile our deepest ambiguities and uncertainties, "are the essence both of music and of spiritual perception" (p. 59). Given the "arid, confrontational, dualistic age" we live in, Harvey concludes, we could use more of this kind of unifying music, for "[w]here there is unity, there is compassion: sympathy and solidarity with suffering" (p. 82).[7]

Bringing together the ideas we have been considering over the course of these last several pages, what we seem to have in (certain) music is an intelligibility, even a meaningfulness, that can be profound and moving, perhaps touching on our deepest metaphysical and moral concerns, that also provides intimations of harmony and unity, spiritual oneness, which in turn translates into solidarity with others and, perhaps, with the non-human world too. Not bad! It could be that all of this is just a matter of psychophysiological "coincidence" and that, while we can feel good about it, there is no need to get spiritually gushy, and certainly no need to posit some sort of "ghostly existence outside of space and time," as Anthony Storr (1992, p.148) puts it. Along with the others from whom we have heard, Storr is well aware of the apparent "mystery" of musical meaning: "How is it," he asks, "that an art which promulgates no doctrine, which preaches no gospel, which is often entirely dissociated from verbal meaning, can yet be experienced as making sense of life?" (p. 168). And how can we explain the suddenness and spontaneity of those intimations of unity that are so frequently felt? "Since these new patterns appear spontaneously,... it is understandable that the religiously inclined describe themselves"—or at least may—"as being inspired by a deity" (p. 182). Who knows? Perhaps it's so. But for the likes of Storr, there

---

6. Harvey also speaks of "the transcendence of the narrow ego" (p. 36), suggesting that the harmony at hand is registered internally, culminating in a more harmonious mode of being. For related comments, see, again, Higgins (1991).

7. It should be noted that much contemporary music eschews the very harmony and unity Harvey is considering, opting instead to express the disharmony and disunity characteristic of much of contemporary life. As I have indicated several times throughout the pages of this book, the connection that Harvey is positing here—between the felt unity brought about by musical works and compassion—remains a tenuous one. Less tenuous, however, is the idea that the violent, decidedly disunifying music we frequently hear generally works *against* such compassion. Perhaps this music is more "realistic." Whatever our thoughts may be on the matter, one thing is clear: this is hardly the age of Aquarius.

is no good reason to go there. "Great music invariably has something beyond the personal about it," he explains, "because it depends on an inner ordering process which is largely unconscious and therefore not deliberately willed by the composer" (p. 187). Listening to such music, in turn, resonates with our own unconscious processes, revealing aspects of ourselves that go beyond our ordinary experience, tapping into regions that feel more whole, perhaps more real. Storr therefore has no problem at all saying that music has "incomparably enriched [his] life," even that it is an "irreplaceable, undeserved, transcendental blessing" (p. 188). But this "transcendental" is not quite the same as the "true" transcendental that Murdoch and others posit, for the "otherness" in question would appear to be a purely internal matter.

Storr could be right about this. It could very well be that musical "mystery" really isn't mysterious at all and that there are ways of accounting for its wondrous power in a purely internal way. At the level of sheer felt experience, it may not *matter* what the ultimate sources are anyway, for the "irreplaceable, undeserved, transcendental blessing" remains in any case. But Storr could be wrong too, and the question of ultimate sources may in fact matter a great deal. George Steiner, whom we met toward the end of the introductory chapter, may be considered one of the strongest contemporary proponents of such sources, his foremost question in his book *Real Presences* (1989) being "whether a hermeneutics...of valuation—the encounter with meaning in the verbal sign, in the painting, in the musical composition, and the assessment of the quality of such meaning in respect of form—can be made intelligible, can be made answerable to the existential facts, if they do not imply, if they do not contain, a postulate of transcendence" (p. 134). But of what sort? In beginning to answer this question, Steiner goes on to consider the reality of aesthetic "enchantment" and "the inviolate enigma of the otherness in things and in animate presences" (p. 139). He speaks of the "radical flinching" that can occur in the face of this otherness, even a kind of "embarrassment," somehow tied to the sudden upsurge of emotional and spiritual life. And this "embarrassment we feel in bearing witness to the poetic, to the entrance into our lives of the mystery of otherness in art and in music, is of a metaphysical-religious kind" (p. 178).

Music looms especially large in Steiner's account. "The energy that is music," he writes, "puts us in felt relation to the energy that is life; it puts us in a relation of experienced immediacy with the abstractly and verbally inexpressible but wholly palpable, primary fact of being. The translation of music into meaning...carries with it what somatic and spiritual cognizance we can have of the core-mystery (how else is one to put it?) that we are. And that this energy of existence lies deeper than any biological or psychological determination" (1989, p. 196). The experience of music, Steiner continues, "mocks analytic rationalization" and "rebukes the arrogance of positivism, of the demand for a quantifiable, for a psychologically evidential or sociologically mapped explanation of things" (p. 217). In carrying intimations within it of a "radical 'non-humanity,'" as he puts it, it immediately outstrips any wholly secular, scientific account of it we might give. Not unlike Levi-Strauss, for this reason, Steiner notes, "I know of no deeper, more neglected conundrum in epistemology, in semiotics and the cognitive *sciences de l'hommes*" (1997, p. 78), and "[t]he more captive our delight, the more insistent our need of 'answering to' a piece of music, the more inaccessible are the reasons why" (p. 83).

This "inaccessibility" of reasons, one might counter, does not necessarily mean that the processes at work are mysterious, beyond the purview of psychological or sociological explanation. For one, such inaccessibility may simply be a function of the kinds of unconscious processes Storr had talked about. For another, reasons that might be inaccessible now could very well emerge at some future time. The history of science provides ample testimony about exactly this. Steiner, however, resists moving in this direction, and the way he does so is through the phenomenology of the musical experience itself, particularly "the reality of a presence, of a factual 'thereness' which defies either analytic or empirical circumscription." In addition, he speaks of a "pressure" of presence, of a sort that is elusive and ineffable enough as to be "extra-territorial to explanation" (Steiner, 1989, p. 84). He might also have spoken of the *priority* of this presence and how it felt to be *Other*, "extra-territorial" not only to explanation but to the self. As Steiner surely knows, there can be no proof here. He might even avow that his "wager on transcendence," as he calls it, is a function of a kind of faith—or what James refers to as an "over-belief" (1982 [1902], p. 516).[8] But this faith, rather than being tied to metaphysical or religious convictions brought to experience ahead of time, owes its

---

8. This notion of an over-belief is examined in much greater detail further on in the present chapter.

existence to experience itself, for it is this, above all else, that bespeaks the priority of the Other.[9]

The Mystical Other

Mystical phenomena, by most accounts, also entail an encounter with an Other of some sort. That is to say, they entail the apprehension, on the part of the experiencing subject, that there exists some object—whether person, thing, or unnamable power—that serves to draw forward the movement of subjectivity such that there results an experience of ecstatic oneness, a felt union and unity with the world. As we have seen, this movement, according to some, embodies the effacement, or even annihilation, of the self; it becomes annulled through the power of the object in question. For others, this movement is better construed as a kind of dispersion or expansion, wherein the self loses its quality of encapsulation and becomes spread out "ex-centrically" into the world. For present purposes, it is unnecessary to choose between these alternatives. What is most important to emphasize is the magnetic presence of some forceful object, some *Other*, which in some way "takes hold" of the self, capturing not only its attention but its very being. Taking this set of ideas one step further, I also want to suggest that mystical experience entails what I have here been calling the *priority of the Other*—in this context, a sense that this Other being encountered is larger than me, and that it embodies a dimension of reality that is *prior* to the more mundane sphere ordinarily inhabited. William James (1982 [1902]) puts the matter well: "It is as if there were in the human consciousness *a sense of reality, a feeling of objective presence, a perception* of what we may call *'something there,'* more deep and more general than any of the special and particular 'senses' by which the current psychology supposes existent realities to be originally revealed" (p. 58).

---

9. Some simply refuse to move in this direction. "Works of art do exercise a powerful effect on me," Freud (1953 [1914]) admits. The challenge is to figure out why. "Wherever I cannot do this, as for instance with music, I am almost incapable of obtaining any pleasure. Some rationalistic, or perhaps analytic, turn of mind in me rebels against being moved by a thing without knowing why." Consequently, we come face to face with "the apparently paradoxical fact that precisely some of the grandest and most overwhelming creations of art are still unsolved riddles to our understanding" (p. 211). Perhaps "this state of intellectual bewilderment is a necessary condition when a work of art is to achieve its greatest effects," Freud muses. But, "It would be only with the greatest reluctance that I could bring myself to believe in any such necessity" (p. 212). We each have our own special brands of faith.

As James (1982 [1902]) immediately goes on to note, "The most curious proofs of the existence of such an undifferentiated sense of reality as this are found in experiences of hallucination" (p. 58)—that is, in situations in which psychical realities are projected outward with such force and clarity that they assume the illusory guise of the wholly Other. "The person affected will feel a 'presence' in the room, definitely localized, facing in one particular way, real in the most emphatic sense of the word, often coming suddenly, and as suddenly gone; and yet neither seen, heard, touched, nor cognized in any of the usual 'sensible' ways" (p. 59). From the very start, therefore, James acknowledges that what *feels* like the priority of the Other may in fact refer to nothing more than the hallucinatory imagination. In this respect, James's perspective on the power of psychical reality is not unlike Freud's: whether assuming the form of hallucinations or fantasies, *psychical* reality is such that it can acquire an experiential presence that rivals and indeed mimics *material* reality. But none of this detracts from the distinct possibility that the "something there" of which James speaks is *not* a product of the psyche at all.

For the time being, in any case, two points warrant emphasis. First, James is referring explicitly to something not "here" but "there"; it is "a sense of reality, a feeling of objective"—rather than subjective—"presence." Hence my use of the term "Other." Second, this "something there" of which James speaks, by virtue of its appearing "more deep and general than any of the special and particular 'senses' by which the current psychology supposes existent realities to be originally revealed," is to be considered primary, phenomenologically. Hence my use of the term "priority." Another way of speaking about these phenomena is precisely to invoke the idea of *transcendence*. By this, I refer not simply to a feeling—akin, for instance, to the oceanic feeling about which Freud (1962 [1930]) speaks—but to an experience of *that which is assumed to exist outside ourselves, in a realm that is beyond the more ordinary one that houses most of everyday life*.[10] I emphasize the word "assumed" here. As suggested a short while ago, whether in fact there *is* such a realm cannot ever be determined

---

10. I am not quite sure whether to use the word "beyond" here. As noted earlier, to speak of the transcendent is not necessarily to invoke a realm entirely separated from the one we ordinarily inhabit. Indeed, one of the great challenges involved in thinking through the idea has to do with the fact that what is felt to be transcendently Other is encountered within ordinary life, enchanting it, infusing it with new meaning and value. For the time being, then, let us take "beyond" to refer not so much to a metaphysically separate realm as to an intuition or intimation of "beyondness," signifying that there is *more* to the world, and to us, than we frequently assume. I believe this position to be consistent with James's own.

definitively, but mystical experience as such is unthinkable outside of the experiential conviction that some such realm exists and that it has been constitutive of the experience in question. In the present context, therefore, the Other may be framed as *an extra-ordinary object of attention that, for the experiencing person, carries within it the magnetic force of a realm that is felt and assumed to be transcendent.*

In much of what follows, I shall try to articulate the meaning and significance of the priority of the Other as it pertains to the issue of transcendence. In doing so, I shall abide by the customary aims of inquiry in the psychological study of mysticism and religious experience and limit my analysis mainly to phenomenological considerations. That is to say, I shall deal mainly with the felt reality of the Other, setting aside those sorts of ultimate questions that are more appropriately considered in theology.[11] But there are two significant challenges to be faced along the way, one from "below," as it were, and one from "above."

The first challenge has to do with the fact that, however powerful the objects of mystical experience may be and however much their power may be localized wholly outside the confines of the self, these same objects are frequently *local* in nature; they embody meanings that are thoroughly circumscribed by prevailing beliefs, values, and ideals (e.g., Hollenback, 1996; Katz, 1978; Proudfoot, 1986; see also Chapter Four). For this reason, many of the objects that incite mystical experiences in one person or group of people would not, and could not, do so in another. Whatever mystical power these objects possess, therefore, has somehow been "acquired" in and through culture and history; they are part of *this* world, not some other, and their power resides in this very belongingness. How might we make sense of this situation? Does it not imply that, finally, mystical experience is a learned phenomenon, tied to the projection of meaning onto to the objects in question? How else could these objects have acquired their magnetic power?

---

11. This doesn't mean that I can, or should, set aside these issues completely. Although I do not pretend to be doing theology, I am in fact interested in the question of whether what people *take to be* Other *really is* Other. This very question may be deemed out of bounds in psychology, or simply irrelevant, insofar as psychology "must" remain with experience, alone. To invoke realities beyond the perimeter of the self is inevitably to bring *faith*, of a sort, into the picture. In this very basic sense, I suppose one could say that in raising the question at hand, I have stepped out of psychology and begun to move in the direction of theology. The other option is to think differently about the very boundaries of psychology. This is more my purpose here.

The second challenge not only is different but, in important respects, seems to run entirely counter to the first. As Louis Dupré argues in his book *Religious Mystery and Rational Reflection* (1998), "All living religion centers around a nucleus that its believers consider to be transcendentally *given*. To exclude that nucleus from phenomenological reflection means to abandon what determines the religious attitude" (p. 6). Dupré also realizes that there is no way of knowing, for sure, whether what believers consider to be transcendentally given really *is* so given. This, again, is a matter of *faith*.[12] "But," he quickly adds, "whatever the final conclusion may be, the religious act certainly displays a distinct quality in the passive attitude that the subject of this act adopts with respect to its object. That object," Dupré tells us, "appears as providing its own meaning rather than receiving it from the meaning-giving subject" and thus "resists all attempts to define its meaning exclusively as actively projected" (p. 7). The religious *as such*, therefore—and, by extension, the mystical—is by its very nature bound up with the positing of the transcendent, and this positing of the transcendent *precludes* the notion that meaning is merely projected onto the world.[13]

On the one hand, therefore, the cultural specificity of many of those objects that incite mystical experience points us toward a theoretical perspective that remains, or appears to remain, grounded in the meaning-giving human subject, largely as a function of what he or she "brings" to experience by way of preparation, readiness.[14] On the other hand, the "passive attitude that the subject...adopts with respect to its object" and the felt conviction that this object is "transcendentally given" point us toward a quite different

---

12. Dupré is undoubtedly referring to religious faith here. But as noted in the previous section, there is a broader meaning to the idea, akin to the aforementioned (Jamesian) notion of an "over-belief." Is more "faith" required to posit the reality of the transcendentally given than not to? From my perspective, faith, of a sort, is operative whether our convictions lead us in the direction of "true transcendence" or away from it. Along these lines, phenomenological data, while vitally important in considering these issues, can never dictate definitive conclusions.

13. Dupré also speaks of "disclosure" in this context. He writes, "Religious insight enriches all facets of the real with a new ontological density.... This insight appears as given gratuitously, an unearned disclosure of truth. However much the religious mind is aware of its own creative part in concretizing this all-comprehensive vision in rituals, myths, and institutions to express its new symbolic richness," therefore, "the Source is experienced as surpassing the mind" (1998, p. 18). See also Marion's (2008) discussion of "revelation" for related comments.

14. See Chapter Four for a discussion of related issues.

perspective, one that entertains the possibility that mystical experiences are *not* a product of the subject at all but instead bona fide *revelations* of what is truly Other. In one sense, James (1982 [1902]) notes in the chapter on conversion, psychology and religion are "in perfect harmony...since both admit that there are forces seemingly outside of the conscious individual that bring redemption to his life." But psychology, "defining these forces as 'subconscious,' and speaking of their effects as due to 'incubation,' or 'cerebration,' implies that they do not transcend the individual's personality." At this point, "she diverges from Christian theology"—among other theologies—"which insists that they are direct supernatural operations of the Deity." James then goes on to propose "that we do not yet consider the divergence final, but leave the question for a while in abeyance" (p. 211). By book's end, this question is still in abeyance, though there are some provocative clues about how he would be inclined to address it.

Are there any alternatives to the positions James has laid out? Can there be a psychological approach to mystical (and other such unifying) experience *not* grounded in the human subject? Framed another way, can there be a psychological approach to mystical experience that preserves its ostensibly transcendent core by locating the power of the object *outside* the confines of the self? And if so, does this entail the further supposition that this power has a (truly) transcendent source?

To the first set of questions, I am prepared to answer in the affirmative. Drawing on some basic principles of hermeneutics (e.g., Gadamer, 1976, 1982), I shall try to show that it is perfectly possible to adopt a psychological approach to mystical experience that is not grounded in the human subject and that preserves its ostensibly transcendent core by locating the power of the object outside the self. As for the second question, the answer is, no, not necessarily. Emphasizing the priority of the Other does not *rely* on the idea of transcendence qua supernatural realm; it simply recognizes that the meaning that inheres in objects, including those that incite mystical experience, often does "transcend the individual's personality." While my own prejudices undoubtedly condition the meaning I derive from a given object, this in no way entails the further supposition that I merely foist meaning onto it, that it is ultimately a blank screen onto which I project my various designs and desires. We can therefore speak of the priority of the Other qua *Other*, as a reality whose meaning transcends me, without necessarily going the route of a supernatural account. In a related vein, we can also speak of *self*-transcendence without positing some wholly other realm of being.

Martha Nussbaum's (1990) reflections on "internal" versus "external" transcendence may be useful in this context. If we look, for instance, at Homer or Sophocles, "with their keen interest in a specifically human heroism and its natural conditions," we see that many of the attributes and activities we have come to prize in people "will not figure in a divine life" (p. 372). The social life of the Olympian gods, Nussbaum notes, is often portrayed as "free-floating, amorphous, uninspired by need"—characterized by "lightnesses," as she calls them. Their love life is similar: "There is a kind of playfulness and lack of depth about the love of the gods" (p. 376), the implication being that striving to be godly, to transcend the everyday world, is precisely to move *away* from, even to relinquish, one's humanity, in all of its earthly messiness. As Nussbaum hastens to point out, there is still plenty of room in the perspective she is offering for a certain kind of desire and ability to transcend our ordinary humanity. For it is clear, she acknowledges, that "most people are much of the time lazy, inattentive, unreflective, shallow in feeling" (p. 378). In other words, the very fact that we are as flawed as we are and that attaining virtue is as difficult as it is means that there remains ample opportunity, within the confines of *this* life, to transcend ourselves. If we wish to speak of transcendence at all, therefore, we would do best, she believes, to speak of it in internal rather than external terms.

Nussbaum's own heroes in regard to the present issues are people like Henry James and Marcel Proust, both of whom claim "that the artist's fine-tuned attention and responsiveness to human life is paradigmatic of a kind of precision of feeling and thought that a human being can cultivate, though most do not" (1990, p. 379). Neither of them, she maintains, "has the slightest interest in religious or other-worldly or even contemplative transcendence," yet "both aim at transcendence nonetheless and exemplify it in their writing." Nussbaum has in mind works "like angels that soar above the dullness and obtuseness of the everyday, offering their readers a glimpse of a more compassionate, subtler, more responsive, more richly human world" (p. 379). The bottom line, then, is that there is so much to be done in our day-to-day lives, as messy and risky and incomplete as they are, that if we really concentrate on them and how they can be improved rather than on what might exist *beyond* them, we will be a whole lot better off.

Nussbaum goes on to acknowledge that the line between internal and external transcendence can never be a sharp one. She thus asks, "When does the aspiration to internal transcendence become the aspiration to depart from human life altogether?" (p. 380) Let me pose a parallel question here: when can we say—when *should* we say, if at all—that this experience in which we are immersed has indeed moved beyond the human world into one that is *other* than human? On one level, one might simply say, "Who cares? Call it what it you want; the main thing is that it's deep and good!" When it starts to matter, however, is when we try to conceptualize human nature and human experience—whether we do so in what are, finally, purely natural, material terms or whether instead we allow for the possibility that there are other dimensions, other regions of being, at work.

It might be reiterated that, according to some, the question of "true transcendence" cannot and should not even be broached by psychologists. Flournoy's (1903) "Principle of the Exclusion of Transcendence" says as much: insofar as psychology is understood in essentially naturalistic terms, it can only address these phenomena anthropologically, in reference to the "purely human" (see also Belzen, 1997b; Wulff, 1997).[15] But again, the question that needs to be posed here is precisely whether psychology must be understood in this way. In one sense, the principle of exclusion is innocuous enough, amounting essentially to a kind of agnosticism vis-à-vis transcendence. Surely, the task of determining whether true transcendence exists (not to mention God) ought not to be left to psychologists! Moreover, there is, arguably, a potential danger in *not* following the rule of exclusion; more than likely, there will be those who will wish to smuggle the divine in through the back door, as it were, justifying their own faith commitments along the way (see Proudfoot, 1986). But there are at least two reasons, considered in greater detail later on, for questioning the exclusion of the principle of transcendence *if* it derives from an a priori commitment to naturalism.[16] The first is that the principle, defined

---

15. It should be emphasized that Flournoy did not set forth this principle out of an a priori commitment to naturalism. Following Vergote (1996), the notion of "exclusion" is, perhaps, better formulated as "bracketing" the question of transcendence. As he puts the matter, "Psychology neither denies nor confirms for itself the reality of the divine, but abstains from the analysis of those relational intentionalities that are either carried out or discarded by the subject under consideration." Along these lines, "Psychology is authorized neither to disprove nor discount specific religious propositions" (p. 27).

16. As just noted, this was not Flournoy's perspective. For many others, however, the reason for this exclusion is derived from what is, arguably, the "default" perspective of contemporary academic psychology—namely, that psychology, as an aspiring science, must adopt as a foundational assumption the idea that human beings, as purely natural beings, operate according to purely natural principles. Without this assumption, it may be argued, we leave the world of science altogether.

in this way, reflects a faith commitment of its own; it is a methodological stance that is itself inseparable from certain ontological and metaphysical convictions regarding the nature of the human being. When questioning it, therefore, one has in hand a valuable tool for prying open some of the foundational assumptions of the discipline. The second and related reason has to do with the potential value of entertaining the possibility that transcendence is something other than a purely natural phenomenon, rooted, finally, in the constitutive faculties of the self.

In positing the priority of the Other in my own attempt to think about these matters, I want ultimately to suggest that mystical experience, along with other areas of (ostensibly) transcendent experience, represents a profound challenge to the legacy of the self.[17] This is so whether or not one abides by the Principle of the Exclusion of Transcendence: the simple phenomenological fact that mystical experience is contingent on the *felt* priority of the Other itself entails a decentering of the self, a shift in the direction of psychical energy. At the same time, entertaining the possibility that transcendence is something other than a purely natural phenomenon deepens mysticism's challenge to the legacy, and putative primacy, of the self. For if the power of the Other bears within it *other* than natural forces, the self we have come to know through scientific psychology needs radically to be rethought. Indeed, so too does the very project of scientific psychology itself.[18]

Beyond Selfhood

As James (1982 [1902]) goes on to suggest in his exploration of the "something there" referred to earlier, "We may now lay it down as certain that in the distinctively religious sphere of experience, many persons (how many we cannot tell) possess the objects of their belief, not in the form of mere conceptions which their intellect accepts as true, but rather in the form of quasi-sensible realities directly apprehended" (p. 64). It is interesting and curious that James frames the issue this way. On some level, it seems, he remains caught in a framework that subjectivizes these objects, rendering

---

17. See Freeman (2004b) for an explicit treatment of this very issue.

18. In some recent work (Freeman, 2013), I suggest that, rather than moving beyond naturalism, we move toward an expanded form of it, one that essentially acknowledges the possibility that the very nature of *human* nature points *beyond* nature, at least as customarily conceived. Whether this move works, I cannot say quite yet.

them "possessions" of the experiencing person. Following his own line of thinking, it would be more phenomenologically accurate to say that it is the *objects* that possess the person. Indeed, when he moves on to the lecture on mysticism, James makes exactly this move via his notion of "passivity": the story of mystical experience, rather than being one of possession or ownership by the self, turns out to be one of *dis*possession, of the self, by the Other—or so it seems to the persons involved:

> Although the oncoming of mystical states may be facilitated by preliminary voluntary operations, as by fixing the attention, or going through certain bodily performances, or in other ways which manuals of mysticism prescribe; yet when the characteristic sort of consciousness once has set in, the mystic feels as if his own will were in abeyance, and indeed sometimes as if he were grasped and held by a superior power. (p. 381)

Whether this "feeling" on the part of the mystic bears within it any reference to an *objective* superior power, James acknowledges, remains to be considered. For the time being, he simply wishes to note the subjective dimension involved.

Another move James makes in the chapter on mysticism comes in the pages that immediately follow. Having sketched out what he considers to be the defining characteristics of mystical experience, his next step is to explore some typical examples. In line with the method of serial study, he begins with "phenomena which claim no special religious significance," after which he moves on to "those of which the religious pretensions are extreme" (1982 [1902], p. 382). Right away, then, we see two important features to James's approach to mysticism. Phenomena with "no special religious significance" are continuous with those that have it in the extreme. Furthermore, these phenomena are not a function of discrete practices and the like (fixing the attention, etc.) but are instead woven into the fabric of everyday life, as lived by mystics and non-mystics alike.

"The simplest rudiment of mystical experience," James (1982 [1902]) continues, "would seem to be that deepened sense of the significance of a maxim or formula which occasionally sweeps over one. 'I've heard that said all my life,' we exclaim, 'but I never realized its full meaning until now' " (p. 382). The paragraph to follow develops this line of thinking most eloquently:

> This sense of deeper significance is not confined to rational propositions. Single words, and conjunctions of words, effects of light on land and sea, odors and musical sounds, all bring it when the mind is tuned aright. Most of us can remember the strangely moving power of passages in certain poems read when we were young, irrational doorways as they were through which the mystery of fact, the wildness and the pang of life, stole into our hearts and thrilled them. The words have now perhaps become mere polished surfaces for us; but lyric poetry and music are alive and significant only in proportion as they fetch these vague vistas of a life continuous with our own, beckoning and inviting, yet ever eluding our pursuit. We are alive or dead to the eternal inner message of the arts according as we have lost this mystical susceptibility. (pp. 382–383)

Mystical susceptibility, James suggests, is there for *all* of us, from childhood on up; the mystery of existence steals into our hearts and thrills us, for reasons that remain utterly obscure. This mystery, he tells us, is part and parcel not only of mystical or religious experience but of *human* experience. And it is precisely when we "lose" this susceptibility, when we succumb to forgetfulness about the mystery of being, that we set apart the religious realm and come to regard it as a separate province, outside the scope of everyday life.

But what exactly are we to make of those "vague vistas of a life continuous with our own" to which James refers? And where are they to be located? Marcel (1973) calls attention to the "aggressive anthropocentrism" that generally characterizes thinking about these matters and encourages us to move in the direction of that which lies outside the orbit of the self. Not unlike ideas put forth by James, however, this move does not entail the further supposition that the "outside" being considered exists in a metaphysically separate world. Indeed, Marcel offers, the process by which the world becomes *illuminated* reveals the "primordial, secret, and…inviolable integrity" (p. 210) that rests in the heart of everyday life.[19] So it is that "each of us is invited…apart from any appeal to faith, which does not concern us here, to restore the traces of a world which is not superimposed from without ours, but is rather this very world grasped in a richness of dimensions which ordinarily we are simply unaware of" (p. 212).

---

19. See Chapter One for a preliminary discussion of this notion of "illumination."

Merleau-Ponty offers a similar idea in his discussion of painting. For all of the attention he devoted to art, especially to painting, and for all that he revered the great artist—his essay on Cezanne (1964a) is especially noteworthy—Merleau-Ponty wants to keep things earthbound. "One admires as one should," he writes,

> only after having understood that there are not any supermen, there is no man who does not have a man's life to live, and that the secret of the woman loved, of the writer, or of the painter, does not lie in some realm beyond his empirical life, but is so mixed with his mediocre experiences, so modestly confused with his perception of the world, that there can be no question of meeting it face to face apart from his life.... The painter himself is a man at work who each morning finds in the shape of things the same questioning and the same call he never stops responding to. (p. 58)

Each painting, in turn, is "a response to what the world, the past, and the completed works demanded..." (p. 59). "To live in painting," therefore, "is still to breathe the air of this world—above all for the man who sees something in the world to paint. And there is a little of him in every man" (p. 64).

There is an interesting dilemma here for those exploring these issues. It probably strikes most people as audacious to claim that we, ordinary folks, have what the great painter has. Without establishing this continuity, however, we would seem to be forced back to the notion of the special gift one either has or does not have—the notion of the "superman," as Merleau-Ponty puts it. More significant still, we would be forced to take the very phenomenon of painting out of the realm of the everyday, the life-world.

> The difficult and essential point here is to understand that in positing a field distinct from the empirical order of events, we are not positing a Spirit of Painting which is already in possession of itself on the other side of the world it is gradually manifested in. There is not, above and beyond the causality of events, a second causality which makes the world of painting a "suprasensible world" with its own laws. Cultural creation is ineffectual if it does not find a vehicle in external circumstances. (Merleau-Ponty, 1964b, p. 68)

This last statement is undoubtedly true, at least as a general rule. But do we in fact *know* that there is not, above and beyond the causality of events, *another* mode of causality altogether? In experiencing beauty, Scarry (1999) told us, the object in question not only "fills the mind" but "invites the search for something beyond itself, something larger or something of the same scale with which it needs to be brought into relation" (p. 29). As she goes on to acknowledge, whether or not this "something" truly exists in some immemorial sphere is, in a certain sense, irrelevant. "Even when the claim on behalf of immortality is gone, many of the same qualities—plenitude, inclusion—are the outcome.... What happens when there is no immortal realm behind the beautiful person or thing is just what happens when there *is* an immortal realm behind the beautiful person or thing: the perceiver is led to a more capacious regard for the world" (pp. 47–48).[20]

In line with what was said earlier regarding musical experience, there are at least two ways of understanding this process. For Bollas (1992), you may recall (see Chapter One), certain objects are like "psychic 'keys' " that "open doors" to unconscious dimensions of self, releasing us into "intense inner experiencings which somehow emphasize us." Such experiencings transpire in a way that is only partly thinkable, Bollas emphasizes: "The experience is more a dense condensation of instinctual urges, somatic states, body positions, proprioceptive organizings, images, part sentences, abstract thoughts, sensed memories, recollections, and felt affinities, all of a piece" (p. 28). Hence, perhaps, the condition of ineffability that is often seen to characterize this sort of experience. For Jones (1991), similarly, the experience of the sacred has a transcendental quality "not because the sacred is a wholly other object but because such experiences resonate with the primal originating depths of selfhood" (p. 125). Not unlike Marcel, therefore, Jones is reluctant to consider the sacred as existing in some separate metaphysical realm. Where they part company is in their understanding of what happens during the course of such encounters. It could be, Jones suggests, that these encounters are as powerful as they are because they somehow tap into "the primal originating depths of selfhood." As he explains in a later (1998) work, those defenses that function

---

20. Scarry's point here is reminiscent of the one brought forth by Storr (1992), which we encountered earlier in this chapter. That music has greatly enriched his life, even that it is an utterly "undeserved" gift, is unarguable. Whether it has ultimately issued from beyond is another matter entirely—and not, he implies, an altogether important one.

as barriers to connection to ourselves and to others can also prevent access to the sacred. "When these barriers are broken through and the real self emerges," Jones writes, "a sense of connection with or concern about the transcendent often surfaces" (pp. 183–184). This is a variant of the same idea. "Transcendence," such as it is, is a function of release, of defenses being broken down, revealing the "real self" in its primal givenness; it is the "sense" one may get upon realizing the full depth and measure of one's inner life.

There are also accounts that are more ambivalent about what might be going on but that also, in the end, look essentially within. Harvey (1999), for instance, in his reflections on music, draws on the familiar "vessels" notion, the idea that we are somehow moved by what is beyond us. "So, being 'vessels,' " he writes,

> brings us back as "selves" into the picture, but at a deeper level, that of the unconscious, or intuition, or inspiration. The question must now be asked to what degree the unconscious is individual or collective. Is it "me," *my* unconscious, as Freud thought? Or is there some deeper connection, some seabed connecting the little individual islands we see poking up above the surface, some archetypal structure that is inherent in the mind, an innate grammar, a participatory epistemology resolving the self's despair at being cut off from knowing the world "in itself," as Jung and his followers posited? Whatever the answer, the place from which inspiration comes is undeniably unconscious. We cannot easily know much more than its borderlands. (p. 20)[21]

If taken as a description, an acknowledgment that there are things that affect us about which we are utterly unconscious, this statement is unassailable. If taken as a proclamation that inspiration ultimately derives from within, from the unconscious corridors of the originating self, it seems much more questionable.

Marcel's understanding of this process, along with Scarry's, takes us in a quite different direction. Phenomenologically, it is not the self that

---

21. It may be interesting to ask why, in a book called *In Quest of Spirit*, the main reference is to the inner rather than the outer, to self rather than Other. Phenomenologically, the latter would appear more suited to the phenomena at hand. This strikes me as a prime example of the potential value of fashioning a new language for considering the kinds of experiences Harvey and others are describing.

is felt to have priority; it is the *Other*. Otto's critique of Schleiermacher in *The Idea of the Holy* (1958 [1923]) addresses exactly this shift in location. Schleiermacher's emphasis on the idea of "dependence," Otto argues, "is merely a category of *self*-valuation, in the sense of self-depreciation." As such, "the religious emotion would be directly and primarily a sort of *self*-consciousness, a feeling concerning oneself in a special, determined relation, viz. one's dependence" (p. 10). According to Otto, however, this way of conceptualizing things "is entirely opposed to the psychological facts of the case," which entail an "immediate and primary reference to an object outside the self" (p. 10). Whatever the ontological status of such an object might be, Otto continues (in a footnote directed to James, actually), the feeling of its presence must be considered "a primary datum of consciousness" (p. 11). Its effects on the self must, in turn, be considered secondary. "The latter presupposes the former" (p. 11). That the self may in fact come to realize some of its own inner depths during the course of mystical experience is surely true. But it is the revelation, and priority, of the Other that makes this possible. How else can the "release" about which Bollas speaks or the "resonance" about which Jones speaks be explained?

Along the lines being drawn here, mysticism's challenge to the legacy of the self is perhaps to be tied not so much to that sort of self-dissolution that is often said to accompany mystical experience as to the existential displacement the Other's priority provokes. The priority of the Other entails the *de*-prioritization—or what I earlier called the *secondarity*—of the self. It is a movement wherein, via the operation of the Other, the self is rendered "ex-centric." The priority of the Other thus leads beyond self qua bounded, encapsulated being. At the same time, it opens up the possibility of conceiving of a kind of "self-beyond," or what I earlier referred to as a larger, more expansive Self, one that acquires its very nature through its relation to those objects that draw it outward. From this perspective, one may still speak of the revelation and realization of the "real self," à la Jones and others, but this real self is being revealed and realized precisely in its secondarity and ex-centricity.

So it is that certain poets, for instance, "have the power to awaken their readers to an implicit answering power, to a previously unfelt sense of possibilities for the self" (Bloom, 1996, p. 15). Bloom also speaks of a sense of "possible sublimity," which Wordsworth had referred to as an intimation of "something evermore about to be" (quoted in Bloom, p. 15). The poet and critic Yves Bonnefoy (1989), from whom we heard earlier, likewise speaks of the "impression of a reality at last fully incarnate, which comes to us, paradoxically, through words which have turned away from incarnation" (p. 164). But that is not all. The reader of poetry, Bonnefoy had reminded us, does not merely "analyze." Rather, he or she, having experienced the intensity of the poetic word, makes a "pledge" to live out this intensity in his or her life. This pledge is a weighty one, for such readers may also have had the opportunity "to bear witness to an existence beyond, to a being, to a plenitude they don't even know how to name" (p. 167). On one level, the Other here is poetry, its "answering power." On another level, however, the Other is reality itself, now revealed in its unnamable bounty. It is precisely this revelation of the Other that gives rise to the Self. We are speaking here not of two processes but of one. In bearing witness to the priority of the Other, I also bear witness to heretofore-undisclosed depths of Self. It might therefore be said once again that the very movement beyond selfhood, brought forth by the priority of the Other, is, at the same time, a movement inward, into the heart of that larger Self, which owes its very being to what exists beyond it.

Transcendence "from Below" and "from Above"

The question nevertheless remains: what is the status of such experiences? The perspectives we have been exploring have varied considerably in their respective degrees of subtlety and in their respective willingness to preserve the possibility of transcendence. In the case of the psychoanalytic perspectives referred to, there was the sense that, finally, the primary object of concern was the self, its quality of experience. As a result, the question of the *other*-than-self was essentially excluded. In the case of Nussbaum and Merleau-Ponty, there seemed to be more of an attempt to wrestle with the other-than-self and, in turn, more of an attempt to truly entertain the possibility of transcendence qua other realm. However, there remained a sense in these latter perspectives too in which the idea was essentially, if not entirely, excluded. I emphasize the word "excluded": intentionally or not, Flournoy's Principle seems to have been taken to heart. Indeed, to the extent that these perspectives have included the possibility of transcendence at all, they have adhered to what might be termed "transcendence from below"—which is to say, a form of transcendence that, in the end, annuls its very otherness.

The question now is whether there is any sensible way to speak of transcendence from *above*. James is again very useful here. What he suggests in *The Varieties of Religious Experience* (1982 [1902]), basically, is that whenever we are dealing with a dimension of experience that feels like a visitation from without, we should, first of all, "make search whether it not be an explosion, into the fields of ordinary consciousness, of ideas elaborated outside of those fields in subliminal regions of the mind." From his perspective, then, it makes sense to stay with the thesis of transcendence from below as far as possible, which usually will mean exploring the subconscious or unconscious life of the individual. This is very much in keeping with the psychoanalytic perspectives just considered. Having said this, James quickly goes on to add that, *"if there be* higher spiritual agencies that can directly touch us, the psychological condition of their doing so *might be* our possession of a subconscious region which alone should yield access to them" (p. 242). More simply put, "If there be higher powers to impress us," James maintains, "they may get access to us only through the subliminal door." In other words, the subconscious may serve as a kind of lightning rod for receiving spiritual agencies, if they exist. As such, there is no necessary incompatibility between transcendence from below and transcendence from above. "The notion of a subconscious self," James says, "certainly ought not... be held to *exclude* all notions of a higher penetration" (p. 243). But again, the question is, how might we begin to think about this idea of transcendence from above?

The easiest way is simply to bring the divine into the picture. In *Phaedrus* (Plato, 1995), Socrates speaks of "the recollection of the things our soul saw when it was traveling with God, when it disregarded the things we now call real and lifted up its head to what is truly real instead" (p. 37). Most people, Socrates continues, forget the sacred objects they had once seen; there are only a few whose memory is good enough, and they are "startled when they see an image of what they saw up there. Then they are beside themselves, and their experience is beyond comprehension because they cannot fully grasp what it is they're seeing" (p. 38). This is a classic statement of the doctrine of recollection.[22] There is also Steiner's more phenomenological perspective, which essentially says that the sheer moving power of certain forms of experience, aesthetic especially, seem to call forth, spontaneously and directly, a certain above-ness, a felt conviction of unity and belonging that is "is of a metaphysical and indeed religious kind" (1989, p. 178). As noted earlier, there is, however, a challenge brought forth by Steiner's position on this set of issues, namely,

---

22. Book Six of *The Republic* (Plato, 2003) takes up similar issues, especially in relation to the form of the good.

that the very objects Steiner cites in order to provide evidence in support of his claims—for instance, Western classical music—are local ones, that could not have possessed a comparable degree of power at other times or in other places. James, you will recall, spoke in a similar way about "the strangely moving power" of passages in certain poems and told us we are "alive or dead" to their "eternal message...as we have kept or lost this mystical susceptibility" (1982 [1902], p. 383). But these very poems are composed of words, language, the meaning and significance of which is largely a function of the concrete, cultured world in which one lives. The meaning of poems is neither forever nor for everyone. And the same may be said of the variety of other objects that might awaken mystical susceptibility. However *unmediated* the resultant experiences feel, they may in fact be mediated by a vast range of values, expectations, and beliefs regarding the objects in question. Indeed, and again, these values, expectations, and beliefs may be the very conditions through which such experiences emerge (e.g., Belzen, 1997a; Hollenback, 1996).[23]

As Belzen (1997a) has suggested, "Human subjectivity in its totality is always subject to specific historico-cultural conditions.... Accordingly, psychology of religion, like history, anthropology and linguistics, is an interpretive science: it focuses attention on meanings and searches out the rules according to which meaning originates in a cultural situation" (p. 111).[24] What is striking about Belzen's rendition of the psychology of religion is its insistence that religious phenomena be located within the context of "specific historico-cultural conditions." In order for conduct to be deemed "meaningful," he goes on to argue, it must be "culturally constituted." Even those arenas of experience that aspire to make contact with the transcendent, therefore, are, on some level, to be tied back to their local moorings. Language is central here. Following Ricoeur (1995), "whatever ultimately may be the nature of the so-called religious experience, it comes to language, it is articulated in a language, and the most

---

23. Individual factors must of course be taken into account as well. Referring once more to Harvey (1999), "As listeners, we respond from our own past memories, the shrapnel fragments embedded in our own buried psychic world that are summoned to life by sympathetic resonance with the vibrations of the music. They awaken and form a dance together, gathering around a nucleus of connecting imaginative energy" (p. 31). Bollas's (1992) comments regarding the fact that certain objects act as "psychic keys," opening up religions of experience that resonate with our own particularities, also highlight this idea.

24. See also Belzen's recent (2010) book *Towards Cultural Psychology of Religion: Principles, Approaches, Applications* for a comprehensive and sophisticated treatment of these issues.

appropriate place to interpret it on its own terms is to inquire into its linguistic expression" (p. 35). In short, then, whatever might exist *beyond* culture and personal history must on this account be manifested *within* it, through language.

Hollenback (1996) conveys similar ideas in his own "contextualist" critique of the "essentialist" view of mystical experience. According to Hollenback, "the contextualist thesis implies that mystical experience in its 'pure' state (free from all context-dependent influences) simply does not exist.... [T]here is never a moment, from the time that a mystical experience begins to form until the time that it is over, when it is not being shaped by context-dependent elements" (p. 10).[25] Hollenback goes on to speak of the capacity of mystical experience "to exhibit an almost infinite plasticity in reifying and rendering concretely present the beings, objects, and spiritual locales posited by the mythology of any given religious tradition" (p. 77). He also speaks of "the amazing sensitivity of the mystical experience to the subject's religious and philosophical assumptions" (p. 79). According to Hollenback, these experiences are thus "anything but spontaneous" (p. 78). But this last assertion does not follow. The contextuality of mystical experience, Hollenback has told us, is necessarily correlative with its lack of spontaneity. But why can't there be true spontaneity *within* the discursive confines of culture and history?[26] As has been suggested already, we are often moved by objects that are local in nature, objects whose very meanings are mediated by and enmeshed within culture. But this says nothing whatsoever about the spontaneity of our response.

I maintain that there is ample room for true spontaneity within a theoretical perspective that recognizes the contextuality of mystical experience. In a related vein, people do not need to "leave" everyday life in order to experience the priority of the Other; oftentimes, the Other emerges in and through the fabric of everyday life itself. What this implies, again (see

---

25. See Katz (1978) and Proudfoot (1986). For a helpful review of the various theoretical possibilities, with particular reference to psychoanalytic theory, see Parsons (1999).

26. One reviewer, on encountering my rendition of Hollenback, indicated that his thinking is "more subtle and dialectical" than I have implied. That may well be so. He does, for instance, ask, "Is it possible that these supernormal accompaniments of mystical experience might bring forth data that challenges the validity of psychologism, the view that everything in a mystical state of consciousness originates from within the mystic's own mind?" (p. 20) In raising this question, Hollenback does entertain the possibility of there being phenomena that somehow go beyond what one brings to experience. I would nevertheless question his thoughts on spontaneity, at least as articulated here.

Chapter Four), is that we are somehow hermeneutically prepared for such experience, that its very condition of possibility is our own existence in tradition (e.g., Gadamer, 1982). This point is important for several reasons. First, it suggests that the category of the Other is to be located not outside of history but within it. Second, it suggests that the existence of the Other, despite pointing straightaway to the "outer" rather than the "inner," retains a connection not necessarily to the "subconscious" or "psychical apparatus" but to *a particular way of life*, one that finds in certain local objects—aesthetic, religious, and otherwise—revelatory points of contact with existence as it is lived and known.

One may nevertheless ask, how is it possible for local objects to acquire the power to incite mystical experience? Consider again what Marcel (1973) said regarding that process by which we are able to behold a world that "is not superimposed from without ours, but is rather this very world grasped in a richness of dimensions which ordinarily we are simply unaware of" (p. 212). Ordinarily, Marcel implies, there is a kind of inertness to the objects encountered throughout the course of everyday life. They are merely "there," to be observed, used, or ignored; they are part of the familiar furniture of things. In certain circumstances, however, this very familiarity becomes undone, revealing in turn what James Edwards (1997) has referred to as "the continual possibility of the familiar's sacramental transformation into the alien" (p. 212).[27] For Edwards, poetry is one prominent site of such transformation.[28] "The power of poetry," he writes, "is not only that it lets us see; it lets us see the seeing, thus lets us see the possibility of even more surprises as the unknown god yields to its alien element, to the sights and sounds that appear against the bright background of the sky" (p. 212).

It is possible that Edwards has overemphasized the notion of the "alien." In many ecstatic experiences, we noted earlier, there can also be a profound sense of recognition. We might recall in this context James's consideration of the "simplest rudiment" of mystical experience, wherein we are able to realize the "full meaning" of that which we may have heard our whole life. Alongside the alienness to which Edwards refers, then, is the

---

27. This notion is not unlike Marion's (2002b, 2008) notion of saturation, which itself entails a kind of sacramental transformation wherein the ordinary phenomena of the world are rendered extraordinary, their potential, previously inert, having become realized. Also relevant are Buber's (1970) comments about the movement from I–It relations to I–Thou.

28. See also Heidegger (1971).

dimension of familiarity and recognition of which James speaks. The experience of encountering the familiar-made-alien, I suggest, is another way of speaking about encountering the *Other*. The simultaneous experience of familiarity and recognition may in turn be understood in terms of the Other's *priority*. This world that comes before me is infinitely larger than me, the mystic might say, but it is also one to which I belong. Mystical experience thus understood becomes a kind of *homecoming*, wherein one's very belongingness in and to the world is revealed in and through its otherness. Perhaps it is this experience of belongingness that can begin to explain the ecstatic quality that frequently characterizes mystical experience. Insofar as the world is revealed as home, as the place where I belong, I am "at one" with it, able, if only momentarily, to move beyond the condition of ordinary oblivion against which the experience is juxtaposed.

Mystical experience may thus be understood to embody a kind of dialectical tension between the ordinary and the extraordinary. The notion of the extraordinary itself reflects this tension; there is reference to a world or a sphere of reality that is *other* than the one ordinarily inhabited. However other-worldly mystical experience may feel, therefore, the condition of this other-worldliness is its relation to, and difference from, the "this-worldly" experience that surrounds it. In this respect, there is a *metaphorical* dimension to mystical experience: the "old" world and the "new" one that supersedes it are somehow held together, resulting in the aforementioned co-presence of the familiar and the alien.[29] The world is *refigured* and, through this refiguring, *remade*, such that it appears *realer* and *truer*. The sudden irruption of mystical experience may thus be tied to the rapture of discovery, wherein the hidden potentiality of ordinary life is disclosed.[30]

---

29. See especially Ricoeur's remarkable essay "The Metaphorical Process as Imagination, Cognition, and Feeling" (1981b). For a more comprehensive treatment, see also his *Rule of Metaphor: Multi-disciplinary Studies of the Creation of Meaning in Language* (1977).

30. Insofar as context remains central to the perspective being offered, some may find it insufficiently "absolute." John Horgan, for instance, following James in broad outline, notes that "a sense of absolute knowledge is the *sine qua non* of mystical experiences." Bearing this in mind, he goes on to suggest that the contextualist thesis is actually "more compatible with atheism than with belief. It implies that mysticism can tell us nothing about ultimate matters; mystics make divergent, inconsistent, and even contradictory claims about the nature of ultimate reality, which reflects mystics' prior conditioning." Given this, "[t]he logical conclusion would be that all mystical visions are illusions" (2003, p. 48). Horgan may be right, at least about extreme versions of the contextualistic thesis, but there is no necessary contradiction between "prior conditioning" and the (possibly) non-illusory nature of mystical experience. I shall try to explain why shortly.

By all indications, James adhered to a similar point of view in his treatment of religious experience. By virtue of his avowed interest in the *varieties* of religious experience, James effectively rejects not only a monolithic conception of transcendence but one that leaps entirely out of the earthly world. Oftentimes this issue is posed in either/or terms: either there is some sort of projection involved in the genesis of mystical experience or there is something completely transhistorical and transcultural going on. To some extent, James himself succumbs to this mode of either/or thinking. But he also seems to want to give us another option in this context.[31] "As a rule," he notes, "mystical states merely add a supersensuous meaning to the ordinary outward data of consciousness. They are excitements like the emotions of love or ambition, gifts to our spirit by means of which facts already objectively before us fall into a new expressiveness and make a new connection with our active life" (1982 [1902], p. 427). To speak about the possibility of transcendence, James implies, is not necessarily to step completely out of history and culture. Indeed, as Gadamer, Heidegger, and others have suggested, particularly via the aforementioned notion of tradition, it is exactly our immersion *in* history and culture that opens the possibility of our being as captivated as we often are by certain objects that may have no universal appeal whatsoever. In keeping with what was said earlier, we might therefore speak of *historically conditioned* or *historically prepared* transcendence, the main idea being that it is perfectly possible to speak about transcendence, of a sort, within the fabric of society, history, and culture.

In localizing the transcendent realm in the way that I have, I certainly do not wish to close off the possibility that "higher spiritual energies," as James puts it, play a vitally important role in the process. Finally, then, let us consider whether in fact there is any justification, within psychology, for moving in this direction.

---

31. According to Barnard (1998), "James has an interactive, dialectical understanding of the dynamics of mystical experience in which mystical experiences are understood to be neither the direct, authoritative revelations of a transcendent Absolute nor simply linguistically structured, culturally produced natural phenomena." As such, "mystical experiences are best understood as the dynamic fusion of cultural and transcultural components [and] as both natural and transnatural in origin" (p. 162). Along these lines, James is offering a perspective "that avoids the rigidity and dogmatism of an objectivist perspective, while at the same time he wants to leave a space in his philosophical model for the existence and power of the translinguistic and transcultural modes of reality that relativism denies" (p. 173).

The Claims of Experience

We have already heard from Murdoch (1970) that there exists "a tiny spark of insight"—at least for those inclined to see it—in support of the conviction that the "there is more than this" that sometimes happens people's way is not only subjectively but objectively real. The very term "goodness," Murdoch suggests, "refers us to a perfection which is perhaps never exemplified in the world we know...and which carries with it the ideas of hierarchy and transcendence." In the course of everyday life, "[w]e see differences, we sense directions, and we know that the Good is still somewhere beyond." At one and the same time, it becomes clear that "[t]he self, the place where we live, is a place of illusion. Goodness," therefore, "is connected with the attempt to see the unself, to see and respond to the real world in the light of a virtuous consciousness" (pp. 90–91). Murdoch's first way of addressing the issue at hand thus has to do with those intimations of the "beyond" we often receive in the course of encountering differences and gradations, of meeting up with people and things, some of which draw us outward, magnetically, by virtue of what they simply are.

Murdoch's second way of dealing with the issue of transcendence is more explicitly phenomenological in nature. For Murdoch, the reality of the Other and the reality of the Good are one, and far from being encountered in art alone, they are encountered in virtually anything that incites *love*.

> People speak of loving all sorts of things, their work, a book, a potted plant, a formation of clouds. Desire for what is corrupt and worthless, the degradation of love, its metamorphosis into ambition, vanity, cruelty, greed, jealousy, hatred, or the parched demoralising deserts of its absence, are phenomena often experienced and readily recognised.... People know the difference between good and evil, it takes quite a lot of theorising to persuade them to say or imagine that they do not. The activity of Eros is orientation of desire. Reflecting in these ways we see "salvation" or "good" as connected with, or incarnate in, all sorts of particulars, and not just as "an abstract idea." "Saving the phenomena" is happening all the time. (1993, pp. 496–497)

According to Murdoch, therefore, "The ordinary way is the way. It is not in that sense theology, and the 'mysticism' involved is an accessible experience" (pp. 508–509). It should be reiterated that for Murdoch, none of what is being said bears on the question of the existence of God. Indeed, much of what she seeks to do in her work is figure out a way of talking about goodness and transcendence without bringing God into the picture. Finally, it is experience itself that is the primary concern, and it is fidelity to experience, following where it leads, that is the primary goal. This does not mean uncritical acceptance of what experience *seems* to reveal. As Murdoch, along with James, was well aware, some of what feels like a visitation from without may actually be a visitation from within, tied to wishes and fantasies and other such vehicles for obscuring the Other. But there is no reason to assume that this is what is *really* happening, for it could very well be that experience is speaking the truth.

Enter James (1982 [1902]) once again. On a "purely subjective" level, "[r]eligion must be considered vindicated...from the attacks of her critics," for it simply does too much—indeed, does too much *good*—to be cast aside as "mere anachronism and survival." Rather, it "must exert a permanent function, whether she be with or without intellectual content, and whether, if she have any, it be true or false." In the end, however, James finds it necessary to "pass beyond the view of merely subjective utility." Not unlike Murdoch, he therefore asks, "Ought we to consider the testimony true?" In the Introduction, you may recall, I referred to James's description of that sort of experience in which the individual recognizes the existence of a "higher part" of being. It is one in which the individual "*becomes conscious that this higher part is conterminous and continuous with a MORE of the same quality, which is operative in the universe outside of him, and which he can keep in working touch with, and in a fashion get on board of and save himself when all his lower being has gone to pieces in the wreck*" (p. 508). As he goes on to state,

> The part of the content concerning which the question of truth most pertinently arises is that "MORE of the same quality" with which our own higher self appears in the experience to come into harmonious working relation. Is such a "more" merely our own notion, or does it really exist? Does it act, as well as exist? And in what form should we conceive of that "union" with it of which religious geniuses are so convinced? (pp. 509–510)

From the standpoint of the various religions, there is generally agreement that this "more" really exists, "though some of them hold it to exist in the shape of a personal god or gods, while others are satisfied to conceive it as a stream of ideal tendency embedded in the eternal structure of the world"

The Possibility of Transcendence

(p. 510). In line with what Dupré (1998) told us earlier, all "living religion" entails the existence of a "nucleus" that is assumed to be "transcendentally *given*," and to exclude this nucleus "means to abandon what determines the religious attitude" (p. 6). Neither James nor we, however, can rest content with this point of view, for what it amounts to is little more than a restatement that this religious attitude is ultimately based on *faith*.

Can we go any further? In considering the idea of the "more," the idea of the "subconscious self"—"nowadays a well-accredited psychological entity"—reenters the picture. Could it be that this is all that's needed? Perhaps: "Apart from all religious considerations, there is actually and literally more life in our total soul than we are at any time aware of" (James, 1982 [1902], p. 511). Much of what is there, James notes, is trivial. But in addition, "many of the performances of genius seem also to have their origin; and in our study of conversion, of mystical experiences, and of prayer, we have seen how striking a part invasions from this region play in the religious life." *There*, James essentially says; we have an answer.

> Starting thus with a recognized psychological fact as our basis, we seem to preserve a contact with "science" which the ordinary theologian lacks. At the same time the theologian's contention that the religious man is moved by an external power is vindicated, for it is one of the peculiarities of invasions from the subconscious region to take on objective appearances, and to suggest to the Subject an external control. In the religious life the control is felt as "higher"; but since on our hypothesis it is primarily the higher faculties of our own hidden mind which are controlling, the sense of union with the power beyond us is a sense of something, not merely apparently, but literally true. (pp. 512–513)

But this cannot possibly be enough, for once again, what is being posited here is a kind of *faux* Other and a *faux* priority, dressed up in the captivating garb of the *real* priority of the *real* Other.[32]

---

32. Buber (1970) deals with a similar issue when he states, "The man who steps out of the essential act of pure relation has something More in his being, something new has grown there of which he did not know before and for whose origin he lacks any suitable words." Whatever the "scientific world orientation" may posit in its "legitimate desire for a causal chain," Buber is insistent that "no subconscious and no other psychic apparatus will do. Actually, we receive what we did not have before, in such a manner that we know: it has been given to us" (p. 158). James is a good deal more circumspect in his treatment of the issue, perhaps owing to his own "scientific world orientation." In the end, however, he is not so far away.

It is at this point, by James's own account, that he essentially abandons the role of scientific psychologist and explicitly states that his "hypothesis" to follow must be regarded as an "over-belief"—that is, a belief that falls short of full-blown religious faith but that cannot help but go beyond "the data" at hand. As for the content of this over-belief, it is as follows:

> The further limits of our being plunge, it seems to me, into an altogether different dimension of existence from the sensible and merely "understandable" world. Name it the mystical region, or the supernatural region, whichever you choose. So far as our ideal impulses originate in this world (and most of them do originate in it, for we find them possessing us in a way for which we cannot articulately account), we belong to it in a more intimate sense than that in which we belong to the visible world, for we belong in the most intimate sense wherever our ideals belong. (1982 [1902], p. 516)

On my reading, James backpedals a bit after this dramatic proclamation. This unseen region, he continues, isn't merely ideal, "for it produces effects in the world," and "that which produces effects within another reality must be termed a reality itself, so I feel as if we had no philosophic excuse for calling the unseen or mystical world unreal" (p. 516). At this point, James's perspective sounds less like an over-belief, tied to what experience itself seems to say, than like a somewhat sophistic bit of philosophic maneuvering. He therefore seems to have backed down just as he was rising to the occasion. Is there anything to say beyond this pragmatic point of view?

Strictly speaking, the answer, again, is no. As James (1982 [1902]) avows, "What the more characteristically divine facts are...I know not. But," he quickly adds, "the over-belief on which I am ready to make my personal venture is that they exist." There still remains a pragmatic edge to this perspective: "By being faithful in my poor measure to this over-belief, I seem to myself to keep more sane and true." Finally, however, the reason James subscribes to it is not only that the divinely Other generates real effects or that it keeps him sane. It is that experience, his own and others', tells him that the "something there" so frequently reported feels so palpably real that he is willing to suspend his own rationalistic skepticism.

> I *can*, of course, put myself in the sectarian scientist's attitude, and imagine vividly that the world of sensations and of scientific laws and objects may be all. But whenever I do this, I hear that

inward monitor of which W.K. Clifford once wrote, whispering the word "bosh!" Humbug is humbug, even though it bear the scientific name, and the total expression of human experience, as I view it objectively, invincibly urges me beyond the narrow "scientific" bounds. (p. 519)

No one says it quite like James.

Needless to say, he has not "proved" anything in his book—certainly not the truth of transcendence. In fact, it could be argued that he has done nothing more, ultimately, than offer his over-belief, which, even if short of full-blown religious faith, is surely closer to that than it is to "science," as ordinarily conceived. But this very over-belief, like so many others—including "consciousness" as well as the "subconscious"—may nevertheless deserve a place in psychological inquiry. But what kind of place? Consciousness and the subconscious, intangible though they are, are (hypothetically) at least within the orbit of personal being. Once one begins speaking about the transcendent Other, the situation becomes rather more complicated. What is to be done about this situation? How might it be possible to affirm the priority of the Other in the present context without resorting explicitly to theological principles? The challenge, I stated earlier, is to fashion an approach to these matters that preserves the Other *as Other*. As I have suggested, one relatively uncontroversial way to do so is through hermeneutics, which allows for conceiving the magnetic power of the Other as localized within the object while at the same time recognizing the preparation one brings to the encounter. By conceptualizing mystical experience in this way, it is possible to avoid entirely any and all recourse to the notion of projection and, thereby, to place credence in the otherness of the Other.

As I have also suggested, however, it might be valuable to consider an approach that truly entertains the possibility that the "something more" that has been spoken of refers to just those sorts of "higher energies" that James posited—however reluctantly, given his own scientific commitments. It should be clear that this cannot be done within the confines of a purely naturalistic psychology, a psychology in which there exist firm boundaries between the human and the other-than-human. To put the matter in more positive terms, if indeed there is some validity to positing the *transcendental* priority of the Other, in the context of mysticism and beyond, then a different kind of psychology is called for. At this point, it is difficult to say what this psychology would look like. But whatever name is given to it, it will have to accommodate the distinct possibility that the human person is rooted not only in nature but in what is *beyond* nature. Perhaps this is not the right way to put the matter; the idea remains rough. Perhaps it is better to say that the human person itself partakes of the other-than-human, that it is indeed boundary-less, an opening into the infinite space of the Other. One could, of course, talk about "spirit" as well. But why do so? What advantages might there be to rethinking things along these lines?

The first advantage has to do with the possibility of exposing the operative assumptions that undergird contemporary scientific psychology, particularly in regard to both its thoroughgoing naturalism and its tendency to privatize experience, to keep it within the confines of the subject. There is a curious situation to be acknowledged in this context. As Proudfoot (1986) has noted, many scholars of religion (e.g., Schleiermacher, Otto) have refused to allow "explanation" of religious and mystical experiences, essentially arguing that the subject's own account must be privileged and dealt with on its own terms. According to Proudfoot, this refusal is problematic insofar as it seems to result in "a protective strategy that serves apologetic purposes" (p. 228). But is there not some sense in which excluding the possibility of transcendence from psychology's purview also serves as a protective strategy, effectively ensuring that the doors to other possible frameworks of understanding remain closed? It might, of course, be argued in this context that scientific psychology is not simply "another framework," but a privileged one. This is perhaps why James considers his own conviction in the reality of the "MORE" to be an over-belief, but not his conviction in the reality of the subconscious. Is it possible that scientific psychology's own faith commitments are preventing it from fully coming to terms with certain forms of experience?

The second advantage is more explicitly concerned with the way we understand human selfhood. Although the Principle of the Exclusion of Transcendence is generally understood to be methodological rather than ontological in nature, it is not clear that the two are wholly separable. In adhering to this methodological norm, it would seem, a certain form of ontology cannot help but be perpetuated—one that need not consider whether in fact human beings are anything more than interesting and complex organisms. Let me be clear about this. It is quite possible that this is exactly what we are and that psychology is quite right to continue operating with this basic assumption. But it is also possible that experiences of the sort we have been considering in this chapter tell us something different. Recall once more Dupré's (1976) idea "that the self is *essentially* more than a mere self, that transcendence belongs to its nature as much as the act through which it is immanent to itself, and that a total failure on the mind's part to realize this transcendence reduces the self to *less* than itself" (p. 104). There is no doubt but that Dupré is relying here on an over-belief. As we have seen throughout this chapter, however, there are some compelling reasons to entertain it that have nothing whatsoever to do with one's religious commitments. If we exclude the possibility of "true" transcendence, we cannot help but remain within the orbit of subjectivity and selfhood, and we can cannot help but relegate the ecstatic inspiration that comes the artist's or the mystic's—or *our*—way to the projective infusion of meaning into the Other. Following Nussbaum, this would be remarkable in its own right; "internal" transcendence has its own deep value. Remaining strictly within the scope of the internal may, however, serve to privatize selfhood and to keep theoretical perspectives fundamentally egocentric. It may also serve to perpetuate the kind of "aggressive anthropocentrism" of which Marcel spoke. When experience and selfhood are conceptualized in more *ex*-centric terms, as I have put it, other perspectives—indeed, other kinds of perspectives—may be opened up. This may be valuable both for psychology and for the human beings it seeks to understand.

6

Living Ex-centrically

From Oblivion to Attention

Now that we have made our way through the ethereal reaches of transcendence as well as the rather more terrestrial concerns of academic psychology, it is time to return to everyday life and the question of how we might better live the priority of the Other. Recall the basic premise I put forth in the Introduction: despite our ample capacity for being deeply attentive to the world, human and non-human alike, and despite the fact that we can derive extraordinary meaning and fulfillment from such attentive experience, we often avoid it, electing instead to carry on with our inattentive, preoccupied, egocentric ways. The centrifugal force of the Other thus gets swallowed up in the centripetal force of the self. Being is shrunken. World is hidden. We call this "normal experience." How might it be different?

This will not be a chapter filled with easy fixes. As noted in Chapter Two, the problem of inattention is hardly a newcomer on the human scene. Nor is the existence of those centripetal energies that draw us inward, and at times backward, toward the hungry ego. There have always been misplaced priorities as well, which lead people to seek gratification and fulfillment in the wrong places and fail to accord the Other, human and beyond, the attention and care deserved. This is simply by way of saying that I will not pretend to offer pat solutions to challenges and problems that are part and parcel of the human condition. I shall also try my best to avoid speaking in terms of those sorts of generalities so near and dear to much contemporary social science: if you do this, you're (statistically) likely to be happier; if you do that, you won't be (even though you think you will); and so forth and so on. It is a familiar idea that findings that might apply to the mass really have no bearing at all on *this* particular person, but this simple fact has largely been ignored by those seeking to provide tidy formulas for living. I do not fault them; this is the way of social science research and thinking. In any case, while I shall certainly be offering some generalities in the pages to come, I shall do so cautiously and with all due recognition of the fact that what applies to the group may be utterly irrelevant to the needs, interests, and inclinations of particular individuals. Moreover, what applies to one individual might be irrelevant to another. One additional qualification is in order; I shall put it in the form of a personal avowal: I don't pretend to know how to live. And I certainly wouldn't want anyone to think that I am some sort of exemplar of what I am here calling "ex-centric" living—far from it. Indeed, much of what I have learned about living ex-centrically and what it might conceivably mean has been derived from its inverted expression—that is, from *not* living this way, from falling short of the mark and trying to come to terms with why it might be so.[1] This is no occasion for self-adulation, therefore. On the contrary, it's an occasion for the most profound humility and for candor about what might be done—what *we* might do—about the shape and meaning of our lives.

One very basic thing we might do—the "we" here being not only psychologists and the like but regular folks—is try to think differently about experience. This has largely been the focus of the previous chapters. The fact is, we inhabit a world in which the Other looms large. But we have adopted a way of thinking and speaking about ourselves that frequently runs counter to this fact. It is not thinking alone, however, that is at stake, for the way we think about ourselves can, and generally does, have a profound impact on how we carry out our lives. If we believe that human beings are ultimately "in it for themselves," we might find it that much more justifiable to live out this self-interest, others be damned. If we believe that everything in the world is ultimately a construction, we might resist the very idea of finding intrinsically nourishing objects or see them as mere ideological phantoms, fashioned, no doubt, by those seeking to manufacture our needs and desires. And if we believe that the so-called mystery of being is really not so mysterious at all but an illusion (or delusion), grounded in nothing more than our weakness and susceptibility to wishful folly, we might find it difficult, at times, to find a good reason to live on.

---

1. For a telling example of the great gulf that frequently persists between one's spiritual ideals and the rather less than ideal realities of one's life, see Robert K. C. Forman's *Enlightenment Ain't What It's Cracked Up To Be: A Journey of Discovery, Snow and Jazz in the Soul* (2011). Forman's book is also a good example of the fact that transfer between domains of experience—for instance, from the aesthetic or spiritual to the moral—is hardly automatic.

The classic (Dostoevskyan) "worry," of course, is that with the death of God, "everything is permitted." Worrisome though this may be, I would be more worried about the *void* becoming the default assumption about the world, about the daunting notion that there really may be *nothing* of transcendent enough value to warrant my interest and concern. I am not claiming that God is required for this transcendent value. If truth be told, it is not at all clear to me, still, how to think about God. Having confessed this, I remain extremely concerned about the reigning, largely scientific, ideology that seeks to "materialize" (most often, either evolutionarily or neuroscientifically) any and all human phenomena and relegates the very idea of God to the status of illusion, ready to be superseded by the putatively unvarnished truth about the human condition. That stance is hubris, plain and simple, and it ought to be challenged every step of the way.[2]

More positively, it is imperative, I believe, to think Otherwise about the kinds of issues just referred to. For one, such thinking can serve as a useful counterweight to prevailing views, particularly those that take as axiomatic the primacy of self-interest and the priority of the ego-driven self. For another, and more important, it is (dare I say) *truer* than these views, more consonant with what (much of) our experience is actually like, would that we could see it more clearly.

Having said this, I must add that thinking Otherwise, however necessary, is but one part of the equation, and says precious little about the very difficult project of *living* Otherwise—that is, ex-centrically—and what it might mean. So, let us continue. By "living ex-centrically," I am referring to living in a way that is more oriented toward those objects and activities that work, centrifugally, to move us beyond the centripetal pull of the ego. As we have seen, one class of such objects consists of those catastrophic events that serve to disturb and displace us, shake us awake.[3] I won't be

---

2. Here, I refer especially to those like Dawkins (2008), Hitchens (2009), and Harris (2005), all of whom, albeit for somewhat different reasons, subscribe to this basic ideological position. Having apparently arrived at the truth about reality, human and otherwise, they are often usually eager to take to task those remaining in the dark. For a thoughtful rejoinder, see Terry Eagleton's *Reason, Faith, and Revolution: Reflections on the God Debate* (2011).

3. Sad to say, at the time of this writing another Worcester firefighter, having raced into a burning building thinking someone might still be in there, met his untimely end. Even as I write, the city remains in a state of sorrow and solemnity, lifted mainly by the fact of this man's having honored and upheld the priority of the Other. As was the case with the earlier tragedy (very much on the minds of people, still), there is talk of his act simply being "part of the job." Perhaps it is. But the job itself has the priority of the Other folded into it, and there is no doubting the moral and ethical vision that informs it.

saying much more about these, "functional" though they are; instead, I will be operating on my stated assumption, or at least hope, that they aren't *required* for our coming-into-being. Several times throughout these pages I have mentioned some other candidates as well: meditation, mindfulness, yoga, and other such practices, all of which are in fact designed, in one way or another, to help people live more attentively and fully. I recommend them heartily and have had some very positive firsthand experience with them myself, but I am hardly an authority on them, so I defer to others to sing their praises.[4] What else, then?

Just yesterday, I was back on my bicycle, thinking all this through.[5] For a time, I was oblivious to my surroundings again, lost in the pages of this book. Be assured that I feel some guilt for this. It had been raining for almost a month, the day was absolutely glorious, and there I was, *thinking*. I did eventually manage to break free and actually ended up uttering some "audibles"—basically grunts of joy—as I raced over a rushing river, a beautiful reservoir, and so on. *Fantastic*, worth being alive in its own right. Until that time, I was...inside, cruising, pedaling away, with some awareness of the day, but elsewhere. But here's the good news: I do my best, wide-open thinking on that bicycle. There is something about the sheer practice of it—the rhythm, the sound of the wheels, the wind—that somehow frees me to break new ground. This is exhilarating too. I have actually thought of speaking these new ideas into a recorder while cruising along. But that's too much (not to mention dangerous); if it's important enough, I should remember it later on. I shall be thinking more about this bicycle-induced freedom in this chapter. There's something to it, and I will do what I can to say what.

Another thing happened on yesterday's ride too, that brings us all the way back to that earlier ride I discussed in Chapter Two. While I was lost in thought, something outside me—the blue sky, the play of light on the water—caught my attention, and in the matter of an instant I was *there*. What had been figure became ground; what had been ground became figure. The Other stood forth—which is about when that joyful grunting began. Shifting in this way is not only a function of being disrupted by the

---

4. I hesitate to even begin to lay out the relevant references. Suffice it to say that this literature is vast. So, do some visit some websites, stroll through some bookstores, and, perhaps most important, try out some of the practices. Doing so will surely serve to alert you to the considerable value of this basic orientation to living.

5. Needless to say, perhaps, this "yesterday" was some time ago. (It takes a while for books like this to take shape.)

Other, however; if that were so, all we could possibly do is *wait*, for something disruptive enough to break the spell to come our way. Rather, it is also a function of *memory*. It seems odd to say, but when I am out on that bicycle or for a good meal (or whatever), I need to remember to *be there* for it. Mindfulness practices and the like can certainly help; in training us to attend, and by slowing us down, requiring that we pause, they can bring some helpful habits to our lives.[6]

There are surely other such mnemonic devices as well, vehicles for bringing us back to the world—or, perhaps more appropriately, bringing the world back to us. This process is a freeing process in its own right. "Freedom," Murdoch (1970) had told us (see Chapter Three, Footnote 21), "is not the sudden jumping of the isolated will in and out of an impersonal logical complex, it is a function of the progressive attempt to see a particular object clearly" (p. 23)—that is, the experience of moving ever closer to what is there, in reality, and thereby lifting ourselves beyond the restricted, at times positively blindered, view of things that so often characterizes our relationship to the world. Rather than being "an inconsequential chucking of one's weight about," therefore, "it is the disciplined overcoming of self," entailing a kind of reverential humility.[7] This humility, Murdoch adds, should not be construed as mere "self-effacement, rather like having an inaudible voice, it is a selfless respect for reality and one of the most difficult and central of all virtues" (1970, p. 93).

Murdoch also speaks of *love* in this context. For

> it is in the capacity to love, that is to *see*, that the liberation of the soul from fantasy consists. The freedom which is a proper human goal is the freedom from fantasy.... What I have called fantasy, the proliferation of blinding self-centred aims and images, is itself a powerful system of energy, and most of what is often called "will" or "willing" belongs to this system. What counteracts the system is attention to reality inspired by, consisting of, love. (p. 65)

---

6. It is important to note a further connection between attention and memory. It is only to the extent that I truly pay attention to what's going on in my world that I will remember it. With inattention, there is forgetting. And in forgetting, we deprive ourselves of whatever energy or nourishment the Other in question may have provided.

7. See Kunz (2002) for some helpful ideas regarding humility with particular reference to psychology.

Linking love together with the idea of the Good, Murdoch writes,

> Good is the magnetic centre toward which love naturally moves. False love moves to false good. False love embraces false death. When true good is loved, even impurely or by accident, the quality of the love is automatically refined, and when the soul is turned towards Good, the highest part of the soul is enlivened. Love is the tension between the imperfect soul and the magnetic perfection which is conceived of as lying beyond it.... Love is [thus] the general name of the quality of attachment and it is capable of infinite degradation and is the source of our greatest errors; but when it is even partially refined it is the energy and passion of the soul in its search for Good, the force that joins us to Good and joins us to the world through Good. Its existence is the unmistakable sign that we are spiritual creatures, attracted by excellence and made for the Good. It is a reflection of the warmth and light of the sun. (p. 100)[8]

Following Murdoch's lead, one path toward living ex-centrically is to find objects and activities that are *loveable* enough to inspire our attention and care. Seeing and loving are of a piece for her, serving to free us from self, from those insistent inclinations toward fantasy and willfulness that obscure reality. Of course, it is not only "seeing" that yields this freedom. Listening is important too, as are touching and being touched, both literally and figuratively. I wouldn't want to leave tasting and smelling out of the picture either. As friends who read these words well know, I am quite serious about this. Had I not become a college professor, I said in a recent interview, I would have done something in the area of food and wine. This is mainly because I love them both dearly. More significant for present purposes is the fact that wine, in particular, has come to serve as a mnemonic device for me. Unlike food, which I sometimes plunge through inattentively, wine (good wine at any rate) demands to be noticed, savored. It has therefore come to be not only a real source of pleasure but a vehicle for helping me remember to attend. After a busy day, having been preoccupied with this or that dilemma or crisis, I can get a moment of reprieve

---

8. I have no doubt that this sort of language will strike many readers as alien, too ponderous and abstract. It may also reek too much of Plato, who, as I acknowledged earlier, is often portrayed as a kind of reifying absolutist. Such qualms aside, there is much in these words, I believe, worth thinking about.

once I crack open a bottle and pour myself a glass. Consider once more what Murdoch had said in regard to a hovering kestrel: as she is looking out her window in an anxious and resentful state of mind, the little bird catches her attention, and in a flash her anxiety and resentment are gone, displaced, even if temporarily. She reminds us that we can do this sort of thing deliberately too, "giving attention to nature in order to clear our minds of selfish care" (1970, p. 82). She might have added good wine to the equation as well.

I don't want to take this example too far. For me, wine remains a relatively simple pleasure, and I would be hard-pressed to build a strong case for living ex-centrically based on its place in my life. If I had more money, this might well change, for the development of connoisseurship involves much the same attention to matters of excellence as is found in the appreciation of painting or music or theater. One could argue that it does not, and cannot, involve the same degree of *meaning*; quaffing good wine can edify one just so much. But it is legitimately Other in its own right, and for some, it contains every bit as much disruptive force as those ostensibly "higher" pursuits generally associated with the arts. Bearing this in mind, it may be useful to return briefly to an issue introduced earlier, concerning the fact that the particular object of one's attention matters. As Csikszentmihalyi (1990) has pointed out in his examination of the flow experience, numerous objects and activities can serve to take us out of ourselves, but they are by no means equally flow inducing. I can be taken out of myself by mindlessly watching television, but the result is more likely to be stupor than rapture. I will have been entertained in this instance, perhaps even enough so that some of my "selfish care" will have been cleared away. But surely no larger Self will emerge from the experience, no sense of my own inner depths or kinship with the world. On the contrary, there is a good chance that the self that emerges in the aftermath of the show will actually be smaller than the one that was there to begin with.

Again, therefore, it's not just any Other that will do but one that is generative in some way, that enlivens rather than deadens me. For Csikszentmihalyi, the flow experience occurs mainly in the context of increasingly complex challenges that are met with increasingly complex skills. He therefore explores activities such as rock climbing and surgery, and insofar as one proves to be "up to the task," given the extraordinary challenges at hand, the experiential consequences may be nothing short of ecstatic. The challenge/skill dynamic that characterizes the flow experience is, however, but one pathway to living ex-centrically. There are others that are more oriented toward simplicity than complexity and have as their aim the quiet contentment of being rather than the "louder" excitement of becoming, of mobilizing one's skills and strengths. Some people will be drawn in the direction of flow experiences. Others will be drawn to these quieter routes to the Other. Others still will want both—for instance, bicycles and wine (though not together!)—and may wish to explore different pathways entirely. This is one of those relatively few places where I am tempted make a recommendation: *do one thing at a time.* Not too long after I finished this very section of this chapter, I sat down to some lunch. The main dish was some chicken in a nice sauce that had come from a local Japanese restaurant. Wonderful. But of course I had to check out the just-arrived *New York Times Book Review* too, and midway through the meal I realized that I hadn't tasted a thing.[9] There are of course some things that work nicely together, enhancing the experience rather than detracting from it—food and wine, for instance! These exceptions to the rule notwithstanding, we would do well, in this age of multitasking, to be more single-minded in our relation to the Other than we often are.

What I have been talking about thus far in this section, especially regarding my own relationship to bicycles and wine, is perhaps best considered under the rubric of "pastimes," vehicles of recreation and refreshment that are of value in disrupting some of life's routines and regularities and reorienting our energies. These can be vitally important in their own right, particularly for those among us who are harried, who have much to do, and who, during the course of a given day or week, simply need to take a break from the action. It should be reiterated that others' relationships to these particular objects may go far deeper; the true bicycling enthusiast, not unlike the wine connoisseur, will move from the more momentary modes of attention I have been addressing to "dedication." I thumb through *Bicycling* magazine and *Wine Spectator*. These people are likely to be decidedly more feverish in their pursuits, and they are also likely to derive a measure of meaning and fulfillment from these pursuits that well surpasses the likes of my own. Although the object of one's attention very much matters, therefore, what this object ultimately

---

9. As Seneca (2005) reminds us, "no activity can be successfully pursued by an individual who is preoccupied...since the mind when distracted absorbs nothing deeply, but rejects everything which is, so to speak, crammed into it. Living is the least important activity of the preoccupied man [or woman]; yet there is nothing harder to learn" (pp. 9–10). The good news is, "life is long if you know how to use it" (p. 2). The not-so-good news is, "the preoccupied find life very short" (p. 14). Attention is of the essence.

is for the experiencing person remains thoroughly contingent on what he or she brings to it, by way of knowledge, commitment, care, and so on. Christopher Bollas (1992) puts the matter well.

> [A]s we encounter the object world we are substantially metamorphosed by the structure of objects; internally transformed by objects that leave their traces within us, whether it be the effect of a musical structure, a novel, or a person.... To be a character is to enjoy the risk of being processed by the object—indeed, to seek objects, in part, in order to be metamorphosed. (p. 59)

To be a character, then, is to be "a bearer of an intelligent form that seeks objects to express its structure" (p. 65), discovering those features of the world that somehow give form to one's interests and desires.

Let me go out on a limb and offer another recommendation here (directed especially to students, trying to fashion their futures): *do what you love*—as long as it is *worthy* of your love. By this I mean pursue what you are most passionate about, as long as it enlivens and expands rather than deadens and contracts. This is emphatically not a call for hedonism. Nor is it a call for pleasure or happiness (though these may at times result). Rather, it is a call to find those objects, those *Others*, that "metamorphose" one in such a way that a more attentive, and loving, relationship to the world is formed. In this respect, doing what one loves, within the boundaries of worthiness, not only is consonant with living ethically but supports and strengthens the very project of doing so.

From Attention to Devotion

I used the word "dedication" above mainly to underscore the sort of sustained attention that is found in the enthusiast or the connoisseur. How does "devotion" enter the picture? Earlier on, I suggested that devotion might be understood as a kind of compound of attention and care, the cognitive dimension and the ethical dimension. Indeed, devotion would seem to entail a level of responsibility and commitment to an Other in a way that attention and dedication do not (or do not necessarily). The term also has religious overtones, the "devotional life" generally being understood as one of sustained commitment to some religious object, some divine being or sphere of activity. How important is this devotional dimension? It surely isn't *necessary* to include this devotional dimension in one's life;

there are plenty of people who get along just fine without it. And for those who do include it in their lives in some way, it surely isn't necessary that they do so in a religious or spiritual way; there are people who are strenuously devoted to the cause of justice, to the well-being of the planet, and to numerous other non-religious objects, and they are getting along just fine as well. Having offered these qualifications, it is clearly the case that including the devotional dimension in one's life can be, and often is, an important vehicle for strengthening and enlarging the Self. How might we understand this?

Louis Dupré (1976) argues forcefully that "[b]y some strange law man must attend to what surpasses both what he is or can ever hope to be in order to gain true humanity. In restricting his scope to what he is, he will not only fail to grow but, as the unhappy receiver of the one talent, lose what he possesses." For Dupré, therefore, "[t]he ultimate paradox of the good life is that it must be defined in terms of what is more than good" (p. 41). For James Edwards (1997), likewise, it is imperative that we reach beyond ourselves if we are to realize and fulfill our humanity: "[A]lthough we don't need gods, we do still need sacraments: deliberate occasions for a particular sort of grace.... Such sacraments, were we to discover and to develop them, would both liberate unforeseen energies for change and modulate that change so as to control our tendency to limitlessly aggrandize the human" (p. 56).

It should be noted that both Dupré and Edwards see a significant measure of loss in the contemporary religious scene. According to Dupré (1976),

> In the present situation, the very reality of the transcendent is at stake.... Theology in the past could count on some *direct* experience of the sacred. Such an experience can no longer be taken for granted. The religious attitude of Western men and women has largely become what it never was before, a matter of existential choice. If they believe, they do so not because of an inherited tradition and seldom because of a direct religious experience, but rather because of an accumulation of experiences confronting them with various choices, one of which they must make their own by a personal decision. (pp. 142–143)

Unfortunately, Dupré continues, "They will soon turn into empty shells unless they are constantly replenished by a rather intensive and deliberate spiritual awareness. The search for a deeper spiritual life, then, means more than a passing phenomenon on today's religious scene; it is a movement for religious survival" (p. 143). Edwards's perspective is somewhat different, the problem at hand being not so much the increasing "privatization" of religion as that "our lives are constituted by self-devaluating values" (1997, p. 46). To a greater or lesser extent, this leaves many of us, both religious and non-, "normal nihilists," saddled with the "rueful recognition...of [our] own historical and conceptual contingency" (p. 47). The resultant "mood of loss" is, ultimately, nothing less than the felt loss of the sacred Other, redoubled by the perceived impossibility of its return.[10]

Needless to say, perhaps, both Dupré and Edwards are open to the charge of nostalgia, of pining for a way of life—or an imagined way of life—that has been left behind. There are many who would reject the "loss" of which they speak, seeing it as little more than a stale remnant of thinking about the world that is better left behind. Given the kind of "spiritual self-seeking" (James, 1950 [1890]) frequently found in today's world, however, they are more than likely on to something quite real. But it really isn't *self*-seeking that's going on in this context. Rather, it is *Other*-seeking brought on, I would suggest, by the relative scarcity of those sources of existential and spiritual nourishment that allow one to grow and flourish.

James, in my view, gets this situation very nearly right in his discussion of the "rivalry and conflict of the different selves" in *The Principles of Psychology* (1950 [1890]). Indeed, he provides a good model of a new and improved evolutionary psychology. Contra those who would consider our more "animal" self-interest primary, James presents a *"hierarchical scale, with the bodily Self at the bottom, the spiritual Self at top, and the extracorporeal material selves and the various social selves between."* As he goes on to explain,

> A certain amount of bodily selfishness is required as a basis for all the other selves. But too much sensuality is despised....He is esteemed a poor creature who is unable to forego a little meat and drink and warmth and sleep for the sake of getting on in the world. The social self as a whole...ranks higher than the material self as a whole. We must care more for our honor, our friends, our human ties, than for a sound skin or wealth. And the spiritual self is so

---

10. Some recent exchanges with Frank Richardson and Brent Slife have been most valuable in helping me think through these issues. I am extremely grateful to both of them.

supremely precious that, rather than lose it, a man ought to be willing to give up friends and good fame, and property, and life itself. (p. 315)

James is not merely preaching here; he is positing the priority of the spiritual self over both the material and the social. Framed differently, James is positing what I have herein been calling the priority of the Other. So it is that he goes on to speak of "an ideal social self, of a self that is at least *worthy* of approving recognition by the highest *possible* judging companion, if such companion there be. This self is the true, the intimate, the ultimate, the permanent Me which I seek. This judge is God, the Absolute Mind, the 'Great Companion' " (pp. 315–316).

What James says next in this portion of the book is downright prophetic: "We hear, in these days of scientific enlightenment, a great deal of discussion about the efficacy of prayer; and many reasons are given us why we should not pray, whilst others are given us why we should. But in all this very little is said of the reason why we *do* pray, which is simply that we cannot *help* praying" (1950 [1890], p. 316). Bearing this this in mind, "[i]t seems probable that, in spite of all that 'science' may do to the contrary, men will continue to pray until the end of time, unless their mental nature changes in a manner which nothing we know should lead us to expect" (p. 316). I would frame these issues somewhat differently as well. It is not at all clear that we cannot help praying; nor is it clear that we will continue to do so until the end of time. What is clear, or at least clearer, is the idea that some Other—some sphere of being and reality greater than us—is vitally important for the nourishment and, indeed, the very *survival* of the soul. Is it *necessary?*

Must one be so oriented toward the Other? No; we can be oriented toward money and prestige and any number of other objects. It is also true that some people may not be able to quite "afford" this Other-seeking. If their main goal is to put food on the table or to avoid dying or being killed, there may be little time or energy for such "higher" pursuits. But none of this negates the priority of the Other; on the contrary, it affirms it. It also helps to explain the aforementioned mood of loss spoken of by Dupré, Edwards, and others. There are many "gods" out there, to be sure, but unless they are truly nourishing or can call forth our sense of responsibility to something larger than ourselves, we will likely feel *some* sense of loss akin to that which we have been considering. It is not the loss of self—not primarily, at any rate. It is the loss of the Other.

What is needed in the face of this spiritually depleted landscape, according to Edwards, is the development of a discipline, "a way of training one's attention" (1997, p. 213) that reorients one's energy in a manner not unlike that which we might find in prayer. As Christopher Dustin and Joanna Ziegler (2007) add, this sort of discipline or "practice," as they put it, "originates in and promises to yield a loving awareness of that which we ourselves do not make," and "[i]t is this realization, if we are capable of it, that makes us fully human" (p. 6). Dustin and Ziegler's work, it should be noted, is less about devotion per se than about what they call "contemplative seeing," a practiced mode of beholding the world with "wondering eyes" that allows for both the unconcealing of reality and, through it, the realization of the Self. But this very seeing, they imply, must itself be undertaken devotionally, that is, with precisely that sort of sustained attention and responsiveness to the Other—to "that which we ourselves do not make," which is the hallmark of the devotional life.

There are some loaded terms in the preceding paragraphs. Dupré spoke of the possibility of gaining "true humanity" through some form of the devotional life; Edwards spoke of our need for "sacraments"; and Dustin and Ziegler, bringing these two ideas together, essentially spoke of the connection between beholding such sacraments—or beholding the world in such a way as to see its sacramentality—and the project of becoming "fully human." What can they possibly mean by these claims? I am not entirely comfortable with notions like "true humanity" and "fully human"; they imply that those who fall short are somehow...*untrue*, incomplete, *less*. My own discomfort notwithstanding, I still find myself compelled by the main ideas being considered: through certain forms of devotional or contemplative practice, one can learn to behold the world more clearly and, in so doing, realize registers of Self that would otherwise remain unrealized, undisclosed.[11] Here, we return once more to the idea of detachment as well as the idea that part of the process of discerning the priority of the Other entails unselfing, "de-prioritizing" the ego in some way. This process may be carried out by the Other itself; at times, its very presence and power can immediately take the ego down to size. So it is that serving others—caring for them, being there for them—can be unselfing in its own right, giving us a clearer and more enduring sense of their priority. But this process may also be carried out via practices that

---

11. Bearing in mind this idea, we might speak Self-*finding* rather than self-seeking—as long as we realize that this process of finding owes its very existence to the priority of the Other.

systematically dismantle or diminish the ego's energies through detachment. As Farley (1996) had put the matter, our "idolatrous egocentrism is razed" in this manner, "but selfhood itself is not destroyed;" it is only "reoriented from itself to others, to the world." Consequently, "[a]s oneself and one's own interests recede in importance, the reality of others is permitted to gain ground" (p. 84).

Contra Simone Weil, who insisted on the importance of affliction as a preparatory moment in encountering the Other, Farley maintains that such "passionate" detachment must be distinguished from "self-abnegation." "Methodological self-abnegation preserves, rather than cleaves, the structure of egocentrism in which the self occupies the center of the universe.... The very insistence on uprooting self-interest is itself a continuation of fixation on the self" and thus "takes on a self-defeating character" (1996, p. 96). The challenge, therefore, is to pursue practices that foster the necessary detachment from one's egocentric energies without making such detachment an explicit goal. Most important in this context are the practices themselves, whatever they may be, for if Farley and others are right—and I believe they are—the force of our own pervasive egocentricity is such that unless it is defeated in some practiced way, the radiant energies of the Other cannot, and will not, appear. Now, the "refocusing of attention" that is entailed in the kinds of practices about which Farley speaks implies what both she and Murdoch refer to as a "moral discipline." It is precisely this effortful moral discipline, I suggest, that moves one's energies in the direction of *devotion*. It is sustained, practiced, and respectful attention, oriented toward the care and well-being of some worthy reality, whether human or non-human. At times, I have spoken of the "de-prioritization" of the ego and attentiveness to the Other as if they were discrete, separable processes. What we see here, however, is that they are perhaps better understood as analytically differentiable moments of a single, indivisible process. Insofar as I am devoted to the Other—or, more specifically, to the *cause* of the Other—I am engaged in some form or other of disciplined practice directed outward, and it is this disciplined practice that reorients the ego's inward energies.

I use the word "cause" with some trepidation, mainly because it might appear to privilege social and political commitment above all else. As valuable as these particular forms of commitment surely are, they are emphatically not to be privileged in this way. In the Introduction, I noted that students at (Jesuit) colleges and universities such as my own, which emphasize being "men and women for and with others," frequently assume that social justice is the cause of causes. They are thus strenuously committed to a wide variety of service activities, volunteer work, and so on. This is good! The downside, I had indicated, is that they sometimes conclude that other pursuits—becoming a poet, for instance—are somehow less valid. No one is being "served" in quite the same way as when one serves a hot meal to the hungry or builds a new home for the homeless, and there is not the same kind of explicit betterment, *redress*. But there are of course less explicit modes of redress, found in art and other such ostensibly more "obscure" places, and these surely deserve a place at the table of worthy causes.

Seamus Heaney, for instance, has spoken explicitly of the redress of poetry, which "comes from its being a glimpsed alternative, a revelation of potential that is denied or constantly threatened by circumstances" (1995, p. 4). Something similar may be said of our experience with music. As we have observed, it is, perhaps, the least "informative" of the arts, and in that sense the hardest to link to the sorts of issues and ideas generally associated with discrete causes. Here too, however, it is important to think more broadly about the matters at hand. Jonathan Harvey had spoken about music's wonderful capacity to create unity out of ambiguity, a "promised harmony" that provides not only a kind of "answer" to this ambiguity, but also compassion, a sense of unity and solidarity with others. Kathleen Higgins, similarly, had spoken of music as presenting an image of a unified existence, one that supports the idea that we can, in fact, exist harmoniously. She also told us that music can take us beyond ourselves and give us a sense of being connected to and engaged with the larger world. Rather than referring to "devotion," Higgins speaks of "reverence"—for the music itself, for those who created it, for those with whom it may be shared, and for the larger world more generally. Such reverence is incompatible with hostility and defensiveness—so much so, she had said, that were she to kick her dog after listening to Mozart, it would be painfully clear (to the dog especially!) that she hadn't fully undergone the kind of ethico-spiritual transformaton that reverence involves.

I would like to believe that Higgins is right about this, but I remain unsure. It seems to me quite possible that one might adopt a reverential stance vis-à-vis Mozart and still become very annoyed and angry at something the dog has done. In fact, juxtaposed against the reverential rapture induced by Mozart, the dog's behavior, having ruined the mood and brought one back to harsh animal reality, may be that much more annoying. Having offered this minor qualification, there is little question that, generally speaking, I am in a better psychological, ethical, and spiritual place after my listening experience than I was in before. And if, moreover, this sort of listening experience is an integral part of my life, a regular practice I engage in so as to tune myself aright to the world, it is that much more likely to be an integral part of my very being, leading me in turn to a more intimate connection with the larger world—another eminently worthy cause. Here again, then, I simply wish to reiterate that there is no need whatsoever to privilege social or political causes over those having to do with poetically inspired hope, musically inspired connectedness to the world, and other such less-tangibles. What is most fundamental is the intensity of the devotion so inspired and the life-givingness it can bring in tow.

I mean this quite literally. Even if there is no "need" for devotional objects in one's life, such objects may nevertheless prove instrumental not only in one's well-being but in one's very survival. Viktor Frankl (1960), for instance, has argued that those concentration camp prisoners who were able to "keep in mind" devotional objects—a family member, perhaps still alive, a yet-to-be-completed book—were more likely to retain an "inner hold" on their moral and spiritual lives. "A man who becomes conscious of the responsibility he bears toward a human being who affectionately waits for him, or to an unfinished work, will never be able to throw away his life. He knows the 'why' for his existence, and will be able to bear almost any 'how' " (p. 80). It should be noted that for Frankl, what was ultimately responsible for one's either retaining or losing this inner hold was a "free decision." The simple fact that anyone could prevail in such horrific conditions provided ample evidence, in his view, that this capacity "to choose one's attitude in any given set of circumstances, to choose one's own way" (p. 66), is a key feature of the human condition. "It is this spiritual freedom—which cannot be taken away—that makes life meaningful and purposeful" (p. 67).

Perhaps Frankl is right about this capacity to choose. But it is not at all clear whether it is "spiritual freedom" that makes life meaningful. Indeed, even by Frankl's own account, it would seem more accurate to say that it was the devotional objects that did so—not in any mechanical, deterministic way but in a way that called forth one's own sense of responsibility and, in turn, one's freedom. Insofar as such spiritual freedom remained operative, therefore, it was inspired by the Other. Could this freedom be retained in the absence of devotional objects? Perhaps; it could be that in some instances people simply chose, through sheer strength of will, to live rather than die. But following Frankl's own line of thinking, this very mobilization of will was inseparable from recognizing the priority of the Other.

In a similar vein, Tzvetan Todorov, referred to earlier, noted that those concentration camp prisoners who continued to care for the others in their midst—fellow prisoners, in need—were themselves more likely to survive the degradation and horror surrounding them. For Todorov, such caring was testimony to the primordial fact of the Other's priority. For both Frankl and Todorov, there is a sense in which upholding the priority of the Other—being responsible to and for them, caring for them, perhaps loving them—can seem like a *means* to one's own well-being. But this is to misconstrue what they most want to say. That one's own well-being may at times result from one's care for the Other seems true enough. This does not mean, however, that this care has as its ultimate aim one's own well-being. Rather, the latter is a by-product of the former, a salutary, unintended consequence. Let us also not forget that there is another "reason" for being responsible and for caring in the way that Frankl and Todorov, among many others, have specified—namely, that *it is a good thing to do*.

The consequences of this goodness are not always happy ones. "To live life in the camps according to an ethic of care," Todorov (1999) writes, "is to render oneself especially vulnerable, for in addition to one's own suffering, one takes on that of the people one cares about.... One is much more protected if one is fighting for an ideal," he explains: "the loss of one person can then be relativized; one's hopes for the triumph of the cause remain intact. But can one protect oneself by ceasing to care for those one loves, by ceasing to love them?" Surely not. The situation is at once tragic and hopeful. "In choosing to suffer, both for and with one another," as so many did and do, "one adds to the world's misfortunes; yet such actions, through their goodness, make the world as a whole more, not less, acceptable" (p. 90).

As Frankl, Primo Levi, and others have pointed out, it wasn't easy to be good in the camps; there was much working against it, including one's own desire to survive. It may be particularly difficult to care for those one *doesn't* love. It has also been argued that such care is simply unnatural in these circumstances, or at least secondary, one's first priority being oneself. But no one said that living the priority of the Other is easy, and no one said that it doesn't take a special effort, at times, to *make* the Other a priority. Our self-preservative energies run deep, and in dire circumstances, circumstances in which one's very capacity to see and feel the reality of the Other may be blunted, if not effaced, considerable energy and effort will likely be needed to counteract them. The good news, again, is that this very energy and effort, this very will and determination, this very *freedom*, rather than being something I must somehow find within myself, issues from the Other, who calls forth my responsibility and indeed my very being. It is therefore vitally important that we heed the Other's call. Both our survival and, more important, *others'* survival depend on it.[12]

It might be noted that in those situations in which one *doesn't* heed the call, however compelling the reason may be, one may be left with the most abject shame. "Coming out of the darkness," Levi writes in *The Drowned and the Saved* (1989),

> one suffered because of the reacquired consciousness of having been diminished. Not by our will, cowardice, or fault, yet nevertheless we had lived for months and years at an animal level: our days had been encumbered from dawn to dusk by hunger, fatigue, cold, and fear; and any space for reflection, reasoning, experiencing emotions was wiped out. We endured filth, promiscuity, and destitution, suffering much less than we would have suffered from such things in normal life, because our moral yardstick had changed.... We had not only forgotten our country and our culture, but also our family, our past, the future we had imagined for ourselves, because like animals, we were confined to the present moment. (p. 75)

Levi could utter these words only after the fact, in hindsight. This process was often extraordinarily painful. Indeed, Levi continues, "I believe it was precisely this turning to look back at the 'perilous water' that gave rise to so many suicides after (sometimes immediately after) Liberation." There would be "a flood of rethinking and depression," and the reality of what had been—the reality of what *they* had been, what they had been reduced to—would suddenly burst forth. Why shame? There were several reasons. "When all was over," Levi writes, "the awareness emerged that we had not done anything, or not enough, against the system in which we had been absorbed" (p. 76). In addition, there was the shame of having failed

---

12. As one might rightly ask, of Frankl in particular, what if there *is* no Other out there, calling me forth—no person, no project, nothing? What then? According to Frankl, I still remain responsible, if only to life itself. This has always struck me as a somewhat abstract commitment, and although I understand why he holds to it, I am uncertain about its practicability.

one's fellow prisoners. "Few survivors feel guilty about having deliberately damaged, robbed, or beaten a companion," Levi notes. "Those who did so...block out the memory. By contrast, however, almost everybody feels guilty of having omitted to offer help" (p. 78). Levi, not unlike Frankl, realizes that there had been much working against them: "Malnutrition, despoilment, and other physical discomforts, which it is so easy and economically advantageous to provoke and at which the Nazis were masters, are rapidly destructive and paralyze before destroying, all the more so when they are preceded by years of segregation, humiliation, maltreatment, forced migration, laceration of family ties, rupture of contact with the rest of the world" (p. 77). Rationally speaking, then, there wasn't much reason for shame. But it was there, nevertheless, painful and, at times, deadly. Levi knew this firsthand.

What he also knew, or felt, was that in failing to heed the call of the Other, he had essentially been an accomplice to the crimes perpetrated by his captors. As I have suggested elsewhere (Freeman, 2010), "shame" doesn't quite capture what Levi appeared to have felt in the aftermath of his time in the camps. "Sin" seems like the more appropriate term. Whereas the former may be seen as a malady of the self and is something one might be able to work through, the latter, one might say, is a malady of the *soul* and is much more resistant to change, to being worked through and beyond.[13] What an awful, ironic, tragic situation: oftentimes, it was the victims, rather than the perpetrators, who were left bathed in shame and sin. But there is some good news here too, for the very capacity to feel this shame and this sin is itself testimony to one's humanity—one's recognition, indeed, of the priority of the Other. There are no recommendations to be made in the face of such situations; by all indications, Levi and his fellow prisoners had little choice but to act as they did, so there is little reason to look backward to see what might have been done differently. There are other situations, however—numerous ones, in fact—when one does have a choice, when one can, and should, heed the Other's call. By doing so, one can avoid the shame that we have been considering. But that, again, is a secondary matter. By recognizing and upholding the priority of the Other, one also recognizes and upholds the priority of the *Good*.

---

13. There is some evidence that Levi took his own life and that it had to do, in part, precisely with the irrevocable nature of his deeds, misdeeds, and, perhaps most significantly, non-deeds. The issue is a controversial one and, as far as I know, has yet to be definitively resolved. There is no question, in any case, about the depth of Levi's shame in the aftermath of Liberation.

What does this mean? There are, of course, any number of ways of thinking about goodness. But for present purposes, I shall restrict myself to those ways that are in keeping with the priority of the Other. Consider once more Primo Levi's situation. I suggested that the word "sin" might be more appropriate than "shame" for conceptualizing what he and others felt as they looked back on their behavior in the camps. One reason I used this term was to emphasize the sheer depth and intensity of feeling that had emerged. Another reason was to emphasize the felt irrevocability of what had, and had not, been done, the conviction that one could not possibly undo the crimes of the past. But there is another still, and here I refer to the idea that what Levi and his fellow prisoners felt appears to go beyond social norms and ideals. Referring once more to the above-mentioned distinction, it is the self that falls short of, meets, or exceeds such ideals. The soul, in contrast, has on its horizon ideals of another sort, ones that bespeak more *transcendent* concerns. "Are you ashamed," Levi (1989) asks, "because you are alive in place of another? And in particular of a man more generous, more sensitive, more useful, wiser, worthier of living than you?" (p. 81). This question cuts deep. Hovering around it is a recognition of the priority of the Other, in inverted form: although he had little choice in the matter, he had not accorded the Other the priority deserved. Others had been much more devoted to the cause of their brothers and sisters; some of them had even been willing to die on their behalf.

We might think of those firefighters in this context too. As some of them claim, they are simply doing their job; they are dedicated professionals, no more, no less. We could therefore skip all that high and mighty talk about heroism, sacrifice, and so on. Perhaps we should. But there is more than professional dedication involved in what they do. There is also devotion, of a strenuous and enduring sort, precisely to the Other, who comes first. In this respect, they embody a sacred ideal, one that we know to be valid and significant and real. That is surely why we all came out to pay our respects and to honor them. More than etiquette was involved. And there was more at stake than appreciation for their good work, for a job well done. What was at stake, ultimately, was the Good itself. It had come out of hiding, and its appearance proved to be a true tonic for the community. That it had waited to come out of hiding until then was at once uplifting, serving to heal the wounds, and profoundly disappointing. It was a shame we weren't like that more often. The implication: *Do good. Be of service. Remember.*

Need I say what this means? Yes, of course; we all have our own definitions. People vary. Cultures vary. Epochs vary. These differences are important to recognize. But amidst all these real and significant differences, I maintain, is a shared idea and ideal: the priority of the Other. This is most visibly so on the moral plane, the plane of good behavior, of treating others with the respect and care they deserve. But it is also visible on the ethical plane, the plane of *living* well. And living well means living ex-centrically, which in turn means that *whatever* I do in this life—whether it is a life of explicit service to others, a life of inquiry, a life of expression,*whatever*—it ought to include some measure of devotion. Without such devotion, I cannot be sustained, fed, nourished; instead, I am left to my own devices. And if Simone Weil and others are right, these cannot possibly suffice to inspire me and infuse my life with the kind of energy and spirit required for living well. Perhaps more important, I cannot and will not be there *for the Other*, whether human or non-, and will therefore be leaving the world that much more depleted and unjust.[14]

From Devotion to Transcendence

I do not want to be elitist in identifying these sorts of requirements. Many people, I acknowledged earlier, are just trying to survive. They don't have the luxury of living "devotionally," and they may be far more concerned with *actual* nourishment than existential nourishment. Fair enough. But let us not underestimate what may be present in such lives. And let us not *over*estimate what may be present in our own. "Goodness," Murdoch (1970) states, "appears to be both rare and hard to picture. It is perhaps most convincingly met with in simple people—inarticulate, unselfish mothers of large families—but these cases are also the least illuminating" (pp. 51–52). With all due respect to Murdoch, this is a (very) loaded statement. I don't know that goodness is rare. If she's talking about *unvarnished* goodness, then yes; it is not only rare but nonexistent. If she's talking about some sort of character trait, or some sort of overall description of someone's foremost inclinations, then this too may be deemed rare. But goodness as an idea, or as a *form*, a never-to-be-fully-realized-in-this-life regulative

---

14. According to Sam Keen (2010), "amid all the offerings on holistic living, healing, meditation, awareness, opening the heart, oneness, knowing God, and sacred bodywork, there is little or no reference to justice" (p. 167). The situation is a contradictory one: "To be concerned with spirituality but ignore the struggle for justice is as much of an oxymoron as compassionate egotism" (p. 168). Once again, this does not mean that *social* justice—serving others, in some explicit way—is the only "struggle." What it does mean is that being of service, *in some way*, is part and parcel of living the priority of the Other.

intimation, isn't rare at all—even if it is often manifested in inverted form. I am not sure it is hard to picture either. There are some obvious pictures: firefighters racing into burning buildings, searching for those who might be trapped inside; concentration camp prisoners reaching out to others; people delivering penicillin to children in faraway lands who would otherwise die. There are less obvious pictures too, ones less explicitly tied to this sort of intervention: passionate teachers, artists, and scientists; the various guardians of spiritual and religious life; the hard workers, proud of what they do or make; and both inarticulate and articulate mothers and fathers of both large and small families, doing their level best to carve out a life worth living for their charges and for themselves. Attention and devotion loom large for all of them. What about transcendence?

It is a different category of experience altogether. Unlike attention and devotion, both of which entail practices that we might hone and sharpen, transcendence is more of a "result," a quality of being that might issue from these practices. As such, we do not, and cannot, seek it. Simone Weil, once again, provides some helpful insights:

> There are people who try to raise their souls like a man continually taking standing jumps in the hopes that, if he jumps higher every day, a time may come when he will no longer fall back but will go right up to the sky. Thus occupied he cannot look at the sky. We cannot take a single step toward heaven. It is not in our power to travel in a vertical direction. (1973 [1951], p. 194)

"Seeking," therefore, "leads us astray. This is the case with every form of what is truly good. Man should do nothing but wait for the good and keep evil away" (p. 197). This doesn't mean that one's "waiting" is a mere passivity, completely detached and undirected; it means only that the truth and goodness about which Weil speaks are not to be sought willfully, as a discrete end or goal—for if she is right, this mode of willful seeking ultimately undermines the very possibility of their attainment.[15]

---

15. As with many of Weil's statements, it is difficult to know how far to take this. Her point about the problem of those "who try to raise their souls" seems valid, for the very goal-directedness of the process militates against the kind of attentive presence required for the emergence of transcendence. At the same time, it is not entirely clear what "waiting" actually entails. I very much appreciate the ambiguity at hand. While I have made some very modest "recommendations" for living the priority of the Other in this chapter, I have stopped well short of identifying discrete measures. For one, they are not there to be had. For another, they may indeed serve to undermine the very process they most seek to promote.

Generally, transcendent experience emerges in ways that are unbidden. As we have seen, one notable site for such non-willful transformation is the catastrophic. Consider the kind of experience I recounted having and observing in the wake of the Worcester fire. Among other things, it was an experience of profound unity, connection, oneness, one that for many brought intimations of the sacred, the holy. More was involved than a sense of common purpose or community. In addition, there was a sense of the Jamesian "MORE," an excess, at once rooted in what was right there before us and somehow overflowing from it. Let us see whether we can get better hold of this idea. James, you will recall, spoke of those experiences in which the individual becomes conscious not only of a "higher part" of his or her being, but also of the sense *"that this higher part is conterminous and continuous with a MORE of the same quality, which is operative in the universe outside of him, and which he can keep in working touch with, and in a fashion get on board of and save himself when all his lower being has gone to pieces in the wreck"* (1982 [1902], p. 508). It is a kind of saving grace, therefore, bearing within it a promise of redemptive reconciliation, not unlike that which we encountered in our discussion of music: ambiguity, complexity, and chaos are contained and reconciled in harmony. James himself explicitly considers this idea of harmony when he raises the question of truth: "the part of the content concerning which the question of truth most pertinently arises is that 'MORE of the same quality' with which our own higher self appears in the experience to come into harmonious working relation" (p. 510).

The MORE, therefore, is experienced both *within* and *without*, the "higher part" that is felt to exist within us being, at one and the same time, intimately and necessarily related to what is Other, resulting in just that state of "union" that "religious geniuses" and the like so often recount. Now, there is no questioning the MORE we feel within; it is simply a phenomenological fact. So too is the MORE felt to be outside of ourselves, beyond us, with which we find ourselves in contact. It too is a phenomenological fact, and at the level of sheer lived experience it is unassailable. We can, of course, go on to ask with James whether it "really exists"—that is, whether what is *felt* to be there is *actually* there—and, as we saw in the previous chapter, the kind of answer we provide has important implications for how we think about the human condition. Here, however, I am more interested in the phenomenology and the question of how such experiences might emerge.

It is not entirely clear to me still why the kinds of transcendent experiences James and others have considered emerge so readily in the wake of catastrophes, tragedies, and maladies, but it surely has something to do with the redemptive reconciliation discussed above. Ordinarily, we exist in state not only of ordinary oblivion but of what might be called a kind of *monadic dispersion*. We go about our own business, intersecting with others—at the dinner table, the department meeting, wherever—but basically doing our own thing (perhaps with a smartphone nearby). There is no particular reason to condemn this state of affairs; it is what it is. What catastrophes do is interrupt and massively disrupt this dispersion and pervasive internality by providing a common object, as it were. In this very basic and colloquial sense, this object therefore *transcends* us and can become a focus of shared attention and care. By being a focus of shared attention and care, wrapped in one another, it can also become an object of devotion, calling forth a kind of sustained being-there-for that is also shared. One may be reminded here of Émile Durkheim's classic, *The Elementary Forms of Religious Life* (2008 [1912]), in which he posits the centrality of the social dimension of religious life, specifically, the idea that, at its base, religious life emerges in connection to shared sacred objects, shared *Others*—totem animals, perhaps—that serve to orient and direct the moral and spiritual energies of a given community. I am not claiming that what is felt in the wake of catastrophes such as the Worcester fire is explicitly religious; this would be to take the idea of the religious a step too far. What I certainly would claim is that such experiences contain the rudiments of religious life—rudiments that, for many, can and do in fact assume explicitly religious form.

Can there be shared objects of this sort that are non-catastrophic in nature? In a way—coronations, royal weddings, some elections. Wondrous and joyous though these occasions may be, however, they generally do not yield the same kind of *communitas*[16] as the catastrophic. In part, this is because they are not "unbidden," as I put it before, but anticipated, and usually through the multicolored filter of the media. As such, they generally do not have quite the same degree of power that a collective "surprise"

---

16. By "communitas," I refer essentially to the experience of togetherness and belonging that sometimes emerges in the context of social life. Durkheim's work is again relevant here. So too are the anthropological investigations of Victor Turner (e.g., 1982). For an examination of the exuberant side of communitas, see also Barbara Ehrenreich's *Dancing in the Streets: A History of Collective Joy* (2007).

has, whether a fire, a tsunami, or a mass killing.[17] What also differentiates the catastrophic and the tragic from these more joyous communal events is that the former tend to call forth our moral and ethical energies in a way that the latter do not.[18] Finally, and perhaps most important, catastrophic events tend to have a social "leveling" effect, which is to say, their effects tend to be shared among categories and classes of people that ordinarily remain apart. Put another way, such events call forth our common *humanity*, and in doing so they can provide an image of oneness, of sharing and belonging and solidarity, that is all too rare. Moreover, this sharing, belonging, and solidarity, infused by the aforementioned moral and ethical energies, have as their ultimate object others' vulnerability and need, their pain and their suffering. They therefore have as their object the priority of the Other, and it is this very priority, so real and clear and self-evident, that makes these experiences as powerful, and in some ways incomparable, as they are.

As I have stated several times, I am reluctant to posit the *necessity* of the catastrophic or tragic in fostering our self-awakening. The simple fact that the birth of a child (for instance) can yield something similar is evidence that our recognition of the priority of the Other may emerge in decidedly "happier" contexts. *Natality* can be every bit as powerful, and transformative, as mortality. With this idea, we return to a question posed back in

---

17. Tragically enough, there have been several mass killings since I initially wrote these words. The most recent one, in Newtown, Connecticut, provides an all too apt example of just this aspect of communitas being considered. It is interesting to ask why this event seemed to call forth much more attention than the one before it, in Aurora, Colorado. One likely reason is the sheer magnitude of it. More likely is the fact that children were involved, many of them, their innocence serving to unite people that much more intensely and forcefully.

18. As Ehrenrich notes in her (2007) book, there are numerous examples of collective celebration and revelry that one might point toward as counter-instances. One might also look toward such various comings-together as the hippie-laden 1960s and gargantuan sports arenas where athletes (generally under the banner of some totemic animal) frequently whip fans into ecstatic frenzies, both wonderful and horrible. In the case of collective celebration and revelry—for instance, politically motivated "dancing in the streets" of the sort witnessed during the Arab Spring—there does of course remain an explicit moral and ethical component; so too with the hippie movement (though it could occasionally be somewhat hazy). As for the kind of exuberance found in conjunction with sports, extraordinary though it sometimes is, I am reluctant to accord it the kind of transcendent status we have been considering, partly because the moral/ethical dimension is largely absent, partly because the experiences in question don't involve comparable "realizations" (e.g., of our humanity or mortality, or of true priorities), and partly because whatever "oneness" they might provide tends to be restricted to the community of fans rather than some larger one. Having said this, I must say that the New England Patriots game I saw just last night was pretty amazing and generated some nice fellow-feeling at the local bar.

Chapter Two, when we asked what sorts of options for unselfing there might be beyond the catastrophic. What sorts of objects or experiences might do a comparable kind of unifying, reconciling, morally and ethically infused work? I have been wrestling with this issue for some time—so long, in fact, that I postponed completing this very chapter. Could there be a happy ending to this book? *Should* there be? Were there things to be said, by way of directives or directions, that weren't simply truistic, self-helpish bromides for those needing answers (including me)?

I could go the way of numerous others and dig deeper into the possibilities of meditation and other such self-altering practices, but as I noted at the outset of this chapter, others far more knowledgeable about such matters than me have already done so. And, if truth be told, it is not where I am most inclined to play out my own way of thinking and being vis-à-vis the priority of the Other. However much these practices can and do attune one to the priority of the Other, they are largely solitary in nature, the "object" at hand mainly being one's own inner processes. There is also concern for self-care, even self-love, and important though such processes surely are—perhaps serving as prerequisites for caring for and loving the Other—they too are essentially self-directed, inward looking, and are thus in something of a tension with the kind of Other-directed focus I have adopted here. I want to be clear about this. These practices are extremely valuable and important, and people who take them seriously frequently derive great and enduring benefit. I also believe that the world would be a better place if more people pursued them—kinder, gentler, softer, wiser. For the record, then, let me simply say: pursue them if you are at all inclined. I have every intention of doing so more seriously, and in a more disciplined way, than I have thus far. But I am after something different in this book, something that is more explicitly directed to the Other, as both nourishing source and source of ethical energy and desire.

In view of this, I might be led in the direction of more explicitly religious practices, oriented as they generally are toward the Other. Unquestionably, when one takes them seriously and pursues them with the proper discipline, it can have an enormous impact on both oneself and others. There is, however, one obvious problem with moving in this direction—namely, that many people have no interest whatsoever in turning to religion. I myself am ambivalent about it and am in no position to proselytize. Bearing this in mind, one might ask, is there a way to somehow "import" certain aspects of religious practice without bringing in all the dogmatic baggage that, for many, gets in the way? I realize that some may find my asking this question troubling. Religion without religion—the perfect modern solution! He gets to have his "spirituality," clothes it in the language of the Other, which gives it a nice quasi-religious patina, and spares himself the trouble of actually *believing* in something! I confess: this rendition isn't all that far from the truth. And it may be of value to pursue it just a bit further. Consider again the power of prayer. "What becomes of such a technique," Murdoch (1970) asks, "in a world without God, and can it be transformed to supply at least a part of the answer to our central question?" (p. 53) Prayer, she goes on to note, "is properly not petition, but simply attention to God, which is a form of love. With it goes the idea of grace, of a supernatural assistance to human endeavour which overcomes empirical limits of personality. What is this attention like, and can those who are not religious believers still conceive of profiting by such an activity?" (pp. 53–54)

These questions, some might say, hardly help the matter. Not only is Murdoch stripping religious practices of the very substance of religious life, but she is using the language of "profit" to boot. But let us continue on this path, for a while at any rate, "by considering what the traditional object of attention was like and by what means it affected its worshippers" (Murdoch, 1970, p. 54).[19] For starters, we can say that "God was (or is) a *single perfect transcendent non-representable and necessarily real object of attention.*" This doesn't necessarily mean that God is *real*, only that she or he (?) can and does serve, for many, as a real object of attention. Moreover, "that God, attended to, is a powerful source of (often good) energy, is a psychological fact" (p. 54). Where, then, does this leave us? For Murdoch, it leaves us on the lookout for *other* Others that, even if they are not of quite the same value as God, are at least comparable, in the running. For many, including Murdoch, great art is a worthy candidate, performing many of the same functions that God does for believers. For others, however, turning to art may not be deemed a whole lot more valuable than turning to God, and for much the same reason: unless one is a person of faith—in this case, *artistic* faith—it might be difficult to derive the sort of nourishing energy that Murdoch and company do. Indeed, it might seem every bit as illusory, a sham and a scam. This is too easy a criticism, and it is often borne simply out of ignorance. Nevertheless, I do not wish to proselytize about art either. It's just not where most people are, and nothing Murdoch or I or anyone else might say is likely to change that.

---

19. I apologize for Murdoch's use of the past tense. (Explicitly religious "objects of attention" remain alive and well for many.)

At this point, we are finding ourselves in the thick of modernity. I say "modernity" rather than "*post*modernity" for one very basic reason. Even though the advent of postmodernist and poststructuralist thinking promised a certain release from the ostensible strictures of "presence," culminating in the free play of meaning and value, it is not at all clear that this promise has been—or can be—realized.[20] This is because even "in a world without God" (Murdoch's words) and even in a world where the very idea of transcendence may be deemed little more than a (comparably) outdated form of nostalgia for those who need to hold on to "there is more than this" modes of thinking and being, there still remains evidence—powerful evidence—that the movement of our lives remains oriented *in some way* toward a transcendent reality and that attending to it, devotionally, is a vitally important source of both existential nourishment and ethical energy and commitment. Factually speaking, of course, not all people are so oriented; they may be oriented to virtually nothing at all or to those lesser "gods" that have come to serve as surrogates, crude substitutes, for what is truly Other. In this respect, it might be said that our orientation toward the transcendent frequently exists in inverted form. But this too bespeaks its presence, and in its own inverted way provides further testimony for the priority of the Other.

For simplicity's sake, and following Murdoch (and Plato) in broad outline, I will call this transcendent reality *Good*. I urge you not to be frightened or put off by this (admittedly loaded) word. Not unlike "God," it is easily corrupted and too readily leads to both false consolation and, more dangerously, absolutist claims about this or that object and what it *commands* us to do.[21] These very clear and obvious pitfalls and dangers notwithstanding, I would still hold that there is some *sense* to the idea of the Good and that it is mainly a modern prejudice that has blinded us to it. But why G̲ood rather than plain old good? Let me hazard an answer: precisely because it connotes a sphere of meaning and value that is *beyond* me, that I do not *choose*, and that is not merely my preference but that *transcends* me. Whether we locate this sphere in a metaphysically separate

---

20. See Freeman (1994, 2000a) for a more detailed exposition.

21. This point is not unrelated to my earlier comments about the idea of obedience. Important though this idea may be in redirecting our sense of what actually happens in (certain of) our encounters with the Other, it can also feed into a kind of unthinking and uncritical slavishness that can be troubling in its own right. All of these loaded words and ideas, therefore, might well come with a warning: *use with caution.*

realm is, again, a secondary matter. What is primary is the existence—and the *priority*—of the Other.

Shortly, I will be getting ready to go see my mother. As I have already acknowledged, there are all kinds of mundane reasons for my doing so. I avow them. But if I ask whether it is better to be there, with her and for her, than *not* be, the answer seems radiantly and unassailably clear. (Yes.) It is not a command. I am not a hostage. And, as I also acknowledged, other things sometimes take priority, not in some grand sense, but only in the sense that there are plenty of other things to do and that these things sometimes trump going to see Mom. But I have no doubt whatsoever that being there with her and giving her what I can is better than her being alone, in a stupor, feeling little, if anything, in the way of pleasure or meaning or love. Could *anyone* doubt this?

Later on I will be going to a party to celebrate the end of the year. Some of what goes on will likely be superficial and self-serving; other people will become phantoms, used for some purpose, whether conscious or unconscious. Egos will be involved; after all, it will be filled with academics. But if all goes well, some real human contact will be there too, maybe even some modest celebration of our shared interests, commitments, and lives. Perhaps we will feel some gratitude for being there or feel that, through it all, what we have together is a gift. I may be slipping into illusion here! (Office parties can move in just the opposite direction too.) But I also may not be. Is the existence of real human connection, celebration, and gratitude better than their absence?

I am tempted to raise some similar questions about the food and drink that will be there, though much more caution needs to be exercised. I, personally, am quite willing to speak of Good when it comes to wine. This doesn't mean that I didn't require some preparation to get there. Nor does it mean that there is some *ur*-wine that warrants designation as the Absolute Best. Preparation *is* required, and judgments about what is best vary considerably, even among the well-prepared.[22] The same is true of painting, music, and just about everything else. Even within relatively delimited categories—burgundies, abstract expressionism, improvisational jazz—there

---

22. For this reason, I have never been quite comfortable with *Wine Spectator* awarding 100 points for certain wines. That score connotes perfection, and even though the idea of perfection remains important as a standard against which things might be measured, it is not to be found in the earthly world. Having offered this qualification, it is only money (or the lack thereof) that prevents me from rushing out to buy a bottle of one of these near-perfect winners.

is bound to be such variability. Once we include cultural variability, historical variability, and so on, bold proclamations need to be uttered that much more cautiously. Finally, of course, there are personal preferences. Shocking though it is, some people simply don't *like* outstanding burgundies; they might find blush wines better, smoother and sweeter. (They'd just better not bring any to the party!) This is what makes the domains of wine and food (and art, music, etc.) more contestable than the domain of spending time with elderly parents or going to a holiday party. Is it possible that some people find the absence of human connection, celebration, and gratitude better than their presence? I suppose. (I hope they won't be at the party either.)

Recall for a moment what Murdoch said in the previous chapter about the idea of goodness: it involves the "discovery of something independent of us, where that independence is essential," an idea that "most people" (at least "non-philosophical people") "unreflectively hold." Where do we find this idea operative? In lots of places, actually—in the experience of truth, for instance, "which comes to us all the time in a weak form and comes to most of us sometimes in a strong form (in art or love or work or looking at nature) and which remains with us as a standard or vision" (1993, p. 508). Can this be doubted? Sure; anything can. But it takes some serious effort to do so.

Along the lines being drawn, I am not "calling" for anything—anything, that is, except an open and honest recognition of what we generally encounter in the world we inhabit. This in itself underscores the priority of the Other. *Thinking* the priority of the Other, therefore, requires little more than acknowledging the reality of experience and fashioning appropriate concepts in turn. As for *living* the priority of the Other, it has something to do with both awakening and becoming more attentive to what is there, in the fabric of the everyday, and finding those additional objects that might be powerful and loveable enough to expand our horizons and render us that much more compassionately connected to both the human and the non-human worlds. Can the idea of Good help us in any way? Difficulties remain, particularly if we take this idea to include some measure of harmony and unity, some process wherein the irrevocable disparateness of things is reconciled. "The notion that value should be in some sense unitary, or even that there should be a single supreme value concept, may seem, if one surrenders the idea of God, far from obvious," Murdoch (1970) acknowledges. "Why should there not be many different kinds of moral values? Why should all be one here?" In this context too, it is easy to slip into consoling illusions; "the difficulty is how to entertain this consoling notion in a way which is not false" (p. 55). The key, once again, is to look carefully at experience itself. "If we reflect on the nature of the virtues," Murdoch continues,

> we are constantly led to consider their relation to each other. The idea of an "order" of virtues suggests itself, although it might of course be difficult to state this in any systematic form. For instance, if we reflect upon courage and ask why we think it to be a virtue, what kind of courage is the highest, what distinguishes courage from rashness, ferocity, self-assertion, and so on, we are bound, in our explanation, to use the names of other virtues. The best kind of courage (that which would make a man act unselfishly in a concentration camp) is steadfast, calm, temperate, intelligent, loving.... This may not in fact be exactly the right description, but it is the right sort of description. (p. 56)

There *is* no "right description" in a case such as this one, nor can there be. Consequently, it is imperative that we do not "over-tighten" descriptions of this sort. But again, there is *sense* to what Murdoch is saying here. The presence of the suffering Other in the concentration camp calls forth my compassion. As Levi and others well know, this in no way ensures that I will act on his or her behalf; my own needs may be too great, my world too small. Whatever compassion I have might therefore be nullified. But can there be any doubt that being "steadfast, calm, temperate, intelligent," and, most of all, "loving" more closely approximates what we know goodness to be?

According to Murdoch (1970), such goodness is not there to be "seen." Beauty, therefore, is perhaps a clearer clue to transcendence. Paraphrasing Plato, from *Phaedrus*, "It is as if we can see beauty itself in a way in which we cannot see goodness itself.... I can experience the transcendence of the beautiful, but (I think) not the transcendence of the good. Beautiful things contain beauty in a way in which good acts do not exactly contain good," she explains, "because beauty is partly a matter of the senses. So if we speak of good as transcendent"—i.e., Good—"we are speaking of something rather more complicated and which cannot be experienced, even when we see the unselfish man in the concentration camp" (pp. 58–59). How, then, do we arrive at such judgments? "One might be tempted to use the word 'faith' here if it could be purged of its religious associations"

(p. 59). Perhaps: Jamesian "over-belief," revisited. It is true that there is a sensuous dimension to beauty that doesn't quite transfer over to goodness. It is also true, I suppose, that the issues are "rather more complicated" in the case of goodness. The stakes seem to be higher, at any rate. But *can't* we see goodness in that unselfish man or woman in the concentration camp? We don't see it *in the same way* as we do blue or red or green, but it is there right in front of us, visible enough that we ourselves might be inspired and moved, glad that he or she is there, glad that what has been done is a human possibility, glad that amidst horror and degradation and evil, there can still emerge *good*.

Even as this goodness is "right there in front of us," immanent, it is, at one and the same time, beyond us, transcendent. This is because in this very act we see that there exists a kind of penumbra or halo, an ex-centric energy, radiating outward, beyond the boundaries of that singular occurrence, pointing toward something...more.[23] I could be wrong about this. Maybe it simply "is what it is," no more, no less. And maybe that's enough. But I don't think so. If there weren't something more at work, something Other, mysterious though it may be, I wouldn't be inspired or moved or glad in the way just described. Why would I be? It could be more mechanical: when in the presence of such-and-such a stimulus (unselfish person), behave this way (be inspired, moved, glad). Or it might be more conventional: because Society has placed a (positive) value on unselfish behavior, I am led to see this (ultimately neutral) act as emblematic of "goodness," which in turn gets me all inspired, moved, and so on. I want to be clear about this. None of what I am claiming here means that we humans "are" good in some essential sense; it means only, and again, that we often know good when we see it. And this very knowing is unthinkable without there being some more primordial sphere informing this very seeing.

---

23. Robert Hass speaks to a related idea when he notes that "when a thing is seen clearly, there is a sense of absence about it—as if, the more palpable it is, the more some immense subterranean displacement seems to be working in it; as if at the point of truest observation the visible and the invisible exerted enormous counterpressure" (1984, p. 275). See also Maurice Merleau-Ponty's *The Visible and the Invisible* (1969) for related ideas. In reference to theological concerns, see Jean-Luc Marion's *The Visible and the Revealed* (2008). Marion's work, in particular, seeks to demonstrate the legitimacy of that which is not "directly visible." In his view, "phenomenology would be the method par excellence for the manifestation of the invisible through the phenomena that indicate it—hence also the method for theology" (pp. 7–8). His position is a controversial one; for some, making the move from phenomenology to theology is too much of a leap. Criticisms aside, Marion's attempt to clear a space for theological concerns through phenomenology strikes me as a valiant and important one.

Jean-Luc Nancy's (2011) reflections on "naming" the transcendent may be useful here: "God, or the divine, or the celestial, would name the fact that I am in relation not with something but with the fact that I am not limited to all those relations I have with all the things of the world, or even with all the beings of the world. It suggests that there is something else." Nancy refers to this "something else" as " 'the opening,' something that makes me be, that makes us be as humans open to something more than being in the world, more than being able to take things up, manipulate them, eat them, get around in the world, send space probes to Mars, look at galaxies through telescopes, and so on. It suggests that there is all this but also something else" (p. 13). What exactly is this something else?

> We have some idea of this other thing, and perhaps more than an idea, a feeling, through the fact, for example, that we know what it is to feel great joy or great sadness, what it is to feel love or...a feeling that is very far from love. When I have such feelings or moods I sense that there is something immense, infinite, which I cannot simply locate somewhere. For when I feel joy or sadness, love or hatred, force or weakness, there is in all this something that infinitely exceeds what I am, my person, my personality, my means, my location, my way of being someone in a particular place in the world. In all this there is some kind of opening. (p. 13)

For Nancy, "the god of the three monotheistic religions," among others, "represents nothing other than this" (p. 13). How, then, shall we live? More specifically, "What does it mean to be oneself as much as possible, and thus to be as much a human being as possible? It means nothing other than being faithful to this opening or to this infinite going beyond of the human by the human" (p. 16). Whether this being-faithful is directed to God (or "the gods") will of course vary. If Nancy is right, though, being "as much a human being as possible" entails living ex-centrically, finding in "the opening" a central source of our very being.[24]

---

24. See Heschel (1951) on the idea of "radical amazement." In psychology, see Kirk Schneider's *Rediscovery of Awe: Splendor, Mystery, and the Fluid Center of Life* (2004; also Schneider, 2009). Although Schneider's perspective is quite differerent than the one offered herein, there is a good deal of overlap as well. The rediscovery of awe, I suggest, frequently exists in tandem with the process of recognizing and upholding the priority of the Other. Does one of them lead to the other? Perhaps. (I am inclined to say that the former emerges as a function of the latter.) It is also possible, however, that these two terms represent different moments of a single indivisible process.

Practically speaking, all this talk about the Good, the "opening," and so on may be largely irrelevant. Just as the possible existence of some "metaphysically separate world" may be irrelevant to what actually transpires in experience (beauty remains beauty in either case), so too with the ideas under consideration now. Whether the goodness (or beauty or truth) we see before us now bespeaks the existence of some more primordial sphere, some Other, *prior* to this particular instance may not matter one whit. *Who cares, anyway?* And does any of this have anything to do with how we live?

It does, actually. Why? One reason has been adduced already: how we think about the world, and our place in it, very much affects the quality of our relationship to it. The second, more concrete and specific, reason is that a world that is ostensibly one of pure immanence, shorn of transcendent meaning and value, is a less than fully human one. Plus, *it is not where we live*. We are always already in a world radiant with energy, both ego-centric and ex-centric. We have been led to focus our attention more on the former than the latter, the result being a landscape that, for many, seems bereft of the Other's priority. Instances in which it emerges thus seem exceptional, which, on one level, they are. So we wait for those catastrophes to come along. But let us not forget: what these reveal to us had been there in some fashion all along.

To Remember

The challenge is to remember, not in the usual sense of looking backward—important though that is—but in the sense of re-collecting, gathering back, being present to what is already there, before us. Jacob Needleman has some interesting things to say about this challenge in the aforementioned book *Why Can't We Be Good?* (2007). There is a Self, he offers,

> which breaks through in the silence of sorrow or in the unbearable, impersonal outrage in the face of monstrous injustice, or in the adamantine quiet of the awareness of one's own inevitable death or, sometimes, in heartbreaking disappointment; or, always, in the trembling joy of the sensation of wonder in front of great nature or the face of the beloved, or at the birth of a new human life. (p. 183)

Bearing these sorts of experiences in mind, "the essential work of man is to remember the Self" (p. 185). As sympathetic as I am to much of what Needleman says in this spirited, provocative book, I am inclined to frame this "essential work" differently. "Remembering" is key, to be sure. But the challenge is to remember the Other; the Self will follow. Needleman seems to know this. Later on in the book, for instance, he writes,

> We are obliged to love, to care, and there can be no meaning, no real happiness in our lives unless we discover how to serve what is greater than ourselves, and with that how to serve our fellow man, our neighbor. We are not constructed to be happy in selfishness. Many have tried and many have gone to their graves bitterly assured that there was no moral imperative out there, that duty was only to one's little self, or that there was no such thing as duty. But the bitterness itself is ample evidence that they lost their lives to an illusion about life, an illusion often even rooted in the ideals of honesty in front of so obviously immoral and unjust a world. (pp. 244–245)[25]

As Needleman acknowledges, the challenge of remembering is a difficult one. Murdoch and others have told us that we are anxiety-ridden beings whose ego-driven preoccupations frequently obscure the world. This seems at least partially right. More pertinent for present purposes is the fact that we are also "amnesic" beings, prone to forgetting what is most real and true. One might also think of this as a kind of existential *inertia*—a "persistence in being," as Levinas (2001) puts it. It may in fact be "the normal order of things, the natural order of things" (p. 47), the "holiness" with which we might approach the Other thus constituting a "reversal" of this order. Yes and no. Yes: just as inertia in the physical world leads objects "to keep moving the same direction, unless affected by some outside source" (as my trusty *Webster's New World Dictionary* puts it), our existential inertia leads us to do much the same thing. But no: there is nothing "unnatural" about the holiness Levinas is speaking of, and the

---

25. In my view, Needleman's book is another prime example of a work in which there is frequently a contradiction between the "data" and the concepts employed to accommodate them. Much of the book is about the priority of the Other. Much of the theory, however, is about the priority of the Self. I therefore found myself "translating" much of what he had to say into language more applicable to the realities being considered. I will say more about this problem shortly, in the Coda.

only "reversal" is one of priority. The challenge, in any case, is to derail this inertia, take it off the beaten track.[26]

Catastrophes do this particularly well. So do our more routine encounters with people in need, who call forth our compassion and care. And so too do those glorious moments—falling in love, witnessing the birth of a child, feeling the incredible power of great music, with others, outside in the sun on a beautiful day—when something wondrously new emerges, not only derailing our inertia, but also reminding us of the great gift of being alive. We do not and cannot seek these moments; they are unbidden and unsought. Even when we know they are coming, as with the birth of a child, there is an element of surprise, of grace and gift; we cannot ever know what it is like until it happens, and when it does, we can be utterly staggered by its sheer improbable, inexpressible presence. Natality, we noted earlier, can be every bit as powerful as mortality, and the awesome can be every bit as life-changing, and priority-changing, as the awful.[27] Unbidden and unsought though such moments are, it would seem important, at times, to find occasions when they might come our way. This means living a life that is not only attentive and devotionally practiced, but also open and welcoming, of both large and small moments, the ones that shake us awake and the ones that gently come to us in our sleepy repose, inviting us to begin the day.

---

26. In a related vein, the meditation teacher and scholar Sharon Salzberg has spoken of "breaking the momentum." She uttered this phrase during the course of a retreat I went on last year. It strikes me still as a very apt description of the challenge at hand.

27. Rudolf Otto connects the two—the awe-inspiring and the "aweful"—in *The Idea of the Holy* (1958 [1923]) via the idea of "*mysterium tremendum*," which can "come sweeping like a gentle tide, pervading the mind with a tranquil mood of deepest worship" or "burst in sudden eruption up from the depths of the soul with spasms and convulsions, or lead to the strangest excitements, to intoxicated frenzy, to transport, and to ecstasy." It also has "its wild and demonic forms and can sink to an almost grisly horror and shuddering." Finally, and perhaps most centrally, "[i]t may become the hushed, trembling, and speechless humility of the creature in the presence of—whom or what? In the presence of that which is a *mystery* inexpressible and above all creatures" (p. 13). As for the idea of "the holy," Otto considers it as both an "*a priori* category of mind" and "as manifesting itself in outward appearance" (1958 [1923], p. 175). Should the same be said of "the Other"? As always, there is more thinking to be done.

Coda

A NEW LANGUAGE FOR PSYCHOLOGY AND BEYOND

FOUR WONDERFUL THINGS happened on today's bicycle ride (actually, there were more, but I will keep it at four). The first, which didn't so much "happen" as simply exist, was the day: December 22, in New England, famous for its harsh, unforgiving winters, 55 degrees, sunny and breezy! I don't have to watch morning shows on my spinning bike; I can go outside and ride on a real one! It was amazing, and everybody was feeling it. So, there I was, cruising along, through and then beyond the city streets, past a beautiful reservoir and up into the stillness of the woods. I always look forward to one particular spot where there is a lovely farm perched on a rolling hill, frequently dotted with horses and donkeys, grazing. This time, there was also a young woman standing just off the side of the road, holding a child, a baby, her wavy black hair blowing in the breeze. She looked at me and smiled as I whizzed by. I did the same. *Good God*. It was a vision, mythical. As I rode away, I found myself thinking something strange: I hope I never see her again. And on I rode. Eventually I descended from the hills and returned to the city streets. At one point, I encountered the shiny food truck that is always parked in an empty lot around lunchtime. For the first time, there was a blackboard sign perched on the gravelly shoulder of the road: "Eat here or we both starve." What a great sign! Then there was that intersection where I almost always stop completely and wait until all the cars and trucks, heading this way or that, have moved on. Talk about persistence in being. It sometimes takes a while for me to get going again; people sometimes deal with me as if I'm not even there. But today, there was one of those little yellow school buses, and the driver slowed to a crawl a solid hundred feet from the intersection, essentially inviting me to go first. Cars coming from other directions also stopped; that slowed-down bus had apparently served as a model for them. I was grateful to, and for, all of them.

Even though I said earlier that I wasn't "calling" for anything in this book, I will break my own rule and call for one small thing: *let the other person go first*. Perhaps you do already; if so, I apologize for the call. If you don't, just do it, beginning now; it makes for a better world. It might be interesting to note that one of Levinas's famous examples of the "holiness" referred to a short while ago is just this sort of situation—"the *après vous* before an open door" (2001, p. 47). He sees this as an example of the kind of "reversal" we are sometimes called to perform, his assumption again being that, fundamentally, it runs counter to "the normal order of things, the natural order of things." In view of what happens at intersections in Worcester, I give him the former, but not the latter—especially if he is speaking not only about persistence in being, our inertia, but about the priority of our natural egotism, "me-firstness." We do not step out of the natural order of things to uphold the priority of the Other! "Unnecessary" though it may be for me to extend a courtesy to another person, or go see Mom, or for the concentration camp prisoner to give his or her meager ration of bread to someone hungrier and needier, there is nothing in the least "unnatural" about doing so. This is not a plea for naturalism, for the idea that the natural order is the only one; we have already had reason to question that assumption. Instead, it is a simple recognition of the fact that we, human beings, possess "reserves" of care and love, for both the human and the non-human world.

These reserves, I have said, exist only *in potentia*. Some can access them; others cannot. Nothing is necessary, automatic, or inevitable, only possible. Some effort is required. This effort is not so much a digging-in to my will, my freedom, as it is a remembering, issuing from the call of the Other. Heeding this call involves not only seeing but listening. Neither is easy. There is no prospect of completely removing the veil over the world; Simone Weil's wish—to see the world as it is when she isn't there to disturb it—is not to be granted. Something similar holds true of listening. There is a lot of interference, a lot of noise, so the Other's call is often quite faint. So, yes, there is inertia, and at times alienation; as a result, we fail to derive nourishment from the world and fail to send it back, to "recycle" our good energy, to and for the Other, both human and non-. We can do better.

We can also *think* better. And one way to begin doing so is by fashioning a new language for depicting the human realm. It is not the language of "altruism," of the good presumed (hoped?) to be within us. It is not the language of "happiness." This too refers mainly to me, and although it is hardly stretching things to claim that most people would rather be happy than not, it is not at all clear whether we can, or should, build a psychology around it. Nor is it the language of "agency." Positing agency often serves as a kind of antidote to crudely deterministic thinking. It is also a way of retaining what many, rightly, take to be our essential humanness. The project is a good and worthwhile one. But however sensitively and subtly it is crafted, the focus remains essentially, and irrevocably, ego-centric. Moreover, it tends to occlude the formative and transformative process whereby this agency is called forth—indeed, constituted and brought into being. None of this is to deny agency; far from it. My aim instead is to properly locate it and to underscore the fact that it cannot, and should not, serve as a starting point, much less a foundation, either for psychology or for the world beyond it.

It is not the language of "construction." That much of what we experience and take to be good, true, and beautiful is socially and culturally constructed is surely so, and it has been important for psychology to recognize this. But it can evaporate the world; it can fail to lend it the credence, and the realness, it so palpably has. I cannot be nourished by a construction, but only by something in the world, something apart from me, different from me, *other*. And even if the power and presence of this thing—or person—is purely local, emerging out of this or that specific social-cultural-historical surround, this power and presence remains. Tracing the trajectory of this emergence is also a good and worthwhile thing to do. But it is no substitute for exploring what is there, in the world.

Much the same may be said of neuroscience. People are no doubt busy in their labs at this very moment, trying to locate those sorts of biochemical processes that are thought to "give rise" to agency, will, consciousness, the seemingly sovereign (but in reality not so sovereign) *I*. The location will be somewhere in the meaty folds of the brain. Homage will be paid, and rightly so, to this extraordinary organ. I very much hope this good work continues. It is immensely important—the brain is the "that without which" there can *be* no agency, will, consciousness, or anything else: no brain, no mind. Not unlike what was just said about "construction," tracing the trajectory of the emergence of these notable human characteristics is thus a good and valuable thing to do. But it says absolutely nothing about the world of experience itself, and it would be a grave mistake for psychology to come to believe that the language of neuroscience will somehow allow it, finally, to come into its own. In reality, the opposite is more likely: the ascendancy of neuroscience spells the possible demise of psychology, our attention being shifted ever inward, ever *brain*-ward, toward the microscopic realities at hand.

In moving ever inward in this way, it is not only "experience itself" that is left behind but the *Other*. It's true: when I am moved by a gorgeous piece of music or a beautiful day, or when I feel another's pain and am moved to be there for her, there is unquestionably something going on internally, microscopically, that makes it possible. The problem, however, is that thinking this way about experience tends to render the Other— the music, the day, the other person—virtually incidental. And the fact of the matter is that it is not. *The Other comes first.* Only by encountering it, before me, can I be moved—with the help of all those microscopic processes. One may be reminded here of the process of photosynthesis. Just as plants "make their own food," we, it is sometimes said, make our own world. But these are partial truths at best. Plants require sunlight. And we require the world, which is there, given and giving, well before our arrival, before our constructions, and before our brains kick into gear. Acknowledging the priority of the Other might therefore be considered "first psychology." It is another form of the "that without which" there can be no agency, no will, no consciousness, no *anything*.[1] This time, however, we can remain with experience, with our relation to the world. We can remain within psychology as well.

But how? Bearing this last idea in mind, it might be argued that this approach, too, spells the possible end of psychology as we know it. This is true. The challenge is therefore to know it differently. Fashioning a new language is key. This language is the language of the Other. It is a language, I believe, that better accommodates the world of meaning, value, and existential nourishment, as well as the world of ethical comportment and commitment, better than the one we currently have. Meaning, value, and nourishment do not, and cannot, come from me. Nor can the energies that lead me to be there for other people or the environment or the countless other "causes" that exist, calling forth my care and devotion. These energies also derive from what is Other. By speaking and thinking

---

1. Plato's metaphor of the sun in *The Republic* (2003), referred to earlier, is of course relevant here as well. Just as the sun is that without which there can be no life, the Good is that without which there can be nothing at all. In this respect, Plato's musings were very much about the priority of the Other.

Otherwise, we may have in hand both a more truthful account of the human situation and a more adequate foundation for imagining how we might live.

What exactly does this mean, though? How might such speaking and thinking be enacted? One very basic way is by translating some of the language currently being employed into different—that is, Other—terms. As I suggested early on, we have been bequeathed a language that is largely ego-centric in its outlook and perspective. As I have also suggested, this language is frequently belied by experience: we use the language of self when that of the Other is more fitting, or we posit the priority of freedom when responsibility actually comes first. There are numerous such examples, and we would do well to look at them anew and see whether the language of the Other might do better to describe them. I see this as a practical matter. Sometimes it will not work; the "old" language may still seem more fitting and appropriate. But it seems worthwhile to shift our view and see where it gets us. I am convinced the process will be a productive one.

In narrative psychology, for instance, the main focus still tends to be the self. This self might be framed relationally or dialogically, and it might even be argued that there *is* no self apart from its conversations and interactions with others. Nevertheless, the stories that emerge are still seen to issue largely from one's own narrative processes. This makes good sense: my story is a story like no other, and however much others might have contributed to it, there is no escaping its "mineness," its belonging, fundamentally, to me. At the same time, this story, in its very mineness, receives its form and meaning from what exists beyond it—from my sense of what is good and worthwhile to be and do, my commitments, the various spheres of otherness to which I am devoted. All this can change: what I had once taken to be good becomes less so, and so I shift my sense of what it's all about. I make new choices, new commitments. But these choices have been inspired by the Other, by new devotional objects, ones that better articulate the goods that draw me forward, if only for now. This process is frequently referred to as "individual development"—which, on some level, it is (e.g., Freeman, 2010). But this very developmental process is unthinkable without invoking the priority of the Other. Indeed, in a very real sense, "my story" issues from the Other, and undertaking the kind of translational work I am proposing may help us see such transformational processes anew.

A second way in which speaking and thinking Otherwise might be enacted is phenomenological: we should do what we can—as researchers, therapists, and human beings—to preserve the otherness of other people. This is at once obvious and, given the nature of contemporary psychology, all too rare. Buber (1970) puts the matter well: "Even as a melody is not composed of tones, nor a verse of words, nor a statue of lines—one must pull and tear to turn a unity into a multiplicity—so it is with the human being to whom I say You. I can abstract from him the color of his hair or the color of his speech or the color of his graciousness; I have to do this again and again; but immediately he is no longer You" (p. 59). This is largely the way of the discipline. We have categories and constructs aplenty, inventories and other such sortings. They can be useful. But they tend to obscure the person, the You, with whom we might be engaged. One way of enacting the priority of the Other is to make our way more readily from the I–It mode to the I–You mode. A number of current practices move in this direction—for instance, certain strands of phenomenological psychology, narrative psychology, and relational psychology, including relational psychoanalysis. But much more can, and should, be done. It is a matter of *respect*. It is also a matter of *truth*, of being adequate to the phenomena (Freeman, 2004a). Academic psychology, in its very (manifest) scientificity, frequently obscures the truth, substituting for it its countless categories and constructs. Speaking and thinking Otherwise can help restore it, on a deeper, more real and secure plane.

Third, there might be more attention devoted to the specific kinds of concerns that have been addressed throughout the pages of this book: the sources of existential nourishment and of ethical energy and commitment; the meaning of transcendence; the mysterious power of both the visible and the invisible, in art, religion, and beyond. It is time, I propose, to bring these concerns more fully into view, not just as purely subjective experiences or "variables" but as meaningful human phenomena in their own right, phenomena that might in fact open up our very idea of what is *real*. The challenges are large, indeed. Speaking cogently about the visible is difficult enough; how are we to speak about the *in*visible and other such elusives? How, for that matter, are we to speak about the *Other*? At least ego-centric language has kept things close to home. Ex-centric language moves away from this home—or, put differently, extends it out into the world. What kind of psychology can possibly deal with this? And what kind of philosophy?

Gabriel Marcel's words come to mind: "It should by now be very clear," he writes, "that a philosophy of this sort is essentially of the nature of a kind of appeal to the listener or reader, of a kind of call upon his inner resources. In other words, such a philosophy could never be completely embodied into a kind of dogmatic exposition of which the listener or reader would merely have to grasp the content" (1950, p. 262). Murdoch conveys a similar idea when she considers how to speak about the Good. "If someone says, 'Do you then believe that the idea of the Good exists?' I reply, 'No, not as people used to think that God existed' "—that is, as some sort of "entity," *thing*. "All one can do is appeal to certain areas of experience pointing out certain features, and using suitable metaphors and inventing suitable concepts where necessary to make these features visible" (1970, p. 73). The project is an artful one, for "it is the height of art to be able to show what is nearest, what is deeply and obviously true but usually invisible" (Murdoch, 1993, p. 90).

These statements seem right to me. Indeed, not only is there no room here for "dogmatic exposition," but there may be no room for *theory*, at least as we know it. This doesn't mean completely abandoning it, however. Again, it means knowing it differently—less as a vehicle of capture and containment, wherein one seeks to "grasp the content," and more as one of articulation, making-visible, *poiesis*. Bearing this in mind, let me take the liberty of citing a piece of my own (Freeman, 2000a) that addresses this idea explicitly:

> The project of theory, which "entraps the real and secures it in its objectness" (Heidegger, 1977, p. 168), is correlative with the primacy of the sovereign subject, the Cartesian *cogito*, seeking to represent the world qua object, thing, *It*. The displacement of emphasis from the *cogito* to the Other, in turn, requires the movement beyond theory, toward the poetic, where truth becomes less a matter of adequacy to the object than fidelity—phenomenological *and* ethical—to others, particularly those in need, who call forth our responsiveness and care. (p. 76)

Hence the idea of what I then referred to as a "poetics of the Other." Having spoken up to this point in the piece exclusively of people, I went on to consider those non-human regions of otherness found, among other places, in aesthetic and religious experience. "These too entail the displacement of the *cogito* and, arguably, require different modes of thinking and writing than those ordinarily associated with theoretical reflection" (p. 76).

The challenge at hand has intensified. This is because insofar as we deal with these domains of experience vis-à-vis the priority of the Other—that is, in their potentially invisible, ineffable otherness—we will have stepped beyond the bounds of theory, as we know it, into the realm of the "untheorizable." Traditionally, the untheorizable has been banished from psychology, given over to philosophers, theologians, and artists, those more willing to speak to these amorphous, uncontainable realities. This, however, is a serious mistake, for this banishment has excluded from our purview some of those very phenomena that are the heart of human existence. The implication? There is the need to somehow *theorize the untheorizable*, as I had put it—that is, include within the scope of the theoretical enterprise precisely those regions of experience that appear to exceed theoretical representation.

How is this possible? George Steiner has suggested that "The word 'theory' has lost its birthright. At the source it draws on meanings both secular and ritual. It tells of concentrated insight, of an act of contemplation focused patiently on its object" (1989, p. 69). The idea of attention is surely relevant here, as is devotion. Sometime during the latter half of the 16th century, "with the inward shift and displacement of understanding into the ego," the term became associated with a "subjective speculative impulse" to be "tested and proved by corresponding facts, by the mirroring evidence of empirical reality" (p. 70). Heidegger (1977) has also noted that the Greek idea of *theōria*, which he translates as "the reverent paying heed to the unconcealment of what presences" (p. 164), has largely been superseded—indeed, "buried"—by the modern version. Theory "at the source" thus sounds much more like the making-visible we now associate with *poiesis*. "The movement toward a poetics of the Other, therefore," I concluded, "far from representing the wholesale abandonment of the theoretical enterprise, may more appropriately be framed as an attempt to fashion *theory beyond theory*" (Freeman, 2000a, p. 77).

I can still sign on to this idea today, but with one small change: rather than speaking of theory "beyond" theory, we would do better to speak of theory *before* theory, as we have come to know it. I am not merely referring to the "older" version that Steiner and Heidegger are thinking of. I am referring instead to one that is *prior* in a deeper way and that is directed to the Other, to what comes before me, igniting my desire to know and to be, to care and to love. This too calls for a new language, one that is more poetic in nature, better able to articulate those dimensions of experience that are drawn forth by the Other. I refer to the poetic here not for the sake of ornamentation or flourish, but for the sake of using language, using *words*, in a way that is adequate to experience. I have come to call this basic project *poetic science*. My hope is that it will make for a more human, and humane, psychology as well as a more adequate vehicle for recognizing the priority of the Other in the shaping of our lives.

References

Ackerman, D. (1999). *Deep Play*. New York: Random House.
Antelme, R. (1992). *Human Race*. Evanston, IL: Marlboro Press.
Antonaccio, M. (2000). *Picturing the human: The moral thought of Iris Murdoch*. New York: Oxford University Press.
Antonaccio, M. & Schweiker, W. (Eds.). (1996). *Iris Murdoch and the search for human goodness*. Chicago, IL: University of Chicago Press.
Arendt, H. (1965). *Eichmann in Jerusalem: A report on the banality of evil*. New York: Penguin Classics.
Armstrong, K. (2011). *Twelve steps to a compassionate life*. New York and Toronto: Alfred A. Knopf.
Aron, L. & Mitchell, S. A. (Eds.). (1999). *Relational psychoanalysis, Vol. 1: The emergence of a tradition*. London and New York: Routledge.
Bakhtin, M. M. (1981). *The dialogic imagination*. Austin, TX: University of Texas Press.
Bakhtin, M. M. (1986). *Speech genres and other late essays*. Austin, TX: University of Texas Press.
Barnard, C. W. (1998). William James and the origins of mystical experience. In R. C. Forman (Ed.), *The innate capacity: Mysticism, psychology, and philosophy* (pp. 161–210). New York: Oxford University Press.
Baudelaire, C. (1981). *Baudelaire: Selected writings on art and artists*. Translated by P. E. Charvet. New York: Cambridge University Press, p. 256.
Becker, E. (1973). *The denial of death*. New York: Free Press.
Bellah, R., Madsen, R., Sullivan, W. M., & Swidler, A. (1985) *Habits of the heart: Individualism and commitment in American life*. Berkeley, CA: University of California Press.
Belzen, J. A. (1997a). Cultural psychology of religion: synchronic and diachronic. In J. A. Belzen (Ed.), *Hermeneutical approaches in psychology of religion* (pp. 109–128). Amsterdam: Editions Rodopi.

Belzen, J. A. (1997b). The inclusion of the excluded? A paradox in the historiography of psychology of religion. *Teori & Modelli, Rivista di storia e metodologia della psicologia, 2*, 41–64.

Belzen, J. A. (2010). *Towards cultural psychology of religion: Principles, approaches, applications.* New York: Springer.

Benson, C. (1993). *The absorbed self: Pragmatism, psychology and aesthetic experience.* New York: Harvester/Wheatsheaf.

Birkerts, S. (2006). *The Gutenberg elegies: The fate of reading in an electronic age.* New York: Faber & Faber.

Bloechl, J. (2000). *Liturgy of the neighbor: Emmanuel Levinas and the religion of responsibility.* Pittsburgh, PA: Duquesne University Press.

Bloom, H. (1996). *Omens of millennium.* New York: Riverhead Books.

Bollas, C. (1992). *Being a character: Psychoanalysis and self experience.* New York: Hill and Wang.

Bonnefoy, Y. (1989). *The act and place of poetry.* Chicago, IL: University of Chicago Press.

Buber, M. (1965). *Between man and man.* New York: Macmillan Publishing Company.

Buber, M. (1970). *I and thou.* New York: Charles Scribner's Sons.

Buber, M. (1998). *The knowledge of man: Selected Essays.* Amherst, NY: Humanity Books. (Original work published 1965)

Caputo, J. D. & Scanlon, M. J. (Eds.). (2007). *Transcendence and beyond: A postmodern inquiry.* Indianapolis, IN: Indiana University Press.

Coles, R. (2001). *Simone Weil: A modern pilgrimage.* Woodstock, VT: Skylights Paths Publishing.

Cording, R. (1991). *What binds us to this world.* Providence, RI: Copper Beech Press.

Crites, S. (1971). The narrative quality of experience. *Journal of the American Academy of Religion, XXXIX*, 291–311.

Csikszentmihalyi, M. (1990). *Flow: Toward a psychology of optimal experience.* New York: Harper Collins.

Csikszentmihalyi, M. (1994). *The evolving self: A psychology for the third millennium.* New York: Harper Perennial.

Cushman, P. (1990). Why the self is empty. *American Psychologist, 45*, 599–611.

Cushman, P. (1995). *Constructing the self, constructing America: A cultural history of psychotherapy.* Garden City, NY: DaCapo Press.

Darwin, C. (2010). *The descent of man.* New York: Dover. (Original work published 1872)

Dawkins, R. (2008). *The God delusion.* Boston: Houghton Mifflin.

Du Plessix Gray, F. (2001). *Simone Weil.* New York: Penguin.

Dupré, L. (1976). *Transcendent selfhood: The rediscovery of the inner life.* New York: The Seabury Press.

Dupré, L. (1998). *Religious mystery and rational reflection.* Grand Rapids, MI: William Eerdmans Publishing Company.

Durkheim, E. (2008). *The elementary forms of the religious life.* New York: Oxford University Press. (Original work published 1912)

Dustin, C. & Ziegler, J. (2007). *Practicing mortality: Art, philosophy, and contemplative seeing*. New York: Palgrave Macmillan.

Eagleton, T. (2011). *Reason, faith, and revolution: Reflections on the God debate*. New Haven, CT: Yale University Press.

Edwards, J. C. (1997). *The plain sense of things: The fate of religion in an age of normal nihilism*. University Park, PA: The Pennsylvania State University Press.

Ehrenreich, B. (2007). *Dancing in the streets: A history of collective joy*. New York: Metropolitan Books.

Ehrenzweig, A. (1971). *The hidden order of art: A study in the psychology of artistic imagination*. Berkeley, CA: University of California Press.

Epstein, M. (2005). *Open to desire: The truth about what the Buddha taught*. New York: Gotham Books.

Farley, W. (1996). *Eros for the other*. University Park, PA: The Pennsylvania State University Press.

Faulconer, J. E. (Ed.). (2003). *Transcendence in philosophy and religion*. Indianapolis, IN: Indiana University Press.

Fiedler, L. (1951). Introduction. In S. Weil, *Waiting for God* (pp. 3–39). New York: Perennial Library.

Finch, H. L. (2001). *Simone Weil and the intellect of grace*. New York: Continuum.

Flournoy, T. (1903). Les principes de la psychologie religieuse [The principles of religious psychology]. *Archives de Psychologie, 2*, 33–57.

Forman, R. K. C. (1990). Introduction: Mysticism, constructivism, and forgetting. In R. K. C. Forman (Ed.), *The problem of pure consciousness: Mysticism and philosophy* (pp. 3–49). New York: Oxford University Press.

Forman, R. K. C. (1998). Introduction: Mystical consciousness, the innate capacity, and the Perennial Psychology. In R. K. C. Forman (Ed.), *The innate capacity: Mysticism, psychology, and philosophy* (pp. 3–41). New York: Oxford University Press.

Forman, R. K. C. (2011). *Enlightenment ain't what it's cracked up to be: A journey of discovery, snow and jazz in the soul*. Winchester, UK: O-Books.

Frankl, V. (1960). *Man's search for meaning*. New York: Washington Square Books.

Freeman, M. (1993). *Rewriting the self: History, memory, narrative*. London: Routledge.

Freeman, M. (1994). *Finding the muse: A sociopsychological inquiry into the conditions of artistic creativity*. New York: Cambridge University Press.

Freeman, M. (1997). Death, narrative integrity, and the radical challenge of self-understanding: A reading of Tolstoy's *Death of Ivan Ilych*. *Ageing and Society, 17*, 373–398.

Freeman, M. (2000a). Modernists at heart? Postmodern artistic breakdowns and the question of identity. In D. Fee (Ed.), *Pathology and the postmodern: Mental illness as discourse and experience* (pp. 116–140). Beverly Hills, CA: Sage.

Freeman, M. (2000b). Theory beyond theory. *Theory & Psychology, 10*(1), 71–77.

Freeman, M. (2002). Charting the narrative unconscious: Cultural memory and the challenge of autobiography. *Narrative Inquiry, 12*, 193–211.

Freeman, M. (2004a). Data are everywhere: Narrative criticism in the literature of experience. In C. Daiute and C. Lightfoot (Eds.), *Narrative analysis: Studying the development of individuals in society* (pp. 63–81). Beverly Hills, CA: Sage.

Freeman, M. (2004b). The priority of the Other: Mysticism's challenge to the legacy of the self. In J. Belzen & A. Geels (Eds.), *Mysticism: A variety of psychological approaches* (pp. 213–234). Amsterdam: Rodopi.

Freeman, M. (2007). Narrative and relation: The place of the Other in the story of the self. In R. Josselson, A. Lieblich, & D. McAdams (Eds.), *The meaning of others: Narrative studies of relationships* (pp. 11–19). Washington, DC: APA Books.

Freeman, M. (2008). Life without narrative? Autobiography, dementia, and the nature of the real. In G. O. Mazur (Ed.), *Thirty year commemoration to the life of A.R. Luria* (pp. 129–144). New York: Semenko Foundation.

Freeman, M. (2009). The personal and beyond: Simone Weil and the necessity/limits of biography. In J. A. Belzen & A. Geels (Eds.), *Autobiography and the psychological study of religious lives* (pp. 187–207). Amsterdam/New York: Rodopi.

Freeman, M. (2010). *Hindsight: The promise and peril of looking backward*. New York: Oxford University Press.

Freeman, M. (2012). Thinking and being otherwise: Aesthetics, ethics, erotics. *Journal of Theoretical and Philosophical Psychology, 32*, 196–208.

Freeman, M. (2013). Listening to the claims of experience: Psychology and the question of transcendence. *Pastoral Psychology*, doi: 10.1007/s11089-013-0528-6

Freud, S. (1953). The Moses of Michelangelo. *Standard Edition XIII*, pp. 211–236. London: Hogarth. (Original work published 1914)

Freud, S. (1962). Civilization and its discontents. *Standard Edition XXI*. London: Hogarth. (Original work published 1930)

Gadamer, H.-G. (1976). *Philosophical hermeneutics*. Berkeley, CA: University of California Press.

Gadamer, H.-G. (1982). *Truth and method*. New York: Crossroad.

Gadamer, H.-G. (1986). *The relevance of the beautiful and other essays*. Cambridge, UK: Cambridge University Press.

Gallagher, W. (2009). *Rapt: Attention and the focused life*. New York: Penguin.

Gantt, E. E. & Williams, R. N. (Eds.). (2002). *Psychology for the other: Levinas, ethics and the practice of psychology*. Pittsburgh, PA: Duquesne University Press.

Gass, W. (1999) *Reading Rilke: Reflections on the problem of translation*. New York: Alfred A. Knopf.

Geertz, C. (1973). *The interpretation of cultures*. New York: Basic Books.

Geertz, C. (1983). *Local knowledge*. New York: Basic Books.

Gergen, K. J. (1992). *The saturated self: Dilemmas of identity in contemporary life*. New York: Basic Books.

Gergen, K. J. (2009). *Relational being: Beyond self and community*. New York: Oxford University Press.

Gilligan, C. (1982). *In a different voice: Psychological theory and women's development.* Cambridge, MA: Harvard University Press.

Goodman, D. M. (2012). *The demanded self: Levinasian ethics and identity in psychology.* Pittsburgh, PA: Duquesne University Press.

Goodman, D. M., Dueck, A., & Langdal, J. P. (2010). The "Heroic I": A Levinasian critique of Western narcissism. *Theory & Psychology, 20,* 667–685.

Guignon, C. (2004). *On being authentic.* London: Routledge.

Harris, S. (2005). *The end of faith: Religion, terror, and the future of reason.* New York: W. W. Norton.

Harvey, J. (1999). *In quest of spirit: Thoughts on music.* Berkeley, CA: University of California Press.

Hass, R. (1984). *Twentieth century pleasures: Prose on poetry.* Hopewell, NJ: The Ecco Press.

Heaney, S. (1995). *The redress of poetry.* New York: The Noonday Press.

Heidegger, M. (1962). *Being and time.* New York: Harper & Row. (Original work published 1927)

Heidegger, M. (1971). *Poetry, language, thought.* New York: Harper Colophon.

Heidegger, M. (1977). *The question concerning technology and other essays.* New York: Harper Torchbooks.

Hermans, H. J. M. (1996). Voicing the self: From information processing to dialogical interchange. *Psychological Bulletin, 119,* 31–50.

Hermans, H. J. M. & Kempen, H. J. G. (1993). *The dialogical self: Meaning as movement.* San Diego, CA: Academic Press.

Heschel, A. J. (1951). *Man is not alone: A philosophy of religion.* New York: Farrar, Straus and Giroux.

Higgins, K. M. (1991). *The music of our lives.* Philadelphia, PA: Temple University Press.

Hitchens, C. (2009). *God is not great: How religion poisons everything.* New York: Twelve.

Hollenback, J. (1996). *Mysticism: Experience, response, and empowerment.* University Park, PA: Pennsylvania State University Press.

Horgan, J. (2003). *Rational mysticism: Dispatches from the border between science and spirituality.* Boston, MA: Houghton Mifflin.

Inertia. (1978). In *Webster's New World Dictionary* (second college ed.). Cleveland, OH: William Collins/World Publishing.

James, W. (1950). *The principles of psychology.* Cambridge, MA: Harvard University Press. (Original work published 1890)

James, W. (1982). *The varieties of religious experience.* New York: Penguin. (Original work published 1902)

Jauss, H. R. (1989). *Question and answer: Forms of dialogic understanding.* Minneapolis, MN: University of Minnesota Press.

Jones, J. W. (1991). *Contemporary psychoanalysis and religion.* New Haven, CT: Yale University Press.

Jones, J. W. (1998). *In the middle of this road we call our life*. San Francisco, CA: HarperCollins.

Jourain, R. (1997). *Music, the brain, and ecstasy*. New York: William Morrow & Company.

Jung, C. G. (1933). *Modern man in search of a soul*. San Diego, CA: Harcourt Brace Jovanovich.

Kabat-Zinn, J. (2005). *Coming to our senses: Healing ourselves and the world through mindfulness*. New York: Hyperion.

Kandinsky, W. (1977). *Concerning the spiritual in art*. New York: Dover. (Original work published 1914)

Katz, S. T. (1978). Language, epistemology, and mysticism. In S. T. Katz (Ed.), *Mysticism and philosophical analysis* (pp. 22–74). New York: Oxford University Press.

Keen, S. (2010). *In the absence of God: Dwelling in the presence of the sacred*. New York: Harmony Books.

Kegan, R. (1998). *In over our heads: The mental demands of modern life*. Cambridge, MA: Harvard University Press.

Kerr, F. (1997). *Immortal longings: Versions of transcending humanity*. Notre Dame, IN: University of Notre Dame Press.

Kirschner, S. (2012). How not to other the other (and similarly impossible goals): Scenes from a psychoanalytic clinic and an inclusive classroom. *Journal of Theoretical and Philosophical Psychology, 32*, 214–229.

Kivy, P. (1990). *Music alone*. Ithaca, NY: Cornell University Press.

Kohn, A. (1990). *The brighter side of human nature: Altruism and empathy in everyday life*. New York: Basic Books.

Kripal, J. J. (2011). *Authors of the impossible: The paranormal and the sacred*. Chicago, IL: University of Chicago Press.

Kunz, G. (1998). *The paradox of power and weakness: Levinas and an alternative paradigm for psychology*. Albany, NY: SUNY Press.

Kunz, G. (2002). Simplicity, humility, patience. In E. E. Gantt & R. N. Williams (Eds.), *Psychology for the other: Levinas, ethics and the practice of psychology* (pp. 118–142). Pittsburgh, PA: Duquesne University Press.

Lasch, C. (1991). *The culture of narcissism: American life in an age of diminishing expectations*. New York: W. W. Norton.

Lear, J. (1998). *Open-minded: Working out the logic of the soul*. Cambridge, MA: Harvard University Press.

Leary, M. R. (2004). *The curse of the self: Self-awareness, egotism, and the quality of human life*. New York: Oxford University Press.

Levi, P. (1984). *The periodic table*. New York: Schocken.

Levi, P. (1989). *The drowned and the saved*. New York: Vintage.

Levinas, E. (1969). *Totality and infinity*. Pittsburgh, PA: Duquesne University Press.

Levinas, E. (1985). *Ethics and infinity*. Pittsburgh, PA: Duquesne University Press.

Levinas, E. (1994). *Outside the subject*. Stanford, CA: Stanford University Press.

Levinas, E. (1996a). God and philosophy. In A. T. Peperzak, S. Critchley, & R. Bernasconi (Eds.), *Emmanuel Levinas: Basic philosophical writings* (pp. 129–148). Bloomington, IN: Indiana University Press.

Levinas, E. (1996b). *Proper names*. Stanford, CA: Stanford University Press.

Levinas, E. (1996c). Substitution. In A. T. Peperzak, S. Critchley, & R. Bernasconi (Eds.), *Emmanuel Levinas: Basic philosophical writings* (pp. 80–95). Bloomington, IN: Indiana University Press.

Levinas, E. (1996d). Transcendence and height. In A. T. Peperzak, S. Critchley, & R. Bernasconi (Eds.), *Emmanuel Levinas: Basic philosophical writings* (pp. 11–32). Bloomington, IN: Indiana University Press.

Levinas, E. (1998). *Otherwise than being or beyond essence*. Pittsburgh, PA: Duquesne University Press.

Levinas, E. (1999a). *Alterity and transcendence*. New York: Columbia University Press.

Levinas, E. (1999b). *Of God who comes to mind*. Stanford, CA: Stanford University Press.

Levinas, E. (2000). *Entre nous*. New York: Columbia University Press.

Levinas, E. (2001). *Is it righteous to be?* Stanford, CA: Stanford University Press.

Levi-Strauss, C. (1970). *The raw and the cooked*. London: Jonathan Cape.

Lifton, R.J. (1993). *The protean self: Human resilience in an age of fragmentation*. New York: Basic Books.

Marcel, G. (1950). *The mystery of being, Vol. 1: Reflection and mystery*. New York: Henry Regnery Co.

Marcel, G. (1973). *Tragic wisdom and beyond*. Evanston, IL: Northwestern University Press.

Marion, J.-L. (2002a). *Being given: Toward a phenomenology of givenness*. Stanford, CA: Stanford University Press.

Marion, J.-L. (2002b). *In excess: Studies of saturated phenomena*. New York: Fordham University Press.

Marion, J.-L. (2007). *The erotic phenomenon*. Chicago, IL: The University of Chicago Press.

Marion, J.-L. (2008). *The visible and the revealed*. New York: Fordham University Press.

Martin, J., Sugarman, J. H., & Hickinbottom, S. (2009). *Persons: Understanding psychological selfhood and agency*. New York: Springer.

McKibben, W. (2004). *Enough: Staying human in an engineered age*. New York: Henry Holt and Company.

Merleau-Ponty, M. (1964a). *Sense and non-sense*. Evanston, IL: Northwestern University Press.

Merleau-Ponty, M. (1964b). *Signs*. Evanston, IL: Northwestern University Press.

Merleau-Ponty, M. (1969). *The visible and the invisible*. Evanston, IL: Northwestern University Press.

Midgley, M. (2010). *The solitary self: Darwin and the selfish gene*. Durham, UK: Acumen.

Miles, S. (Ed.). (1986). *Simone Weil: An anthology*. New York: Grove Press.

Mitchell, S. (1988). *Relational concepts in psychoanalysis: An integration.* Cambridge, MA: Harvard University Press.

Murdoch, I. (1970). *The sovereignty of good.* London: Routledge.

Murdoch, I. (1993). *Metaphysics as a guide to morals.* New York: Penguin Books.

Murdoch, I. (1998). *Existentialists and mystics.* New York: Penguin Books.

Nancy, J.-L. (2007). *Listening.* New York: Fordham University Press.

Nancy, J.-L. (2011). *God, justice, love, beauty: Four little dialogues.* New York: Fordham University Press.

Needleman, J. (2007). *Why can't we be good?* New York: Tarcher.

Nussbaum, M. (1990). *Love's knowledge: Essays on philosophy and literature.* Oxford, UK: Oxford University Press.

Orange, D. (2011). *The suffering stranger: Hermeneutics for everyday clinical practice.* New York: Routledge.

Otto, R. (1958). *The idea of the holy.* Oxford, UK: Oxford University Press. (Original work published 1923)

Parsons, W. (1999). *The enigma of the oceanic feeling: Revising the psychoanalytic theory of mysticism.* Oxford, UK: Oxford University Press.

Perrin, J. M. (1953). Simone Weil in her religious search. In J. M. Perrin & G. Thibon, *Simone Weil as we knew her* (pp. 11–108). London: Routledge and Kegan Paul.

Plato. (1995). *Phaedrus.* Indianapolis, IN: Hackett.

Plato. (2003). *The republic.* New York: Penguin.

Post, S. G., Underwood, L. G., Schloss, J. P., & Hurlburt, W. B. (Eds.). (2002). *Altruism and altruistic love: Science, philosophy, and religion in dialogue.* New York: Oxford University Press.

Proudfoot, W. (1986). *Religious experience.* Berkeley, CA: University of California Press.

Ratushinskaya, I. (1988). *Grey is the color of hope.* New York: Knopf.

Richardson, F. C., Fowers, B. J., & Guignon, C. B. (1999). *Re-envisioning psychology: Moral dimensions of theory and practice.* San Francisco, CA: Jossey-Bass.

Ricoeur, P. (1970). *Freud and philosophy: An essay on interpretation.* New Haven: Yale University Press.

Ricoeur, P. (1974). *The conflict of interpretations.* Evanston, IL: Northwestern University Press.

Ricoeur, P. (1977). *The rule of metaphor: Multi-disciplinary studies of the creation of meaning in language.* Toronto: The University of Toronto Press.

Ricoeur, P. (1981a). *Hermeneutics and the human sciences.* Cambridge, UK: Cambridge University Press.

Ricoeur, P. (1981b). The metaphorical process as imagination, cognition, and feeling. In M. Johnson (Ed.), *Philosophical perspectives on metaphor* (pp. 228–247). Minneapolis, MN: University of Minnesota Press.

Ricoeur, P. (1995). *Figuring the sacred: Religion, narrative, and imagination.* Minneapolis, MN: Fortress.

Robinson, M. (2010). *Absence of mind: The dispelling of inwardness from the modern myth of the self*. New Haven, CT: Yale University Press.

Sampson, E. E. (1993). *Celebrating the other: A dialogic account of human nature*. Boulder, CO: Westview Press.

Santner, E. L. (2001). *On the psychotheology of everyday life: Reflections on Freud and Rosenzweig*. Chicago, IL: University of Chicago Press.

Scarry, E. (1999). *On beauty and being just*. Princeton, NJ: Princeton University Press.

Schneider, K. (2004). *Rediscovery of awe: Splendor, mystery, and the fluid center of life*. St. Paul, MN: Paragon House.

Schneider, K. (2009). *Awakening to awe: Personal stories of profound transformation*. Lanham, MD: Jason Aronson.

Seneca (2005). *On the shortness of life*. New York: Penguin.

Simão, L. M. & Valsiner, J. (Eds.). (2007). *Otherness in question: Labyrinths of the self*. Charlotte, NC: Information Age Publishing.

Slife, B. (2004). Taking practices seriously: Toward a relational ontology. *Journal of Theoretical and Philosophical Psychology, 24*, 179–195.

Sober, E. & Wilson, D. S. (1998). *Unto others: The evolution and psychology of unselfish behavior*. Cambridge, MA: Harvard University Press.

Steiner, G. (1989). *Real presences*. Chicago, IL: University of Chicago Press.

Steiner, G. (1997). *Errata: An examined life*. New Haven, CT: Yale University Press.

Stolorow, R., Atwood, G. & Orange, D. (2002). *Worlds of experience: Interweaving philosophical and clinical dimensions in psychoanalysis*. New York: Basic Books.

Storr, A. (1992). *Music and the mind*. New York: Ballantine Books.

Taylor, C. (1989). *Sources of the self: The making of modern identity*. Cambridge, MA: Harvard University Press.

Taylor, C. (1991). *The ethics of authenticity*. Cambridge, MA: Harvard University Press.

Taylor, C. (1996). Iris Murdoch and moral philosophy. In M. Antonaccio & W. Schweiker (Eds.), *Iris Murdoch and the search for human goodness* (pp. 3–28). Chicago, IL: University of Chicago Press.

Thibon, G. (1953a). Introduction. In J. M. Perrin & G. Thibon, *Simone Weil as we knew her* (pp. 1–10). London: Routledge and Kegan Paul.

Thibon, G. (1953b). Simone Weil as she appeared to me. In J. M. Perrin & G. Thibon, *Simone Weil as we knew her* (pp. 109–171). London: Routledge and Kegan Paul.

Thibon, G. (1997). Introduction. In S. Weil, *Gravity and grace* (pp. vii–xxxvii). London: Routledge. (Original work published 1952)

Todorov, T. (1996). *Facing the extreme: Moral life in the concentration camps*. London: Weidenfeld & Nicolson.

Tolstoy, L. (1960). *The death of Ivan Ilych and other stories*. New York: New American Library. (Original work published 1886)

Tracy, D. (1996). Iris Murdoch and the many faces of Platonism. In M. Antonaccio & W. Schweiker (Eds.), *Iris Murdoch and the search for human goodness* (pp. 54–75). Chicago, IL: University of Chicago Press.

Turkle, S. (2011). *Alone together: Why we expect more from technology and less from each other*. New York: Basic Books.

Turner, V. (1982). *From ritual to theatre: The human seriousness of play*. New York: Performing Arts Journal Press.

Twenge, J. M. & Campbell, W. K. (2009). *The narcissism epidemic: Living in the age of entitlement*. New York: Free Press.

Vattimo, G. (2010). *Art's claim to truth*. New York: Columbia University Press.

Vergote, A. (1996). *Religion, belief and unbelief: A psychological study*. Amsterdam: Rodopi.

Wallace, A. (2006). *The attention revolution: Unlocking the power of the focused mind*. Somerville, MA: Wisdom Publications.

Weil, S. (1973). *Waiting for God*. New York: Perennial Library. (Original work published 1951)

Weil, S. (1986). Human personality. In S. Miles (Ed.), *Simone Weil: An anthology* (pp. 49–78). New York: Grove Press.

Weil, S. (1997). *Gravity and grace*. London: Routledge. (Original work published 1952)

Westphal, M. (2004). *Transcendence and self-transcendence: On God and the soul*. Indianapolis, IN: Indiana University Press.

Williams, R. N. (2002). On being for the Other: Freedom as investiture. In E. E. Gantt & R. N. Williams (Eds.), *Psychology for the other: Levinas, ethics and the practice of psychology* (pp. 143–159). Pittsburgh, PA: Duquesne University Press.

Worcester Telegram & Gazette (1999a). December 10.

Worcester Telegram & Gazette (1999b). December 17.

Wulff, D. (1997). *Psychology of religion: Classic and contemporary*. New York: John Wiley & Sons, Inc.

Index

Absence of Mind: The Dispelling of Inwardness from the Modern Myth of the Self (Robinson), 7n9
Absolute, 26–28, 104–105, 172n31
absorption, 70–71, 114
Ackerman, Diane, 23–24, 127n7
aesthetics, 136
  ethics and, 9–10, 60, 64, 142–143
affliction, 71, 73–74, 121, 125–127, 138, 193
agency, 218–219
alienation, 11, 14, 43–44, 60, 217
altruism, 82n1, 102, 218
anthropocentrism, 84, 85n4, 161, 179
anxiety, 5, 43, 62, 186, 214
appreciation, 41, 64, 186, 199
  of art, 140–143, 206
  of nature, 15, 114–115, 142–143
Arendt, Hannah, *Eichmann in Jerusalem*, 68
Armstrong, Karen, 48n24
art, works of, 60, 115n3, 221. *See also* music
  attentiveness to, 15–16, 39, 63–64, 71–72
  Freud on, 152n9
  as objects of appreciation, 140–143, 206
  painting, 162
  transcendence and, 4, 10, 135–136

artists, 135–136, 141
attention, 3, 14, 15, 52–53, 117–118, 201, 209. *See also* contemplative practices; *see also* objects of attention
  in daily life, 71–76
  dissolution of the self and, 137–140
  inattention, problem of, 17, 180
  moral life and, 63–70
  to nature, 15, 114–115, 142–143
  practices of, 12, 205
  shifting of, 13, 63, 183–184
  single-mindedness, 187
  sustained, 3, 188
  to works of art, 15–16, 39, 63–64, 71–72
attention deficit disorder, 58
Aurora, Colorado mass killing, 204n17
Auschwitz's "Special Squad," 65–67
authenticity, 27, 33–35, 135
awakening, 14, 20, 93–95, 107, 131, 204, 209
  through catastrophes, 14, 20, 73–74, 100, 107, 109, 182, 213, 215
awe, 212n24, 215

Bach, Johann Sebastian, 16
Barnard, C. W., 172n31
Baudelaire, Charles, 133
beauty, 39–43, 59–60, 163, 210–211

Becker, Ernest, *Denial of Death, The,* 6n8, 14n18
Beethoven, Ludwig van, 16
being-given-by, 37
Being Given: Toward a Phenomenology of Givenness (Marion), 37n19
Bellah, Robert, *Habits of the Heart: Individualism and Commitment in American Life,* 6
belongingness, 57, 72, 76, 171, 203–204
Belzen, J. A., 168
Benson, C., 71
Between Man and Man (Buber), 26–30
bicycle riding, practice of, 52, 70, 72, 183–184, 187, 216
Bloom, H., 165
Bollas, Christopher, 23n2, 45–46, 163, 165, 168n23, 188
Bonnefoy, Yves, 38, 118n5, 165–166
brain, science of, 218–219
breathing, process of, 26
Buber, Martin, 14, 43
  on human nature, 83n3
  I and Thou, 24–25, 47–48
  I–It mode, 61n11
  I–Thou relations, 12–13, 45, 84–91, 95–97, 111–112, 221
  Between Man and Man, 26–30
  on mystery of being, 6
  on relational processes and states, 2n4, 24–30
  on spheres of otherness, 76
  on the subconscious, 175n32

caring, 14, 101–102, 143, 196, 215
catastrophes
  awakening through, 14, 20, 73–74, 100, 107, 109, 182, 213, 215
  community responses to, 53–56, 77–84, 89–91, 98, 202–204
  causes, social and political, 9, 39, 43, 101, 122, 193–195, 219
celebrations, collective, 203–204, 208–209

centrifugal force of the Other, 14, 63, 180
centripetal force of the self, 14, 62, 180
certainty, 40–41, 144–145
Cézanne, Paul, 162
Christianity, 124–129, 156
Civilization and Its Discontents (Freud), 10–11
Coles, Robert, 121, 131
communitas, 203
community, 88–90
compassion, 66–68, 80, 84, 210, 215
concentration camps, 65–69, 101–103, 195–199, 210–211
connectedness, 3, 57, 60, 78, 81, 89, 194–195, 208–209
contemplative practices, 13, 73–73, 141–142, 192, 223. *See also* attention
control, desire for, 7, 97
creativity, 135–136, 139
Crites, Stephen, 136–137
Csikszentmihalyi, Mihaly, 23, 63n13, 186
cultural context, 114, 168–169, 172
culture of narcissism, 17

Dancing in the Streets: A History of Collective Joy (Ehrenreich), 203n16, 204n18
Darwin, Charles, 6, 82
death, 14, 89, 98–99, 114, 138, 204, 215. *See also* killing
  of God, 182
  of the Other, 103
  reality of, 69–70, 84, 213
  Thanatos, 11, 66
Death of Ivan Ilych, The (Tolstoy), 32–36, 97–98
dedication, 187–188
deep play, 23–24, 127
Denial of Death, The (Becker), 6n8, 14n18
dependence, 6, 25n4, 165
depersonalization, 140–141
depression, 5, 43, 62, 197
Descartes, René, 1

Descent of Man, The (Darwin), 82
desire, 4, 43, 56, 68, 73, 75, 156, 181, 188
detachment, 73, 76, 117, 139, 192–193
developmental theory, 25n5
devotion, 36–43, 188–201
   devotional objects, 12, 34, 220
   idea of, 3, 117–118
   to other persons, 88, 109
dialogical thinking, 28, 30
dialogue, in relationships, 84–85, 91
disruption, 19–21
distanciation, 117n4
divine, the, 4, 128, 130, 138, 158, 167, 188, 212
Dostoevsky, Fyodor, 97
Drowned and the Saved, The (Levi), 65–68, 197
drugs, pharmaceutical, 43–44
du Plessix Gray, F., 121–123, 130
Dupré, Louis, 48–50, 87, 175, 179, 189–190
   on devotional life, 192
   Religious Mystery and Rational Reflection, 155
Durkheim, Émile, *Elementary Forms of Religious Life, The*, 203
Dustin, Christopher, 69n19, 192

Edwards, James, 170, 189–190, 192
ego. *See also* self
   de-prioritizing of, 192–193
   desires of, 75
   egocentricity, 87, 193, 218
   ego cogito, 1, 97
   ego-driven self, 182
   orientation toward, 86–88
   status of, 106–107
Ehrenreich, Barbara, *Dancing in the Streets: A History of Collective Joy*, 203n16, 204n18
Ehrenzweig, Anton, *Hidden Order of Art: A Study in the Psychology of Artistic Imagination, The*, 148n5
Eichmann in Jerusalem (Arendt), 68

Elementary Forms of Religious Life, The (Durkheim), 203
Enlightenment Ain't What It's Cracked Up To Be: A Journey of Discovery, Snow and Jazz in the Soul (Forman), 181n1
Epstein, Mark, *Open to Desire: The Truth about What the Buddha Taught*, 73
Eros (love), 10, 11, 66, 116, 173
Eros for the Other (Farley), 10n14
Erotic Phenomenon, The (Marion), 85n5
erotics, 10–11, 57, 60, 116
ethics, 8–9, 14, 96, 102, 200
   aesthetics and, 9–10, 60, 64, 142–143
   challenges in interpersonal relations, 52–58, 64–65
   killing and, 65–68, 97
   before ontology, 94–95, 104, 108
   priority of the Other as ethical imperative, 46–51
evil, 12, 145, 211
evolution, 6–7, 46, 56n4, 66, 182, 190
ex-centric
   living, 16–17, 181–188
   perspective, 2
   self, 165, 179
existentialism, 32
existential nourishment, 4–5, 9, 13, 103–104, 219, 221
   lack of, 11, 43
   music as source of, 59
   Other as source of, 21, 26, 29, 35, 71, 118, 145
   transcendent reality as source of, 207

face of the Other, 8–9, 14–15, 53n1, 65, 66–67, 77–78, 98–99
Facing the Extreme: Moral Life in the Concentration Camps (Todorov), 101–102

faith, 91, 151, 155, 175, 210
  in art, 206
  commitments, 158–159
  religious, 155, 176–177
Farley, Wendy, 116–117, 193
  Eros for the Other, 10n14
Fiedler, L., 122–123, 130
Finch, H. L., 132–133, 135
firefighters, 77–81, 182n3, 199
Flournoy, T., "Principle of the Exclusion of Transcendence," 158, 166, 178
flow experiences, 5, 23, 63n13, 186–187
forgetfulness, 79–80, 83–84
Forman, Robert K. C., *Enlightenment Ain't What It's Cracked Up To Be: A Journey of Discovery, Snow and Jazz in the Soul*, 181n1
Frankl, Viktor, 109n21, 195–196, 197n12
  Man's Search for Meaning, 102
freedom, 50, 108–109, 184–185
Freeman, Mark
  "Charting the Narrative Unconscious: Cultural Memory and the Challenge of Autobiography," 114n2
  Hindsight: The Promise and Peril of Looking Backward, 58n7, 104n19
Freud, Anna, 131
Freud, Sigmund, 28, 62, 135, 152n9, 153
  Civilization and Its Discontents, 10–11
fulfillment, 4–5, 59–61, 110, 117, 187

Gadamer, Hans-Georg, 115n3, 118n5, 147
Gass, William, 71n21
Geertz, Clifford, 136
Gergen, Kenneth, 28n9
giving, 37, 208, 219
  being-given-by, 37
God, 26–28, 76, 89–91, 167, 212
  death of, 182
  dimension of height and, 105–106
  divine, the, 4, 128, 130, 138, 158, 167, 188, 212
  as object of attention, 12, 206–207
  question of existence of, 174
Good, idea of the, 145–146, 185, 207–213
  priority of the Other and, 100, 198–200
goodness, 12, 41, 57, 110, 173–174
  among concentration camp prisoners, 196–198
  as an idea, 200–201
  in community response to catastrophe, 89–91
  Murdoch, Iris on, 200, 209–210, 222
  priority of the Other and, 99–102
  as transcendent, 211
  Weil, Simone on, 90
grace, 13, 132, 137–138, 189, 206, 215
Gravity and Grace (Weil), 137
grief, 53–54, 78, 80

Habits of the Heart: Individualism and Commitment in American Life (Bellah), 6
happiness, 188, 214, 218
harmony, 149, 202, 209
Harvey, Jonathan, 148–149, 149n6–7, 168n23, 194
  In Quest of Spirit, 164n21
Hass, Robert, 35, 46, 211n23
Haydn, Franz Joseph, 16
Heaney, Seamus, 194
Heidegger, Martin, 27, 28n9, 33, 115n3, 136n10, 223
height, dimension of, 105
hermeneutics, 28, 129, 135, 137, 140, 156, 177
Hidden Order of Art: A Study in the Psychology of Artistic Imagination, The (Ehrenzweig), 148n5
Higgins, Kathleen, 64, 194
  Music of Our Lives, The, 59–60
Hindsight: The Promise and Peril of Looking Backward (Freeman), 58n7, 104n19

Hitler, Adolph, 11–12
Hobbes, Thomas, 82
holiness, 202, 214, 215n27, 216
Hollenback, J., 169
Holocaust, 100. *See also* concentration camps
Homer, 157
Horgan, John, 171n30
humanity, 77–84, 192
human nature, 29–30, 82–83
humility, 50, 184

I and Thou (Buber), 24–25, 47–48
Idea of the Holy, The (Otto), 165, 215n27
I–It relations, 6n11, 96–97, 221
illumination, 42, 161
immortality, 40–41, 70, 133, 163
inattention, problem of, 17, 180
independence, 6n8, 7, 92, 209
individualism, 6, 82, 86
in-ness, 31
In Quest of Spirit (Harvey), 164n21
inspiration, 3, 26, 33–34, 164, 179
interpersonal relations, ethical challenges in, 52–58, 64–65
invisible, the, 221, 223
inwardness, 31n13
I–Thou relations, 12–13, 45, 84–91, 95–97, 111–112, 221

James, Henry, 157
James, William, 31–32, 128, 151–153, 166–168
  on evolutionary psychology, 190–191
  on the MORE, 202–203
  on mystical experiences, 159–161, 170–172
  Principles of Psychology, The, 3n5, 190
  on psychology and religion, 156
  on religion, 174–178
  Varieties of Religious Experience, The, 16, 27n7, 166

Jesus Christ, 126–128, 131
Jones, J. W., 163–164, 165
Jourain, Robert, *Music, the Brain, and Ecstasy*, 147n3
Jung, Carl, 135–136, 141
justice, 9, 39, 41, 87, 99, 105, 111, 143, 189

Kabat-Zinn, Jon, 26
Kandinksy, Wassily, 148n4
Keen, Sam, 200n14
Kierkegaard, Søren, 27, 28n9, 32
killing
  ethics of, 65–68, 97–98
  mass, 204
Kirschner, Suzanne, 87n7
Kivy, Peter, *Music Alone*, 147–148
knowledge, 85, 92–93, 96–97, 111, 114, 132, 140

language, 168–169
  of the Other, 219–224
  for psychology, 17–18
  of the self, 6–8
Lear, Jonathan, 44–46
Levi, Primo, 83, 196–199, 210–211
  Drowned and the Saved, The, 65–68, 197
  Periodic Table, The, 103
Levinas, Emmanuel
  face of the Other, 8–9, 14–15, 53n1, 65, 66–67
  on holiness, 214, 216
  hostage, metaphor of, 8, 106–109, 126n6
  on I–Thou relations, 95–96
  on persistence in being, 214
  on priority of the Other, 1n2, 76, 88, 104–112
  on summons to responsibility, 93–100
Levi-Strauss, Claude, 148
Lifton, R.J., 56n4

listening, 33–34, 59, 146n1, 185, 217
   to music, 150, 194–195
Listening (Nancy), 59n9, 146n1
love, 4, 10–11, 116, 173, 184–185, 188

Man's Search for Meaning (Frankl), 102
Marcel, Gabriel, 31, 42–43, 93n10, 96, 132, 164, 221–222
   on aggressive anthropocentrism, 161, 179
   Mystery of Being, The, 6n7
   on objects, 170
   on presence, as term, 2n3
Marion, Jean-Luc, 15–16, 21, 26, 59n9
   Being Given: Toward a Phenomenology of Givenness, 37n19
   Erotic Phenomenon, The, 85n5
   on erotic phenomenon, 11
   on phenomenon, as term, 2n3
   on saturation, 170n27
   Visible and the Revealed, The, 211n23
Marx, Karl, 28
mastery, desire for, 7, 97
meaning, 25, 33–35, 219
   from pastimes, 187
   spiritual freedom and, 195
   of wine, 186
mediation of experience, 114, 168–169, 172
medicalization of experience, 43–44
meditative practices, 12, 26, 29n11, 73, 183
memory, 17, 184
   forgetfulness, 79–80, 83–84
   remembering, 213–215
Merleau-Ponty, Maurice, 162, 166
Midgley, Mary, 25n4, 82, 85
   Solitary Self: Darwin and the Selfish Gene, The, 6–7
mindfulness practices, 3n5, 183–184, 205
modernity, 207
monadic self, 30
monologic self, 28, 30
moral discipline, 193

moral life, 11–12, 63–70
more/MORE, idea of the, 174–175, 178, 202
mortality, 69–70, 98, 114, 204, 215. *See also* death; killing
Mozart, Wolfgang Amadeus, 16, 194
multitasking, 187
Murdoch, Iris
   on art, 10, 15, 39, 71, 141–143, 147n2
   on ego, 11, 62–63, 74–75, 214
   on freedom, 109n21, 184–186
   on goodness, 200, 209–210, 222
   on moral discipline, 193
   on obedience, 36
   on perfection, 91–92
   on prayer, 206–207
   on transcendence, 3–4, 144–145, 173–174
music, 136–137
   listening to, 150, 194–195
   meaning, mystery of, 146–151
   mystical experiences and, 163–164
   otherness of, 59–60
   transcendence and, 16, 150–151
   truth and, 147
   unity and, 194–195
Music, the Brain, and Ecstasy (Jourain), 147n3
Music Alone (Kivy), 147–148
Music of Our Lives, The (Higgins), 59–60
mystery of being, 13
Mystery of Being, The (Marcel), 6n7
mystical experiences. *See also* transcendence
   contextualist critiques of essentialist view, 169
   dispossession of the self, 160
   local objects and, 170
   objects of, 154–155
   ordinary and extraordinary, tension between, 171
   priority of the Other and, 152–159
   susceptibility to, 161, 168
mysticism, 48, 160, 165, 173

Nancy, Jean-Luc, 39n21, 212
  Listening, 59n9, 146n1
narcissism, culture of, 17
narrative
  personal, 2, 125–126
  psychology, 2, 220–221
  unconscious, 128–129
natality, 204, 215
naturalism, 158, 159n18, 178
nature, appreciation of, 15, 114–115, 142–143
nearness and otherness, dialectic of, 113–118
Needleman, Jacob, *Why Can't We Be Good?*, 9n12, 213–214
neighbors, 54–57, 77–81
neuroscience, 218–219
Newtown, Connecticut mass killing, 204n17
Nietzsche, Friedrich, 28
Nussbaum, Martha, 157–158, 166, 179
Nyiszli, Myklos, 65

obedience and necessity, 36–37, 98, 105, 125–126
objects of attention
  art as, 140–143, 206
  devotional, 12, 34, 220
  God as, 12, 206–207
  local, 170
  loveable, 185
  mystical experiences and, 154–155
  specific nature of, 71–72, 129, 140–141, 186–188
  worthiness of, 12–13, 188
oblivion, 11, 14, 52–53, 62, 66–69, 75, 203
On the Psychotheology of Everyday Life: Reflections on Freud and Rosenzweig (Santner), 56n3
ontology, 94–97, 104, 107–108, 159, 178
Open to Desire: The Truth about What the Buddha Taught (Epstein), 73
ordinary oblivion. *See* oblivion

Other
  centrifugal force of, 14, 63, 180
  death or loss of, 103, 191
  face of the, 8–9, 14–15, 53n1, 65, 66–67, 77–78, 98–99
  human, 104–112
  human-to-human relationships, 84–92
  language of the, 219–224
  non-human, 111–113, 123–130
  poetics of, 222–224
  ways of thinking about, 217–224
Other, priority of the
  acknowledgement of, 219
  as ethical imperative, 46–51
  in everyday life, 11–12, 74–76, 169–170, 180–188, 209
  experience of being moved, 21–24
  goodness and, 99–102
  Levinas, Emmanuel on, 1n2, 76, 88, 104–112
  mystical experiences and, 152–159
  necessity of, 191
  priority of the Good and, 100, 198–200
  psychology and, 1–2
  self-altering practices and, 205
  Self and, 165–166
  significance of, 154, 161–162
  tragedy and, 55
  transcendence and, 154–159, 177–178
otherness
  dialectic of nearness and, 113–118
  of music, 59–60
  preservation of otherness of people, 17
  spheres of, 13, 26, 76, 191, 220
Otto, Rudolph, 178
  Idea of the Holy, The, 165, 215n27
over-belief, 151, 176–177, 179, 211

painting, 162
pastimes, 187
perfection, 91–92, 144–145
Periodic Table, The (Levi), 103

personalized depersonalization, 135–143
personhood, 6, 13, 33, 86–87
Phaedrus (Plato), 10, 167, 210
phenomenology, 37, 53, 211n23, 220–222
   transcendence and, 153–155, 159–160, 167, 173, 202
philosophy, 221–223
Plato, 185n8
   Phaedrus, 10, 167, 210
   Republic, The, 57, 144, 219n1
play, 23–24, 127n7
poetic science, 224
poetry, 29, 35, 38, 165–166, 168, 170, 194
poiesis, 222–223
political and social causes, 9, 39, 43, 101, 122, 193–195, 219
postmodernity, 207
poststructuralism, 207
prayer, 191, 206
Principles of Psychology, The (James), 3n5, 190
priorities
   misplaced, 180
   in personal life, 14, 55–63
priority of the Other. *See* Other, priority of the
Proudfoot, W., 178
Proust, Marcel, 157
psychology
   academic, 221
   ego-centric focus of, 1, 4–5
   evolutionary, 190–191
   mysticism and, 154
   narrative, 2, 220–221
   new language for, 17–18, 218–224
   question of true transcendence and, 158
   religion and, 154, 156
   scientific, 158, 176, 177–178
   spirituality and, 132–133, 135
psychotherapy
   practice of, 5, 44
   self-world relationship and, 43–46

reality
   awareness of, 184
   of death, 69–70, 84, 213
   psychical, 153
   social construction of, 28–29, 47, 72n22, 181, 218–219
   ur-reality, 143
Real Presences (Steiner), 150–151
reciprocity, 85–86, 88, 95–97
recognition, 88, 137, 170–171
Rediscovery of Awe: Splendor, Mystery, and the Fluid Center of Life (Schneider), 212
reductionism, 135
relationality, 24–30, 70
religion, 172, 174–175, 178–179, 221
   faith, 155, 176–177
   mood of loss in, 189–191
   practices, 205–206
   religiosity, 27
   religious devotion, 39, 188–189
   religious life, 13, 16
   social dimension of, 203
Religious Mystery and Rational Reflection (Dupré), 155
remembering, 213–215
Republic, The (Plato), 57, 144, 219n1
responsibility, 14, 93–96, 100, 106–109
responsiveness, 14, 36–37
reverence, 42, 64, 194
Ricoeur, Paul, 117n4, 168–169
Rilke, Rainer Maria, 35, 46
Robinson, Marilyn, 31n13, 82n1
   Absence of Mind: The Dispelling of Inwardness from the Modern Myth of the Self, 7n9

sacraments, 192
sacred, the, 4, 163–164
Santner, Eric, *On the Psychotheology of Everyday Life: Reflections on Freud and Rosenzweig*, 56n3

Sartre, Jean-Paul, 27, 33
saturated phenomena, 15–16, 21
Scarry, Elaine, 39–42, 163, 164
Schleiermacher, Friedrich, 165, 178
Schneider, Kirk, *Rediscovery of Awe: Splendor, Mystery, and the Fluid Center of Life*, 212
science, 182, 221
    neuroscience, 218–219
    scientific psychology, 158, 176, 177–178
secondarity of the self, 165
self. *See also* ego; personhood
    being true to, 31–35
    ego-driven, 63
    ex-centric, 165, 179
    as focus of psychology, 4–5
    importance of, 47–50
    narrative psychology and, 2, 220–221
    self–world relationship, 43–46
    spiritual, 190–191
    unselfing, 15, 73–75, 139, 142, 192–193
    ways of thinking about, 213
Self
    beyond Selfhood, 159–166
    realizing of the, 75
    remembering, 213–214
self-actualization, 4
self-altering practices, 205. *See also* contemplative practices
    meditative, 12, 26, 29n11, 73, 183
    mindfulness, 3n5, 183–184, 205
self-awakening, 204. *See also* awakening
self-centeredness, 31
self-destruction, 74–75
self-effacement, 10n14, 74, 119–120, 123, 134, 152, 184
self-emptying, 117, 137–140
self-enclosure, 34, 48
self-esteem, 5, 31–32
self-interest, 182
self-preservation, 196–197

self-realization, 33, 110
Seneca (Lucius Annaeus, the Younger), 69–70, 187n9
shame, 197–199
sin, 198–199
social and political causes, 9, 39, 43, 101, 122, 193–195, 219
social constructionism, 28–29, 47, 72n22, 181, 218–219
social justice, 9, 101, 193–195
Socrates, 144, 167
Solitary Self: Darwin and the Selfish Gene, The (Midgley), 6–7
Sophocles, 157
sorrow, 69, 78, 80, 89, 182n3, 213
spirit, 178
spiritual freedom, 195
spirituality, 13, 27n7, 206
spiritual oneness, 149
spontaneity, 169
sports, 204n18
Steiner, George, 16, 167–168, 223
    Real Presences, 150–151
Stockhausen, Karlheinz, 147n2
Storr, Anthony, 149–150, 151, 163n20
subconscious self, 167, 170, 175, 177–178
subjectivity, 107–108
substitution, 106–107
suffering, 32, 66, 103, 117, 138, 196–197. *See also* affliction
    desire to alleviate, 80–81, 92–93, 204
    medication for, 44
    summons to responsibility, 93–100
supernatural realm, 156
surrender, idea of, 37
survival, 196–197
suspicion, hermeneutics of, 28
symmetry, 41, 85, 96–97

Taylor, Charles, 3, 33–36
Thanatos (death), 11, 66

theology, 154
theory, 222–223
therapy. *See* psychotherapy
Thibon, Gustav, 118–120, 122, 133–135
Todorov, Tzvetan, 82, 196
    Facing the Extreme: Moral Life in the Concentration Camps, 101–102
Tolstoy, Leo, *Death of Ivan Ilych, The*, 32–36, 97–98
Tracy, David, 74n23
tragedies, 53–56, 73, 77–84, 100. *See also* catastrophes
transcendence, 3–4, 16, 49–50, 129, 221. *See also* mystical experiences
    art and, 4, 10, 135–136
    from below and above, 166–172
    culturally and historically conditioned, 172
    emergence of, 201–204
    evidence for, 145–146
    goodness and, 211
    idea of, 144–146, 153
    internal and external, 157–158, 179
    Murdoch, Iris on, 3–4, 144–145, 173–174
    music and, 16, 150–151
    naming of, 212
    orientation toward, 207
    phenomenology and, 153–155, 159–160, 167, 173, 202
    Principle of the Exclusion of Transcendence, 158, 166, 178
    priority of the Other and, 154–159, 177–178
    psychology and question of, 158
    real self and, 164
    seeking of, 201
transformation, 64, 123, 170, 194–195, 202, 220
transmutation, process of, 137
truth, 17, 40–42, 221
    music and, 147
    seeking of, 117

unity, 148–149, 152, 194, 202, 209
unselfing, 15, 73–75, 139, 142, 192–193

value, 5, 9, 21, 30–31, 43, 104, 207, 219
Varieties of Religious Experience, The (James), 16, 27n7, 166
veiledness of the world, 62–63, 140, 217
Visible and the Revealed, The (Marion), 211n23
volunteer work, 101, 194

We, forms of, 88–90
Weil, Simone, 15, 26, 200, 217
    affliction and, 73–74, 121–122, 125–128, 130, 193
    on attention, 137–139, 142n14
    biographical challenges, 133–135
    Catholicism, 125–129
    on devotion, 39n20
    egoism of, 119–120
    on goodness, 90
    Gravity and Grace, 137
    on humility, 2, 50
    mystical and spiritual experiences of, 123–131, 135, 140, 146
    on obedience, 36
    personality of, 118–123
    political attitudes of, 120–123
    on seeking transcendence, 201
    self-effacement, 119–120, 123, 134
    on sources of meaning and value, 30–31
Why Can't We Be Good? (Needleman), 9n12, 213–214
willed ignorance, 68–69
Worcester Cold Storage and Warehouse Co. fire, 53–55, 77–84, 89, 202
    significance of the building, 114
Wordsworth, William, 165

yoga, 183

Ziegler, Joanna (Jody), 64n14, 69n19, 192

BF
321
F817
2014

WITHDRAWN
From Library Collection

Reinsch Library
Marymount University
2807 N Glebe Road
Arlington, VA 22207